SHORTLIST

Barcelona
2009

WHAT'S NEW | WHAT'S ON | WHAT'S BEST

timeout.com/barcelona

Contents

Barcelona by Area

Essentials

Published by Time Out Guides Ltd
Universal House
251 Tottenham Court Road
London W1T 7AB
Tel: + 44 (0)20 7813 3000
Fax: + 44 (0)20 7813 6001
Email: guides@timeout.com
www.timeout.com

Managing Director Peter Fiennes
Financial Director Gareth Garner
Editorial Director Ruth Jarvis
Deputy Series Editor Dominic Earle
Editorial Manager Holly Pick
Assistant Management Accountant Ija Krasnikova

Time Out Guides is a wholly owned subsidiary of Time Out Group Ltd.

© Time Out Group Ltd
Chairman Tony Elliott
Financial Director Richard Waterlow
Group General Manager/Director Nichola Coulthard
Time Out Magazine Ltd MD Richard Waterlow
Time Out Communications Ltd MD David Pepper
Time Out International Ltd MD Cathy Runciman
Production Director Mark Lamond
Group IT Director Simon Chappell
Head of Marketing Catherine Demajo

Time Out and the Time Out logo are trademarks of Time Out Group Ltd.

This edition first published in Great Britain in 2008 by Ebury Publishing
A Random House Group Company
Company information can be found on www.randomhouse.co.uk
Random House UK Limited Reg. No. 954009
10 9 8 7 6 5 4 3 2 1

Distributed in the US by Publishers Group West
Distributed in Canada by Publishers Group Canada

For further distribution details, see www.timeout.com

ISBN: 978-1-84670-098-9

A CIP catalogue record for this book is available from the British Library.

Printed and bound by Firmengruppe APPL, aprinta druck, Wemding, Germany.

The Random House Group Limited supports The Forest Stewardship Council (FSC), the
leading international forest certification organisation. All our titles that are printed on
Greenpeace approved FSC certified paper carry the FSC logo. Our paper procurement
policy can be found at www.rbooks.co.uk/environment.

Time Out carbon-offsets all its flights with Trees for Cities (www.treesforcities.org).

Barcelona Shortlist

The **Time Out Barcelona Shortlist 2009** is one of a new series of guides that draws on Time Out's background as a magazine publisher to keep you current with what's going on in town. As well as Barcelona's key sights and the best of its eating, drinking and leisure options, it picks out the most exciting venues to have opened in the last year and gives a full calendar of events from September 2008 to December 2009. It also includes features on the important news, trends and openings, all compiled by locally based editors and writers. Whether you're visiting for the first time in your life or the first time this year, you'll find the *Time Out Barcelona Shortlist* contains all you need to know, in a format that is both portable and easy to use.

The guide divides central Barcelona into seven areas, each containing listings for Sights & Museums, Eating & Drinking, Shopping, Nightlife and Arts & Leisure, and maps pinpointing their locations. At the front of the book are chapters rounding up these scenes city-wide, and giving a shortlist of our overall picks. We include itineraries for days out, plus essentials such as transport information and hotels.

Our listings give phone numbers as dialled within Spain. From abroad, use your country's exit code followed by 34 (the country code for Spain) and the number given.

We have noted price categories by using one to four euro signs (€-€€€€), representing budget, moderate, expensive and luxury. Major credit cards are accepted unless otherwise stated. We also indicate when a venue is **NEW**, and give **Event highlights**.

All our listings are double-checked, but businesses do sometimes close or change their hours or prices, so it's always a good idea to call a venue before visiting. While every effort has been made to ensure accuracy, the publishers cannot accept responsibility for any errors that this guide may contain.

Venues are marked on the maps using symbols numbered according to their order within the chapter and colour-coded as follows:

❶ Sights & Museums
❶ Eating & Drinking
❶ Shopping
❶ Nightlife
❶ Arts & Leisure

Map key

Major sight or landmark	
Hospital or college	
Railway station	
Park	
River	
Carretera	
Main road	
Main road tunnel	
Pedestrian road	
Airport	✈
Church	✚
Metro station, FGC station	Ⓜ 🌀
Area name	EIXAMPLE

Time Out Barcelona Shortlist 2009

EDITORIAL
Editor Sally Davies
Deputy Editor Edoardo Albert
Proofreader Karen Mulkern
Indexer Rob Norman

DESIGN
Art Director Scott Moore
Art Editor Pinelope Kourmouzoglou
Senior Designer Henry Elphick
Graphic Designers Gemma Doyle,
 Kei Ishimaru
Digital Imaging Simon Foster
Advertising Designer Jodi Sher
Picture Editor Jael Marschner
Deputy Picture Editor Katie Morris
Picture Researcher Gemma Walters
Picture Desk Assistant Marzena Zoladz

ADVERTISING
Commercial Director Mark Phillips
International Advertising Manager
 Kasimir Berger
International Sales Executive
 Charlie Sokol
Advertising Assistant Kate Staddon
Advertising Sales (Barcelona) Creative
 Media Group

MARKETING
Marketing Manager Yvonne Poon
Senior Publishing Brand Manager
 Luthfa Begum
**Sales & Marketing Director,
 North America** Lisa Levinson
Marketing Designers Anthony Huggins,
 Nicola Wilson

PRODUCTION
Production Manager Brendan McKeown
Production Controller Damian Bennett
Production Co-ordinator Julie Pallot

CONTRIBUTORS
This guide was researched and written by Sally Davies, with additional contributions from Katie Addleman, Stephen Burgen, Nadia Feddo, Alex Phillips and Tara Stevens.

PHOTOGRAPHY
All photography by Greg Gladman, except: page 11 Roberto d'Lara, 2007; pages 19, 28, 31, 39, 40, 44, 45, 48, 54, 57, 59, 60, 62, 64, 65, 66, 68, 69, 70, 71, 73, 74, 76, 77, 78, 80, 86, 88, 89, 90, 94, 98, 102, 105, 108, 111, 112, 113, 115, 117, 118, 119, 121, 124, 126, 135, 137, 138, 141, 145, 146, 150, 151, 154, 157, 162, 163, 171, 175, 189 Elan Fleisher; page 27 Metropolis Media Group; page 33 Richard Cugat; page 36 Tracy Gilbertder; page 41 Josep Aznar; page 82 Sascha Burkard Gonzalez; page 85 Metropolis media group; page 95 Sally Davies; page 136 Josep Usano for 'By'; page 166 Enric Ruiz-Geli © Cloud 9

Cover image:Dallas and John Heaton/Spectrum/Imagestate

MAPS
JS Graphics (john@jsgraphics.co.uk).

About Time Out

Founded in 1968, Time Out has expanded from humble London beginnings into the leading resource for those wanting to know what's happening in the world's greatest cities. As well as our influential what's-on weeklies in London, New York and Chicago, we publish more than a dozen other listings magazines in cities as varied as Beijing and Mumbai. The magazines established Time Out's trademark style: sharp writing, informed reviewing and bang up-to-date inside knowledge of every scene.

 Time Out made the natural leap into travel guides in the 1980s with the City Guide series, which now extends to over 50 destinations around the world. Written and researched by expert local writers and generously illustrated with original photography, the full-size guides cover a larger area than our Shortlist guides and include many more venue reviews, along with additional background features and a full set of maps.

 Throughout this rapid growth, the company has remained proudly independent, still owned by Tony Elliott four decades after he started Time Out London as a single fold-out sheet of A5 paper. This independence extends to the editorial content of all our publications, this Shortlist included. No establishment has been featured because it has advertised, and no payment has influenced any of our reviews. And, for our critics, there's definitely no such thing as a free lunch: all restaurants and bars are visited and reviewed anonymously, and Time Out always picks up the bill.
For more about the company, see www.timeout.com.

Don't Miss
2009

Museu de la Música

WHAT'S BEST
Sights & Museums

While 2007 was about new museums, such as the Museu Olímpic i de l'Esport (p114) and the Museu de la Música (p126), 2008 has been about shifting and consolidating existing museums, setting in motion the plans for a grand Museu del Disseny (Design Museum) in the Plaça de les Glòries, along with a future Museu de la Societat (Museum of Society) that will incorporate the archaeological, ethnological and Catalan history museums.

Both have proven highly controversial, and work on the latter may be stalled for some time. Barcelona's new shrine to design, however, is already under way. The idea is that it will incorporate the clothing, ceramics and decorative arts museums, along with several smaller collections, though the country's ceramicists are up in arms at the idea that a painted plate should be considered 'design' rather than 'art'. For the meantime, however, the Museu Tèxtil has moved from its longstanding home in a Born mansion, and reopened in July 2008 under the same roof as the Museu de Ceràmica and the Museu de les Arts Decoratives in the Palau Reial de Pedralbes. Together these now form the Museu de les Arts Aplicades (p156).

Elsewhere, the city's attractions are, as ever, best enjoyed alfresco. There's plenty to do on a rainy day, of course, and fans of the arts won't want to miss the Museu Picasso (p76), the Fundació Joan Miró

SHORTLIST

Best newcomers
- Fundació Suñol (p125)
- Parc Central de Poblenou (p115)

Best revamps
- Fundación Francisco Godia (p125)
- Museu de les Arts Aplicades (p156)
- Palau Güell (p95)

Best churches
- Cathedral (p56)
- Sagrada Família (p126)
- Sant Pau del Camp (p95)
- Santa Maria del Mar (p77)

Best works of Modernisme
- Casa Batlló (p124)
- Hospital de Sant Pau (p125)
- Palau Güell (p95)
- Palau de la Música Catalana (p76)
- Sagrada Família (p126)

Oddball museums
- Museu de Carrosses Fúnebres (p125)
- Museu del Calçat (p56)
- Museu del Perfum (p126)
- Museu Frederic Marès (p56)

Best for kids' stuff
- L'Aquàrium (p106)
- CosmoCaixa (p155)
- Museu de la Xocolata (p74)
- Zoo de Barcelona (p78)

Best alfresco strolls
- Jardí Botànic (p111)
- Parc de Collserola (p153)
- Parc de la Ciutadella (p77)
- Park Güell (p144)

Best views
- Park Güell (p144)
- Spires of Sagrada Família (p126)
- Telefèric de Montjuïc (p116)
- Torre de Collserola (p153)

(p110), or the odd gem of an exhibition at the CaixaForum (p110), but really this is a city to savour from the street. Even its best-known museums, including the MACBA (p89), are really more notable for their exteriors than their holdings. A trip around the inside of the Sagrada Família (p126) is nothing compared to contemplating the excesses of its façade, while the huddle of medieval streets around the cathedral (p56) is as intriguing to explore as the tourist-thronged interior of the church. We do not, however, suggest you extend this approach to Barcelona's most-visited sight, the Nou Camp football stadium (p152), which looks exactly like a football stadium. Even this is set to change, however, with Norman Foster's spectacular overhaul, which will see the stadium sheathed in a Gaudí-inspired shimmering, polychromatic façade. Work begins in 2009 and should take two years.

Fundació Suñol p125

Barrio by barrio

The Old City (Ciutat Vella) is the tangle of streets that make up the Raval, the Barri Gòtic and the Born, with the cathedral at its heart. It is flanked by the peaceful, residential district of Poble Sec to the west, and beyond that the hill of Montjuïc. To the east is the post-industrial neighbourhood of Poblenou, which for many years now has been touted as Barcelona's 'Hoxton'. Its loft apartments are apparently brimming with bright young things overflowing with new ideas, though in truth it can be hard to pick this up at street level.

Cutting straight through the Old City are La Rambla and Via Laietana. La Rambla, once a seasonal riverbed that formed the western limit of the 13th-century city, is now a tree-lined boulevard dividing the medieval buildings and cathedral of the Barri Gòtic from the Raval, home to the MACBA and the CCCB (p88). Via Laietana, driven through in the 19th century to bring light and air to the slums, is the boundary between the Barri Gòtic, and the Born and Sant Pere, which is where you'll find the striking Palau de la Música Catalana (p76), the Museu Picasso and the Parc de la Ciutadella (p77).

Fanning out above these neighbourhoods are the grid-like streets of the Eixample, brought about by the demolition of the medieval walls in 1854. It was to become a showcase for the greatest works of Modernisme, including the Sagrada Familia, Hospital de Sant Pau, Casa Batlló and La Pedrera. When the only traffic was the clip-clopping horse and rattling cart, these whimsical flights of architectural fancy must have been still more impressive; nowadays the Eixample can be noisy and polluted, as almost every road carries four lanes of traffic. Beyond lies the former village of Gràcia, still with a quiet community feel, and beyond that is Gaudí's fantastical Park Güell.

Getting around

Most of Barcelona is easily traversed on foot, although trips to sights such as the Park Güell or the Sagrada Familia are a tedious hike on a hot day. Public transport, however, is cheap and generally excellent. For a map of the metro, see the back flap; the subterranean tourist information office in Plaça Catalunya provides a very good bus map.

The city council runs walking tours on various themes (from Picasso to Modernisme, gourmet to Gothic) at weekends and occasional other days. These tours start in the Plaça Catalunya tourist office, and take 90 minutes to two hours, excluding the museum trip. For more information, see www.barcelonaturisme.com.

A fun and eco-friendly way to get around the city (and to head to the beach) is to hire a bright yellow Trixi rickshaw. Running 11am to 8pm, April to September, and costing €10 per half hour, they can be hailed on the street or booked on 93 310 13 79 and www.trixi.com. Cycling has also seen a boost with the council's new Bicing scheme, by which residents can pick up bikes all over town and use them free for short journeys. There are also plans afoot to make the system accessible to tourists, via a weekly pass; see www.bicing.com. For other places to hire a bike see p180.

There are two tourist buses seen all over town: the orange Barcelona Tours (93 317 64 54, www.barcelonatours.es) and the white Bus Turístic (www.barcelonaturisme.com). The

former is less frequent but less popular, meaning you won't have to queue, while the latter gives a book of discounts for various attractions. Both visit many of the same sights and cost much the same.

One novelty in 2008 has been the introduction of the GoCars (C/Freixures, Born, 93 310 73 83, www.gocartours.com), little yellow 'talking' three-wheel cars that explain the sights as you go, directing you via GPS.

Tickets

A range of discount passes to Barcelona's attractions exists. For details of the new Arqueoticket, see box p62. Also fairly new is the Tiquet Ciència, which allows entry to Cosmocaixa, the Zoo, Museu Marítim, the Jardí Botànic, the Museu de Ciències Naturals and a couple of others outside Barcelona, for a bargain €19. The Articket (www.articketbcn.com, €20) gives free entry to seven museums and art galleries over three months: Fundació Miró, MACBA, the MNAC, Espai Gaudí-La Pedrera, the Fundació Tàpies, the CCCB and the Museu Picasso. All these tickets are available from participating venues and tourist offices.

A word of warning

While the situation has improved of late, Barcelona's reputation for muggings is not completely without justification. You are very unlikely to be physically assaulted, but bag-snatching and pickpocketing are rife, especially in the Old City, on the beach and on public transport. Leave whatever you can in your hotel, keep your wallet in your front pocket, wear backpacks on the front and be wary of anyone trying to clean something off your shoulder, sell you a posy or get you to point something out on a map.

Artkuisine

WHAT'S BEST
Eating & Drinking

As El Bulli, to nobody's surprise, collected the gong for Best Restaurant in the World 2008 at the San Pellegrino awards, the culinary world was again forced to acknowledge that not all great kitchens sit north of the Pyrenees.

The huge challenge for Barcelona has been to raise the gastronomic bar to cater for the El Bulli wannabes; those hopeful foodies who fly in from all over the globe in the hope of securing a last-minute cancellation, but in the meantime spend a hungry week hovering around the city.

This, among other factors, has created a demand for more top-end restaurants, and given rise to new and innovative chef-led joints such as Manairó (p131), Gresca (p131) and Artkuisine (p157), places which can only keep their heads above water thanks to the patronage of reasonably well-off tourists.

At a slightly more modest level many have noted a back-to-basics trend, whereby classic dishes (particularly tapas) are done well and with prime ingredients. Two fine examples of this are Inopia and Tapaç24 (see box p128). Another, the Bar Seco (p118) in Montjuïc, also reflects an awakening interest in the Slow Food movement and organic produce.

Raise a glass

One of the first words in Spanish uttered by many visitors is *cerveza* – but few realise that it applies only to bottled beer. If you want draught

beer, ask for a *caña*, which is a small measure; only a true tourist would ask for a *jarra*, which is closer to a pint. Recently there has been a welcome comeback for Moritz beer, brewed in Barcelona and infinitely superior to the ubiquitous Estrella. Shandy (*clara*) is also popular, made tastier by bitter lemon and untainted by the stigma it has in the UK.

Catalan wines are gaining ground over Rioja and Albariño, even internationally, and it's worth looking out for the local DOs Priorat, Montsant, Toro and Costers del Segre, as well as the commonplace Penedès. Most wine drunk here is red (*negre/tinto*), apart from the many cavas, which run from *semi-sec* ('half-dry', but actually pretty sweet) to *brut nature* (very dry).

Spanish coffee is strong and generally excellent. The three basic types are *solo* (also known simply as café), a small strong black coffee; *cortado*, the same but with a little milk, and *café con leche*, the same with more milk. Cappuccino has yet to catch on; whipped cream as a substitute for foam is not unheard of. Then there's *café americano* (a tall black coffee diluted with more water) and *carajillo*, which is a short, black coffee with a liberal dash of brandy. Decaffeinated coffee (*descafeinado*) is popular and widely available, but specify *de máquina* (from the machine) unless you want instant (*de sobre*).

Tea is pretty poor and generally best avoided. If you can't live without it, ask for cold milk on the side ('*leche fría aparte*') or run the risk of getting a glass of hot milk and a teabag. Basic herbal teas are found everywhere, particularly limeflower (*tila*), mint (*menta*) and chamomile (*manzanilla*, not to be confused with the light sherry of the same name).

SHORTLIST

Best new restaurants
- Artkuisine (p157)
- Gresca (p131)
- Manairó (p131)

Best for fast food
- Fast Good (p130)
- La Paninoteca D'E (p133)

Best for slow food
- Bar Seco (p118)

Best for a Manhattan
- Boadas (p71)
- Dry Martini (p130)
- Gimlet (p80)

Best for outdoor drinking
- Bar Colombo (p105)
- Bar Kasparo (p90)
- Casa Paco (p79)
- La Caseta del Migdia (p116)
- El Jardi (p91)

Best for outdoor eating
- Agua (p106)
- Bestial (p107)
- Cafè de l'Acadèmia (p58)
- La Font del Gat (p116)
- Els Pescadors (p160)
- La Venta (p155)

Best vegetarian
- La Báscula (p78)
- Organic (p96)
- Sésamo (p93)

Best for coffee and cake
- La Granja (p59)
- Granja M Viader (p91)
- Dolso (p130)
- La Nena (p147)

Best for seafood
- Botafumeiro (p145)
- Cal Pep (p79)
- Can Ramonet (p99)
- La Paradeta (p81)

Best for pizza
- La Bella Napoli (p119)
- La Paninoteca D'E (p133)
- Ravalo (p92)

Situated in the heart of Barcelona in the Ribera neighbourhood, you'll find the restaurant Peps Buffet. Close to the emblematic church Santa Maria del Mar and neighbours with the Picasso Museum on Calle Gruñi number 5.

The architecture of the restaurant dates back to the 17th century, and the decor is in a typical Catalan style with a rustic ambience. You can appreciate the building's original features; the most splendid is an antique well with a spiral staircase that leads down to the bathrooms.

Home-made Catalan cuisine — just like grandma used to make.

Tapaç24

Tapas tips

Tapas are not an especially Catalan concept, and with a few exceptions (such as Inopia or Tapaç24, see box p138), they are a pale imitation of those found elsewhere in Spain. The Andalucían custom of giving a free tapa, or just a saucer of crisps and nuts, is almost unheard of.

What has caught on big time in Barcelona are *pintxo* bars – their Basque origin means that the word is always given in Euskera – such as Euskal Etxea (p80). A *pintxo* (be careful not to confuse it with the Spanish term *pincho*, which simply refers to a very small tapa) consists of some ingenious culinary combination on a small slice of bread. Platters of them are usually brought out at particular times, often around 1pm and again at 8pm. *Pintxos* come impaled on toothpicks, which you keep on your plate so that the barman can tally them up at the end. Unfortunately, the British are the holders of the worst reputation for abusing this eminently civilised system by 'forgetting' to hand over all their toothpicks.

Without a decent grasp of the language, tapas bars can be quite intimidating unless you know exactly what you want. Don't be afraid to seek guidance, but some of the more standard offerings will include *tortilla* (potato omelette), *patatas bravas* (fried potatoes in a spicy red sauce and garlic mayonnaise), *ensaladilla* (Russian salad), *pinchos morunos* (small pork skewers), *champiñones al ajillo* (mushrooms fried in garlic), *gambas al ajillo* (prawns and garlic), *mejillones a la marinera* (mussels in a tomato and onion sauce), *chocos* (squid fried in batter), *almejas al vapor* (steamed clams with garlic and parsley), *pulpo* (octopus) and *pimientos del padrón* (little green peppers, one or two of which will kick like an angry mule, in a vegetable Russian roulette).

How it's done

In bars, unless they're very busy or you're sitting outside, you won't usually be required to pay until you leave. If you have trouble attracting a waiter's attention, a loud but polite '*oiga*' or, in Catalan, '*escolti*' is acceptable. On the vexed question of throwing detritus on the floor (cigarette ends, olive pits and so on), it's safest to keep an eye on what the locals are doing.

In restaurants, lunch starts around 2pm and goes on until roughly 3.30pm or 4pm; dinner is served from about 9pm until 11.30pm or midnight. Some restaurants open earlier in the evening, but arriving before 9.30 or 10pm generally means you'll be dining alone or in the company of foreign tourists. Reserving a table is generally a good idea: not only on Friday and Saturday nights, but also on Sunday evenings and Monday lunchtimes, when few restaurants are open. Many also close for holidays, including about a week over Easter, and the month of August. We have listed closures of more than a week wherever we can, but restaurants are fickle.

Costs & tipping

Eating out in Barcelona is not as cheap as it used to be, but low mark-ups on wines keep the cost relatively reasonable for northern Europeans and Americans. All but the upmarket restaurants are required by law to serve an economical, fixed-price *menú del dia* (*menú* is not to be confused with the menu, which is *la carta*) at lunchtime; this usually consists of a starter, main course, dessert, bread and something to drink. The idea is to provide cheaper meals for the workers, but while it can be a real bargain, it is not by any means a taster menu or a showcase for the chef's greatest hits; rather, they're a healthier version of what in other countries might amount to a snatched lunchtime sandwich.

Laws governing the issue of prices are often flouted, but, legally, menus must declare if the seven per cent IVA (VAT) is included in prices or not (it rarely is), and also if there is a cover charge (generally expressed as a charge for bread). Catalans, and the Spanish in general, tend to tip little, but tourists decide for themselves.

Fast Good p15

Vinçon p21

Shopping

The retail world of the Catalan capital has carried on peacefully for centuries, dominated by family-run businesses and shops so specialised that there is one selling only felt, another selling feathers and a third for clothes hangers. In 2007, however, there was a shopkeepers' revolt. Enough! they cried. Enough nodding donkeys, enough bullfighting fridge magnets and enough flamenco dolls.

The argument is not that these things are tawdry but that they are not Catalan. The authorities argued that they couldn't ban the selling of Mexican sombreros, but eventually agreed to promote items and crafts that were more typical of the region. A showcase has been set up in the form of the Artesania

Catalunya (C/Banys Nous 11, Barri Gòtic, 93 467 46 60, www. artesania-catalunya.com), which holds occasional exhibitions of various arts and crafts, along with information on shops such as Art Escudellers (p65), where these items can be bought.

Neighbourhood watch

A walk down Spain's high streets will offer a similar roll call (Mango, Zara, Benetton, Body Shop) to those of other large European cities. At the small scale, however, the city really shines as a shopping destination: the dressmakers and one-off fashion boutiques in the Born, the indie art galleries of the upper Raval, the traditional artesans and antiques stores of the

Barri Gòtic, and the quirky jewellery workshops and vintage clothes shops of Gràcia all attest to the continuing presence of truly local retailers and craftsmen.

Shops in Barcelona match their context so neatly that they can seem to be part of a giant themed architectural park. The Eixample's expansive boulevards and Modernista architecture complement its wealth of upmarket designer furniture, fashion and homeware stores, while the Old City's narrow streets and restored medieval spaces are home to a jumble of small craft shops, antiques dealers and specialist outlets, selling anything from religious candles to carnival masks and anchovy-flavoured bonbons.

Markets

Many of Barcelona's traditional local markets have been overhauled in the last couple of years, most dramatically the Mercat Santa Caterina in Sant Pere and the Mercat de la Barceloneta, and more revamps are due, starting with the Mercat Sant Antoni in 2009. The first two of these were arguably more important as pieces of high-profile architecture acting as catalysts for urban redevelopment than as support for small shopkeepers.

In an attempt to fuse modern and traditional approaches to shopping, the modernised markets tend to hold far fewer actual stalls than before, with more space turned over to supermarkets and restaurants. In 2008 the city council raised the spectre of Sunday opening, arguing that markets could therefore attract a broader and younger clientele, but in the face of vociferous opposition from what tends to be an especially reactionary group of workers, these plans seem unlikely to reach fruition for a while.

SHORTLIST

Best new shops
- Capricho de Muñeca (p84)
- Olive (p84)

Best for books
- Altaïr (p60)
- Casa del Llibre (p135)
- FNAC (p135)
- Hibernian Books (p149)

Best for fashionistas
- Custo Barcelona (p84)
- Giménez y Zuazo (p93)
- Tribu (p67)

Best one-stop shops
- El Corte Inglés (p135)
- Barcelona Glòries (p160)
- Diagonal Mar (p160)
- Maremàgnum (p105)

Best foot forward
- Camper (p135)
- Mango (p135)
- U-Casas (p85)

Best for presents
- Le Boudoir (p65)
- El Ingenio (p67)
- Olive (p84)
- Vinçon (p137)

Best specialist shops
- Arlequí Mascares (p83)
- Caelum (p65)
- Drap (p66)

Best local names
- Camper (p135)
- Custo Barcelona (p84)
- Mango (p135)
- Zara (p67)

Best for wine
- Torres (p97)
- Vila Viniteca (p85)
- Vinus & Brindis (p149)

Most photogenic
- Almacenes del Pilar (p64)
- La Boqueria (p72)
- Herboristeria del Rei (p67)
- Papabubble (p67)

DON'T MISS: 2009

Olive

The best possible taste

As a newly crowned gastro capital, Barcelona is designing itself into its own navel with an ever-growing range of shops that present food as modern art. For classy chocolates in classier packaging, head to Bubó (p84), Escribà (p72) and Enric Rovira (p151). Retro sweet shop chic is the order of the day at Papabubble (p67), whose USP is that the candy is cooked, stretched and rolled out right in front of you.

A new addition to the Born's foodie scene is Olive (p84), a shrine to the golden lifeblood of the Med, which, as well as stocking umpteen flavours of olive oil, has candles, cosmetics and myriad other things made from it. Also in the area is toasting house Casa Gispert (p84), for bags of nuts and coffee, while in the Barri Gòtic is the delightful Herboristeria del Rei (p67).

The fash pack

The success of Barcelona fashion fair Bread & Butter in July and, to a lesser extent, new fashion show Pasarela 080 in March, has created a buzz, throwing a spotlight on the city's fashion scene, particularly the indie labels. This translates in to a rash of tiny boutiques packed with unusual designs and posing of catwalk-like intensity in fashion hotspots such as C/Avinyó in the Barri Gòtic, the upper Raval, around C/Verdi in Gràcia and pretty much all of the Born.

Most famous of home-grown designers is Custo Barcelona, but for a good selection of interesting designers, try boutiques like Tribu (p67) and On Land (p84).

Open for business

Most small independent stores still open 10am-2pm and 5-8pm Monday to Saturday, but more shops are adopting a European timetable and staying open through the siesta period. Don't be surprised to see many shutters down on Saturday afternoons, especially in summer. Many shops close for at least two weeks in August. Except for the run up to Christmas, Sunday opening is still limited to shops in tourist zones such as La Rambla and the Maremàgnum. Many newspaper kiosks, bakeries and flower stalls are open Sunday mornings, and the majority of convenience stores stay open all day. Markets mostly open only until 2 or 3pm, though some stay open into the evening from Thursday to Saturday.

Shop tactics

Sales (*rebaixes* or *rebajas*) run from 7 January to mid February, and again during July and August. Tourist offices stock free Shopping Guide booklets, with a map and advice on everything, from how to get your VAT refund to using the Barcelona Shopping Line bus.

Money matters

With steep inflation and the plunge of the pound and the dollar against the euro, cheap shopping in Barcelona is a thing of the past. There are, however, a few things that are still less pricey here than abroad, including olive oil, cured ham, Spanish wines and home-grown designs like Zara (p67), Mango (p135) and Camper (p135). Bargaining should only be attempted at the Els Encants flea-market or when haggling over unofficial Barça strips on La Rambla; in shops, prices are fixed. As long as you're spending over €10 or so, all but the most cobwebby of places now accept major credit cards, although note that you will have to show ID, usually a passport. Chip-and-pin is slowly being introduced.

Sala Instinto

WHAT'S BEST
Nightlife

The big nightlife story of 2008 was La Paloma, the city's much-loved and long-running dancehall, which seemed to open and close, close and open, and single-handedly acted as a barometer for the Ajuntament's patience with the city's night-owls and, conversely, the most querulous of its citizens. At the time of writing La Paloma was, rather crucially, closed.

It's the same story as most other cities in Europe. Vociferous neighbourhood campaigns and a couple of mayors keen to be seen as giving the city back to its residents have resulted in a raft of closures and a dearth of exciting new venues. The news is not all bad, however. In a city with more DJs than palm trees, many bars and restaurants have employed laptop turntablists to conjure up beats from bytes to enhance the eating and drinking experience. This stems partly from the current impossibility of securing an 'entertainment licence' – which allows a venue to charge an admission fee and stay open until late. These resto-club combinations sometimes result in a certain personality disorder, yet if done well, can make for a unique night.

Other venues have been saved from closure after lengthy campaigns, as with the Harlem Jazz Club, or the little classic London Bar (p94). Some, such as the Sala Jazzroom (see box p79), have simply adapted and now host occasional one-off nights and parties.

SHORTLIST

Best new clubs
- Red Lounge Bar (p106)
- Sala Instinto (p116)
- Sala Monasterio (p102)

Best for big-time bands
- Bikini (p151)
- Razzmatazz (p160)
- Sala Apolo (p120)

Best for intimate gigs
- Jazz Sí Club (p94)
- London Bar (p94)
- Sala Monasterio (p102)
- Sidecar Factory Club (p69)

Best under the stars
- La Caseta del Migdia (p116)
- Danzatoria (p155)
- Elephant (p158)
- La Terrrazza (p117)

Best for spotting WAGs
- CDLC (p107)
- Mondo (p106)
- Shôko (p107)

Best for muscle marys
- Arena (p137)
- Metro (p139)
- Salvation (p139)

Best for tech-house
- Moog (p97)
- Pacha (p159)
- Space Barcelona (p139)
- La Terrrazza (p117)

Best for rare groove
- Diobar (p85)
- Red Lounge Bar (p106)
- Suite Royale (p103)

Best for spotting models
- Buda Restaurante (p137)
- Danzatoria (p155)
- Mondo (p106)

Best for a late drink
- Barcelona Pipa Club (p68)
- Big Bang (p94)
- La Concha (p97)

Moving out

But while the authorities seem intent on pursuing classic venues, they do support the non-traditional clubs outside the city centre. Clubs like Sala BeCool (p159) remain hassle-free in the middle of the financial district, far from nagging neighbours. At the port and far from the earshot of sleeping citizens, Mondo (p106) has been joined by the new Red Lounge Bar (p106).

Taxpayers also seem to be getting some of their money's worth from the über-expensive multifunctional public square in Poblenou called the Fòrum. All of the major music festivals except for Sónar have moved there: Primavera Sound, Wintercase, Summercase and BAM, as well as the new Weekend Dance festival. The metro and bus lines have even extended their weekend operating hours to address the growing demand for late-night transport.

FOOD, DRINK AND MUSIC SINCE 1997

A fusion place in the heart of Ciutat Vella that has always marked new tendencies

The menu has a range of unforgettable "mexiterranean" dishes: fried green tomatoes, guacamole, tamales and fajitas as well as delicious vegetarian dishes

Wonderful cocktails such as Margaritas, Mojitos, Caipirinhas feature on the amazing drinks list

Music of all eras and genres provides an atmosphere with something for everyone

When in Barcelona, visiting Margarita Blue is as essential as seeing the Sagrada Familia

Moving up

Still far from being New York or Paris, Barcelona has recently had a much needed shot of sophistication in the arm. Cocktail bars are popping up everywhere in a city that only a few years ago didn't know a cosmopolitan from a Manhattan, and whose most complicated drink involved ice, gin and tonic. Bars like Xix (p134), Club Mix (p85) and Omm Hotel (p175) strive to outdo each other's cocktail menus to entice the uptown crowd.

Musically, as everywhere, lounge is the new rock 'n' roll, and new clubs like Club Mix, Diobar (p85), and Suite Royale (p103) favour jazz funk and rare groove over four-to-the-floor house beats, which still reign supreme in places like La Terrrazza (p117).

Live music

Though Spanish and Catalan pop is pretty dire, on the whole, jazz, indie and electronica are well represented and local names to look out for at festivals such as BAM, Primavera Sound and Sónar include indie rockers Unfinished Sympathy, electro-popper Iris and 12Twelve,

an unclassifiable quartet bringing together free jazz, psychedelia and cosmic krautrock. Where Barcelona has had most international success is with *mestizaje* – a blend of influences including rock, flamenco, rai, hip hop, and various South American, Asian and African styles. Joining the *mestiza* top draws of Manu Chao, Ojos de Brujo and the Raval's 08001 are Dumballa Canalla, who fuse Catalan and gypsy folk into an electric vaudevillian performance.

The main venue for international names (as well as hotly tipped unknowns and local musicians) is the multi-faceted industrial space Razzmatazz, which in 2008 hosted acts from Megadeth to James Blunt. Moving into fallback position, Bikini used to net plenty of top-notch international names, but in 2008 was hosting acts along the lines of Sultans of Swing, a Dire Straits tribute band.

Old dancehalls Sala Apolo and Luz de Gas host several concerts a week. Global superstars perform in Montjuïc's stadiums, at the sprawling Fòrum, and at the new Espacio Movistar.

Club Mix

Teatre Nacional de Catalunya p31

WHAT'S BEST
Arts & Leisure

For a little town, Barcelona packs a wallop culturally, but it does depend very much on the season. Though some venues, such as the Auditori (p139) or the Palau de la Música (p76), have steady programming of music – world and jazz as well as classical – through the year, the opportunities to see theatre and dance do seem to culminate in late spring and early summer, before the city empties for most of July and August.

Festivals

Late spring is also when some of the sharpest arts festivals happen; the Festival del Grec (p36), which takes place from June to August, is the mother of all Barcelona festivals, attracting musicians, dance troupes and actors from all over the world; its open-air venues are magical on a summer night. The Marató de l'Espectacle (p39) is in June, with two nights of non-stop micro performances. Dies de Dansa (p39) offers three days of national and international dance in June and July, in sites such as the Port, the CCCB or the MACBA. Several music festivals are staged, the foremost of which are the Festival de Música Antiga (p38) and the Nous Sons (p37) festival of contemporary music, both in spring. In summer, the focus moves. Various museums hold small outdoor concerts and there are weekly events in several city parks, particularly as part of July's Clàssics als Parcs season (p39).

Film

After years of resistance to subtitled films (dubbed films, ironically, are often seen as more sophisticated), it's increasingly accepted that watching films in English might actually improve language skills. This is also partly down to the stifling of Castilian Spanish: if a film can't be seen dubbed in Catalan, hell, we'll watch it in English. Whatever the reason, it's good news for foreign filmgoers, who can now add the Casablanca-Gràcia (p140), Casablanca-Kaplan (p140) and Boliche (p159) to the list of cinemas showing *versión original* films.

Subtitled indie flicks are also shown at the Generalitat's new free film night at the Estació de França, Sessió Continua (p103), along with occasional outdoor cinema seasons, such as the Sala Montjuïc (www.salamontjuic.com) or Gandules in the patio of the CCCB (p88), both in July and August.

For undubbed, subtitled films, look for the letters 'VO' (*versió original*) in listings.

Classical music

Classical music was given a fillip recently thanks to the efforts of L'Auditori (p139), which has opened an additional 600-seater auditorium, installed the Museu de la Música (p126) and also overhauled its programming policy in the hope of attracting a new, younger audience. Its excellent concert cycles are worth catching, as are those at the Palau de la Música (p76).

In the world of opera, Barcelona has its own enfant terrible, Calixto Bieito, renowned for his wildly polemical interpretations of *Hamlet* and *Don Giovanni*, and more recently his staging of Michel Houellebecq's *Platform*. Look out,

DON'T MISS: 2009

SHORTLIST

New for filmgoers
- Boliche (p159)
- Casablanca-Gràcia (p140)
- Casablanca-Kaplan (p140)

Best for art-house movies
- FilmoTeca (p140)
- Méliès Cinemas (p140)
- Sessió Continua (p103)

Best concert halls
- L'Auditori (p139)
- Gran Teatre del Liceu (p72)
- Palau de la Música Catalana (p76)

Best for flamenco
- El Tablao de Carmen (p117)
- Los Tarantos (p70)

Best fun for little ones
- The beach (p106)
- L'Aquàrium (p106)
- IMAX cinema (p106)
- Zoo de Barcelona (p78)

too, for another local genius, Carles Santos, who composes, directs and performs in surreal operatic-cum-theatrical performances combining sex, psychology and sopranos.

Theatre & dance

As in so much of Europe, big brash theatrical productions still reign supreme, and in fact Catalan theatre has traditionally been very physical and reliant on spectacle, partly thanks to linguistic censorship under Franco. Born out of this tradition have come groups like La Fura dels Baus, whose focus on the physical has aided their huge success internationally.

There is little theatre performed in English in Barcelona beyond the occasional show as part of the Grec festival (p36), but look out for low-key productions by the local English-speaking group Black Custard.

BIKE TOURS BARCELONA
Daily bike tours

Enjoy the city on two wheels! We offer you daily guided bike tours **in English**. You'll get to see the "musts" in Barcelona off the typical tourist routes.

What you will see: Gothic Quarter, Cathedral, Old Harbour, Ciutadella Park, Sagrada Familia, Pedrera, Olympic Port and much more.

Tour Times
11,00 every day, from Jan 2 to Dec 31 (except 25 & 26 Dec)
16,30 Fri, Sat, Sun & Mon, from April 1 to Sep 15

Duration 3 hours including enough time to take photos and have a drink.

Price 22€ (includes bike, tourist guide and drink)

Meeting point Pl. Sant Jaume - outside the tourist office. ①

Reservations not necessary.
Look out for our guide in a red
t-shirt or our red bike.
If you are a group contact us
for a private bike tour.

bike tours
barcelona

T. (+34) 932 682 105
info@biketoursbarcelona.com
www.biketoursbarcelona.com

BIKE RENTAL
Barcelona at your own pace.

We offer you a **different, original and enviromentally friendly way to discover Barcelona**. At your own pace, stopping whenever and wherever you like. Low prices, child seats available, locks included.

Opening Hours
Open every day from 10 am to 7 pm

Rental Shop
c/Esparteria, 3
(parallel to Passeig del Born) ②

ONE LESS
BIKE TOURS & RENTAL

T. (+34) 932 682 105
info@bicicletabarcelona.com
www.bicicletabarcelona.com

Liceu — Ⓜ
PL. CATEDRAL ③
Jaume I — Ⓜ
LA RAMBLA
C. FERRAN
SANT JAUME ①
C. PRINCESA
VIA LAIETANA
PG. DEL BORN
C. ESPARTERIA ②
PLA DE PALAU
MARQUÈS D'ARGENTERA
PARC DE LA CIUTADELLA
PG. DE COLOM
RONDA LITORAL

TRIXI TOUR

Sit back and relax while one of our drivers shows you the city!

Tour Hours 11:00h - 20:00h
From March to November
Prices (2 people)
1/4 h.....6€
1/2 h.....10€
1 h.....18€
Stop Cathedral ③

www.trixi.com

Although the city has many thriving contemporary dance companies, there are few major dance venues for them to put on shows, and most companies spend a large amount of their time touring. Performers such as Pina Bausch and the Compañía Nacional de Danza (directed by the revered Nacho Duato) have played to sell-out crowds in the Teatre Nacional and the Liceu, while the Teatre Nacional has a resident company led by the indefatigable Sol Picó, and the Teatre Lliure hosts quite a lot of new work. However, it's generally difficult for companies to find big audiences.

Innovative ensembles such as Sol Picó and Mar Gómez usually run a new show every year, as do emblematic, influential companies such as Metros, Mudances and Gelabert-Azzopardi.

Family fun

Boys will be boys and will be entranced by a trip to the Nou Camp stadium (p152), either for a match or a tour of the grounds and museum. Other child-friendly attractions include the IMAX cinema (p106), L'Aquàrium (p106), the zoo (p78), the Font Màgica de Montjuïc (p110) and trips on the cable car (p116). Even the local museums are feeling the pull of small, sticky hands on the purse strings and provide an ever-growing choice of children's activities, from making chocolate figurines at the Museu de la Xocolata (p74) to blowing giant paint bubbles at CosmoCaixa (p155). There's also the beach, of course, and La Rambla (p70), with its entertainers, artists and living statues.

Gran Teatre del Liceu

Calendar

Jamie Cullum at Festival Internacional de Jazz de Barcelona p35

The following are the pick of the annual events that take place in Barcelona, as well as major one-off happenings. Further information and exact dates can be found nearer the time from the new *Time Out Barcelona* magazine, along with flyers and seasonal guides available from tourist offices (p185). For gay and lesbian events, look out for free magazines such as *Nois* and *Shanguide*.

Dates highlighted in **bold** are public holidays.

September 2008

Festival L'Hora del Jazz
Various venues
www.amjm.org
Three-week festival of local jazz acts, with free daytime concerts.

11 Diada Nacional de Catalunya
All over Barcelona
Flags and marches affirm cultural identity on Catalan National Day.

13-14 **Hipnotik**
CCCB (p88)
www.cccb.org
www.hipnotikfestival.com
A two-day festival that celebrates all that is hip hop.

Mid Sept **Festival Asia**
Various venues
www.casaasia.es/festival
Shows, music, workshops and stalls from 17 Asian countries, over a week.

Mid Sept **Weekend Dance**
Parc del Fòrum, Poblenou
www.weekendance.es
One-day electronic dance festival, which featured Faithless and Massive Attack in 2007.

Late Sept **Barcelona Arts de Carrer**
Various venues
www.artsdecarrer.org
Three-day street performance festival.

Week of 24 Sept **Mostra de Vins i Caves de Catalunya**
Moll de la Fusta, Port Vell
Tasting fair of local wines and cavas.

Festa del Tres Tombs

Week of 24 Sept **Barcelona Acció Musical (BAM)**
Various venues
www.bam.es
Around 40 concerts, mostly from local acts, and many free.

Week of 24 Sept **Festes de la Mercè**
All over Barcelona
www.bcn.cat/merce
Barcelona's biggest, brightest festival with fire-running, human castles, giants, concerts, an airshow, fireworks on the beach and more.

24 La Mercè

End Sept **Festa Major de la Barceloneta**
All over Barceloneta
www.cascantic.net
Festival fever fills the fishing quarter.

October 2008

LEM Festival
Various venues, Gràcia
www.gracia-territori.com
Month-long festival of multimedia art and experimental electronica.

11-12 **Caminada Internacional de Barcelona**
www.euro-senders.com/internacional
The International Walk is conducted along several different routes of varying lengths.

12 Dia de la Hispanitat

Late Oct **Festival de Tardor Ribermúsica**
Various venues, Born
www.ribermusica.org
Over 100 free music performances are held in squares, churches, bars and even shops.

23-26 **Art Futura**
Mercat de les Flors (p120)
www.artfutura.org
Digital and cyber art festival.

23-30 **In-Edit Beefeater Festival**
Cine Rex, Gran Via 463 & Aribau Club, Gran Via 565-567
www.in-edit.beefeater.es
Cinema festival of musical documentaries that range from jazz to flamenco.

31-**1 Nov La Castanyada**
All over Barcelona

All Saints' Day and the evening before are celebrated with piles of roast chestnuts and floral tributes at cemeteries.

November 2008

Ongoing La Castanyada (see Oct)

Nov **Wintercase Barcelona**
Sala Razzmatazz 1, C/Almogàvers 122, Poblenou
www.wintercase.com
Big-name indie bands.

1 Tots Sants (All Saints' Day)

1-30 Nov **Festival of Pocket Opera**
Various venues
www.festivaloperabutxaca.org
Contemporary opera. See box p41.

1 Nov-31 Dec **BAC!**
CCCB (p88) & other venues
www.cccb.org
www.bacfestival.com
Contemporary art festival.

14-22 **L'Alternativa**
CCCB (p88)
www.alternativa.cccb.org
Indie cinema festival.

Nov/Dec **Festival Internacional de Jazz de Barcelona**
Various venues
www.theproject.es
Jazz from bebop to big band.

December 2008

Ongoing Festival Internacional de Jazz de Barcelona (see Nov), BAC! (see Nov)

Els Grans del Gospel
Various venues
www.theproject.es
A three-week festival of gospel music.

1-24 **Fair of Sant Eloi**
C/Argenteria, Born
Christmas street fair for artisans, with live music playing from 6-8pm.

1-24 **Fira de Santa Llúcia**
Pla de la Seu & Avda de la Catedral, Barri Gòtic
www.bcn.cat/nadal

Fira de Santa Llúcia is a Christmas market with trees, decorations and nativity-scene figures.

6 Día de la Constitució

8 La Immaculada

16-21 **Drap Art**
CCCB (p88)
www.drapart.org
An international creative recycling festival, with concerts, performances, workshops and a Christmas market.

Late Dec **BAF (Belles Arts Festival)**
Sala Apolo (p120)
One day avant-garde, non-commercial art and performance, with music and DJs until dawn.

25 Nadal (Christmas Day)

26 Sant Esteve (Boxing Day)

28 Día dels Inocents
Local version of April Fool's Day, with paper figures attached to the backs of unsuspecting victims.

31 Cap d'Any (New Year's Eve)
Swill cava and eat a grape for every chime of the clock at midnight. Wear red underwear for good luck.

January 2009

1 Any Nou (New Year's Day)

5 Cavalcada dels Reis
All over Barcelona
www.bcn.cat/nadal
The three kings (Melchior, Gaspar and Balthasar) head a grand parade around town from 5-9pm.

6 Reis Mags (Three Kings)

Mid Jan-Mar **Tradicionàrius**
Various locations, mainly in Gràcia
www.tradicionarius.com
Cycle of concert performances of traditional and popular Catalan music.

17 Festa dels Tres Tombs
Around Mercat Sant Antoni & Raval
www.xarxantoni.net
Neighbourhood festival celebrating St Anthony's day.

Grec is the word

Argentine Ricardo Szwarcer takes over the Grec Festival.

Ricardo Szwarcer

The long-running **Grec Festival** (p39) – named for the spectacular Greek-style amphitheatre that forms its signature venue – is the last big bash of the season before performance spaces close and the city slides into sultry summertime.

In its 32 years it has become such a local institution that the recent appointment of Argentine director Ricardo Szwarcer caused quite a stir. We talked to him about his plans for the festival.

What's your background?
In Buenos Aires I worked in contemporary dance, theatre and opera at the San Martín and Colón theatres. I spent ten years in France with Lille Opera and seven freelancing in London.

Why were you picked for Grec?
They wanted an outsider, a fresh point of view. I don't have any political attachments, so I have no problem changing anything.

Tell us about the festival.
The Grec is eclectic by nature. It started out as a selection of all the best shows of the year and at one time incorporated 160 acts. I'm concentrating on putting about 60

events into five weeks – I need to know exactly with what and whom I'm working; what I'm opening with, and how much support I'm giving to local companies. It's a short festival so I try not to create competition between the shows.

Which is?
The amphitheatre itself: it may not be a real one but the proportions are excellent and Montjuïc mountain at the back creates an intense atmosphere. We're working on projects with the venue in mind, some envisaged for Greek or Roman theatres.

Sell it to us.
We've got more adventurous combinations including contemporary spins on traditional stuff and a big international component. There are Chinese-Belgian and British-Iranian contemporary dance collaborations and an ambitious opera on the agenda. Equally importantly, the Grec is a spotlight for local talent. Quality is key. There are 116 festivals in Barcelona, there's only one Grec.
■ www.bcn.cat/grec

Last weekend **Sa Pobla a Gràcia**
Gràcia, around Plaça Diamant
www.bcn.cat
Two days of festivities drawn from
Mallorcan folk culture.

February 2009

Ongoing Tradicionàrius (see Jan)

Feb **Festival Internacional de Percussió**
L'Auditori (p139)
www.auditori.org
International percussion festival.

Feb-Mar **Nous Sons – Músiques Contemporànies**
L'Auditori (p139) & CCCB (p88)
www.auditori.org
International contemporary music at
the three-week New Sounds festival.

Feb-Mar **Xcèntric Film Festival**
CCCB (p88)
www.cccb.org/xcentric
Avant-garde festival showcasing short
films and videos.

Week of 12 Feb **Santa Eulàlia**
All over Barcelona
www.bcn.cat/santaeulalia
Blowout winter festival in honour of
Santa Eulàlia, co-patron saint of the
city and a particular favourite of children. Expect many kids' activities.

21-24 **Carnival**
All over Barcelona
www.bcn.cat/carnaval
King Carnestoltes leads the fancy dress
parades and street parties before being
burned on Ash Wednesday.

Late Feb **Minifestival de Música Independent de Barcelona**
Les Basses, C/Teide 20, Nou
Barris
www.minifestival.net
One-day festival of eclectic indie
sounds from around the world.

Late Feb **Barcelona Visual Sound**
Various venues
www.bcnvisualsound.org
Ten-day showcase for untried film talent covering shorts, documentaries,
animation and web design.

March 2009

Ongoing Nous Sons (see Feb),
Tradicionàrius (see Jan), Xcèntric
Film Festival (see Feb)

2 **Marató Barcelona**
Starts & finishes at Plaça de
Espanya
www.maratobarcelona.com
City marathon.

3 **Festes de Sant Medir de Gràcia**
Gràcia
www.santmedir.org
People riding decorated horse-drawn
carts shower the crowds with blessed
boiled sweets.

Week of 17 March **El Feile**
Various venues
www.elfeile.com
Irish festival of music, dance and
stand-up comedy for Saint Patrick's.

April 2009

Apr-June **Festival Guitarra**
Various venues
www.theproject.es
Guitar festival spanning everything
from flamenco to jazz.

6-13 **Setmana Santa (Holy Week)**
Palm fronds are blessed at the cathedral on Palm Sunday at the start of
Holy Week, and children receive elaborate chocolate creations.

10 **Divendres Sant (Good Friday)**

13 **Dilluns de Pasqua (Easter Monday)**

23 **Sant Jordi**
La Rambla & all over Barcelona
Feast day of Sant Jordi (St George), the
patron saint of Catalonia. Couples
exchange gifts of red roses and books.

End Apr-early May **BAFF Barcelona Asian Film Festival**
Various venues
www.baff-bcn.org
Digital cinema, non-commercial films
and anime from Asia.

Late Apr **Dia de la Terra**
Passeig Lluis Companys, Born
www.diadelaterra.org
Two-day eco-festival.

Late Apr-early May **Feria de Abril de Catalunya**
Fòrum area
www.fecac.com
Satellite of Seville's famous fair with decorated marquees, flamenco and manzanilla sherry.

Late Apr-mid May **Festival de Música Antiga**
L'Auditori (p139)
www.auditori.org
Cycle of ancient music.

May 2009

Ongoing Festival Guitarra (see Apr), BAFF Barcelona Asian Film Festival (see Apr), Feria de Abril de Catalunya (see Apr), Festival de Música Antiga (see Apr)

1 Dia del Treball (May Day)
Various venues
Mass demonstrations across town, led by trade unionists.

Early May **Festival Internacional de Poesia**
All over Barcelona
www.bcn.cat/barcelonapoesia
Week-long city-wide poetry festival, with readings in English.

Early May **La Cursa del Corte Inglés**
All over Barcelona
www.elcorteingles.com
Over 50,000 participants attempt the seven-mile race.

11 Sant Ponç
C/Hospital, Raval
www.bcn.cat
Street market of herbs, honey and candied fruit to celebrate the day of Saint Ponç, patron saint of herbalists.

18 Dia Internacional dels Museus
All over Barcelona
http://icom.museum/imd.html
Free entrance to the city's museums.

Mid May **Festa Major de Nou Barris**
Nou Barris
www.bcn.cat
Neighbourhood festival famous for outstanding flamenco.

Late May **Festival de Flamenco de Ciutat Vella**
CCCB (p88) & other venues
www.tallerdemusics.com
The Old City Flamenco Festival, with concerts, films and children's activities.

Late May-late June **Festival de Música Creativa i Jazz de Ciutat Vella**
All over Old City
www.bcn.cat/agenda
The Old City Festival of Creative Music and Jazz.

Late May **La Tamborinada**
Parc de la Ciutadella, Born
www.fundaciolaroda.net
A one-day festival of concerts, workshops and circus performances.

Mid May **Loop Festival**
Various venues
www.loop-barcelona.com
Experimental video art festival.

Late May-early June **Primavera Sound**
Fòrum area
www.primaverasound.com
Big-name three-day music festival and the Soundtrack Film Festival.

31 Segona Pascua (Whitsun)

June 2009

Ongoing Festival Guitarra (see Apr), Festival de Música Creativa i Jazz de Ciutat Vella (see May), Primavera Sound (see May)

June-July **De Cajón**
Various venues
www.theproject.es
Series of top-class flamenco concerts.

Early June **Festa dels Cors de la Barceloneta**
Barceloneta
www.bcn.cat

De Cajón

Choirs sing and parade on Saturday morning and Monday afternoon.

Early June **Marató de l'Espectacle**
Mercat de les Flors (p120)
www.marato.com
Anarchic performance marathon, over two nights.

11-13 **L'Ou com Balla**
Cathedral cloisters & other venues
www.bcn.cat/icub
Corpus Christi processions and the unusual L'Ou Com Balla – for which hollowed-out eggs have a dance on specially decorated fountains.

Mid June **Sónar**
Various venues
www.sonar.es
The Festival of Advanced Music and Multimedia Art – electronic music, urban art and media technologies.

Mid June **Festa de la Música**
All over Barcelona
www.festadelamusica
Free international music festival with amateur musicians from 100 countries.

Late June **Gran Trobada d'Havaneres**
Passeig Joan de Borbó, Barceloneta
www.bcn.cat/icub
Sea shanties with fireworks and cremat (flaming spiced rum).

June-Aug **Festival del Grec**
Various venues
www.bcn.cat/grec
Two-month spree of dance, music and theatre all over the city.

23-24 **Sant Joan**
All over Barcelona
Summer solstice means cava, all-night bonfires and fireworks.

July 2009

Ongoing De Cajón (see June), Festival del Grec (see June)

July **B-estival**
Poble Espanyol (p114)
www.b-estival.com
Three weeks of blues, soul, R&B and more in a 'festival of rhythm'.

July **Clàssics als Parcs**
Various venues
www.bcn.cat/parcsijardin
Free alfresco classical music, played by a variety of young performers in Barcelona's parks.

Early July **Dies de Dansa**
Various venues
www.marato.com
Dance performances in public spaces dotted around the city.

Mid July **Festa Major del Raval**
Raval
www.bcn.cat/icub

Over three days, events include giants, a fleamarket, children's workshops and free concerts on the Rambla del Raval.

Mid July **Downtown Reggae Festival**
Camp de Futbol La Satalia,
Passeig de la Exposició, Poble Sec
www.downtownreggae.net
A free Jamaican music festival puts on dancehall reggae from 5pm-2am.

Mid July **Summercase**
Parc del Fòrum
www.summercase.com
A weekend-long music festival that pulls in big indie names.

Late July-early Sept **Mas i Mas Festival**
Various venues
www.masimas.com
The best of Latin music in Barcelona.

August 2009

Ongoing Festival del Grec (see June), Mas i Mas Festival (see July)

Every Wed **Summer Nights at CaixaForum**
CaixaForum (p110)
www.fundacio.lacaixa.es
All exhibitions are open until midnight with music, films and other activities.

Every Wed & Fri **Jazz in Ciutadella Park**
Parc de la Ciutadella, Born
www.bcn.cat/parcsijardins
Free 10pm shows from jazz trios and quartets in front of the fountain.

Every Tue-Thur **Gandules**
CCCB (p88)
www.cccb.org
A series of outdoor films screened to the deckchair-strewn patio of the CCCB.

15 L'Assumpció (Assumption Day)

Week of 16 Aug **Festa de Sant Roc**
Barri Gòtic
www.bcn.cat
The Barri Gòtic's party with parades, fireworks, traditional street games and fire-running.

Late Aug **Festa Major de Gràcia**
Gràcia
www.festamajordegracia.org
A best-dressed street competition, along with giants and human castles.

Late Aug **Festa Major de Sants**
Sants
www.festamajordesants.org
Traditional neighbourhood festival with street parties, concerts and fire-running.

B-estival p39

Pocket watch

November's Festival d'Ôpera de Butxaca i Noves Creacions (**Festival of Pocket Opera**, p35) takes a contemporary, often quirky, slant on chamber opera, featuring small-format, hour-long musical numbers that tend to be solo performances with a handful of musicians.

Director Toni Rumbau's background is in puppetry, while producer Dietrich Grosse worked with Catalan dance company Lanònima Imperial. The two met at a celebratory dinner, having both been awarded the Ciutat de Barcelona prize. Puppets and dancers feature in the festival, and occasionally combine.

The first show was held in 1993 on a 3.5sq m (38sq ft) micro-stage in basement theatre Malic and went down a storm with a packed audience of 60. Since then Pocket Opera has expanded its repertoire into an eight-piece programme. When the Malic closed in 2002, the festival inherited its public funding and began to roam the city looking for likely venues, such as L'Auditori and the former Convent dels Àngels.

About half the pieces are international collaborations. The British Council co-organised a Peter Maxwell Davies cycle in 2006 and German Staatstheater Darmstadt produced Agustí Charles' and Marc Rosich's Catalan opera *La Cuzzoni* in 2007.

Themes reflect today's issues. In 2007, Croatian singer Katarina Livljanić brought medieval texts to life in the Santa Ágata chapel. In 2008, Catalan countertenor Xavier Sabata sings Baroque texts in a piece about *los capones*, the Spanish castrati. In 2009, puppets will take on Jean-Jacques Rousseau.

Local composers Ramón Humet and Héctor Parra, also feature in 2009. The former, winner of the Olivier Messiaen music prize in 2007, provides the score for poet Mario Lucarda's Spanish language homage to choreographer Martha Graham. Parra, meanwhile, puts music to American theoretical physicist Lisa Randall's study on string theory in a show likely to be unique to Barcelona, if not the world.

■ www.fobnc.org

September 2009

Ongoing Mas i Mas Festival
(see July)

Sept **Festival L'Hora del Jazz**
See above Sept 2008.

11 Diada Nacional de Catalunya
See above Sept 2008.

Mid Sept **Festival Asia**
See above Sept 2008.

Mid Sept **Hipnotik**
See above Sept 2008.

Mid Sept **Weekend Dance**
See above Sept 2008.

Late Sept **Barcelona Arts
de Carrer**
See above Sept 2008.

Week of Sept 24 **Mostra de Vins
i Caves de Catalunya**
See above Sept 2008.

Week of Sept 24 **Barcelona
Acció Musical (BAM)**
See above Sept 2008.

Week of Sept 24 **La Mercè**
See above Sept 2008.

24 La Mercè

End Sept **Festa Major de
la Barceloneta**
See above Sept 2008.

October 2009

Oct **LEM Festival**
See above Oct 2008.

12 Dia de la Hispanitat

Late Oct **Caminada Internacional**
See above Oct 2008.

Late Oct **Festival de Tardor
Ribermúsica**
See above Oct 2008.

Late Oct **Art Futura**
See above Oct 2008.

Late Oct-early Nov **In-Edit
Beefeater Festival**
See above Oct 2008.

31-**1 Nov La Castanyada**
See above Oct 2008.

November 2009

Ongoing La Castanyada (see Oct);
In-Edit Beefeater Festival (see Oct)

Nov **Festival of Pocket Opera**
See above Nov 2008.

Nov **Wintercase Barcelona**
See above Nov 2008.

Nov-Dec **BAC!**
See above Nov 2008.

1 Tots Sants (All Saints' Day)

Nov **L'Alternativa**
See above Nov 2008.

Nov/Dec **Festival International
de Jazz de Barcelona**
See above Dec 2008.

December 2009

Ongoing Festival de Jazz de
Barcelona (see Nov), BAC!
(see Nov)

Dec **Els Grans del Gospel**
See above Nov 2008.

1-24 Dec **Fair of Sant Eloi**
See above Dec 2008.

1-24 **Fira de Santa Llúcia**
See above Dec 2008.

6 Día de la Constitución

8 La Immaculada

Mid Dec **Drap Art**
See above Dec 2008.

Late Dec **BAF (Belles Arts
Festival)**
See above Dec 2008.

25 Nadal (Christmas Day)

26 Sant Esteve (Boxing Day)

28 **Día dels Inocents**
See above Dec 2008.

31 **Cap d'Any (New Year's Eve)**
See above Dec 2008.

Itineraries

Picasso's Barcelona

'Barcelona, beautiful and bright', was how Picasso remembered the city where he spent his formative years. He arrived just before his 14th birthday and the seven years he spent here were to be a huge influence on his work, most directly that from the Blue Period, although Barcelona continued to feature heavily even in his later paintings, when he had not been back for many years.

A tour of Picasso's Barcelona is a full-day itinerary; to trace his time in the city in roughly chronological order, start where the Born meets Barceloneta by the Pla del Palau. When Picasso and his family first arrived in the city in the autumn of 1895, they lived here, at C/Reina Cristina 3, on the corner of C/Llauder. Just over the road, at C/Consolat de

Mar 2, is La Llotja, the old stock exchange that, in those days, housed the art school where Picasso's father worked as a tutor. At just 15 years old, Picasso breezed through the entrance exam and shone as a student of realist painter Antoni Caba.

From here, cross over Via Laietana to C/Mercè 3, the next Picasso family home, now destroyed. While still living with his parents, Picasso also rented a series of studios that often doubled up as overnight accommodation; his first, which he shared with his fellow art student and lifelong friend, Manuel Pallares, was almost next door on C/Plata 4. In the 1890s, the whole harbour area was a red-light district filled with drunks, sailors and beggars, and Picasso

Museu Picasso p76

soon developed a fascination with the low life around him. On the right, the once notorious C/Avinyó was lined with brothels and inspired his Cubist masterpiece, *Les Demoiselles d'Avignon* (1907).

Continue along C/Mercè and turn right on La Rambla then left along C/Nou de la Rambla to another of Picasso's bedsit-studios at no.10, which at the time was next door to his favourite sleazy cabaret venue, the Edén Concert. At this point Picasso was living in great poverty and had to resort to burning some of his work to keep warm. His Blue Period (1901-1904) reflects this time of personal hardship and the poverty he witnessed around him: two famous examples include the *Old Guitarist* (1903) and *Life* (1903). This particular studio also happened to be directly opposite Gaudí's newly built Palau Güell. While Picasso was no great fan of Gaudí, art critic Robert Hughes and artist Ellsworth Kelly both suggest that the bright colours and fragmented mosaics of the terrace

chimneys might have sown the seeds of Picasso's cubism, developed several years later.

Back on La Rambla, walk up towards Plaça Catalunya; turn right up C/Cardenal Casañas and then turn left at C/Petritxol. The Sala Parès gallery at no.5 was a meeting point for the fin-de-siècle Barcelona set, hosting debates and concerts, and also exhibited the work of the young Picasso in 1901, along with that of Ramon Casas.

At the top of C/Petritxol turn right on C/Portaferrissa and up the broad shopping avenue of Portal de l'Àngel. About halfway up on the right is C/Montsió, where, at no.3, is the most famous symbol of Picasso's days in Barcelona: **Els Quatre Gats** (p61).

Luxuriantly designed by Catalan Modernista architect Puig i Cadafalch, this tavern was inspired by Le Chat Noir in Montmartre and run by the decidedly eccentric art lover, Pere Romeu. It was the hub of bohemian Barcelona with political debates, poetry readings, music recitals and, of course, countless art exhibitions. From 1899 to the time he left, almost all of Picasso's closest friends were members of the circle he met here, including the writer and artist Carles Casagemas whose suicide in 1901 also coloured the doleful Blue Period. Picasso even designed the menu illustration, which is still used today (the original is displayed in the Museu Picasso) and held his first exhibition here in February 1900 at the age of 19, featuring his portraits of many of the café's prominent habitués. If you stop here for lunch, come as early as possible to beat the queues of tourists; the place is no gastro temple but does serve decent Catalan favourites and has a reasonably priced set lunch (the menu is posted daily online).

After lunch head back down Portal de l'Àngel; on the corner of Plaça Nova, opposite the cathedral, is the Col·legi d'Arquitectes (Association of Architects). Its façade is decorated with a graffiti-style triptych of Catalan folk scenes, from a design drawn by Picasso while in exile in the 1950s and sculpted by Norwegian Carl Nesjar in 1961. Known as the *Three Friezes of the Mediterranean*, the section on C/Capellans celebrates the Senyera (Catalan flag); the section facing Plaça Nova features the *gegants* (giant figures that head traditional processions) and the section facing C/Arcs depicts dancing children. Ask inside to be directed to two interior friezes depicting a *sardana* dance and a wall of arches. The somewhat uncharacteristic style is said to come from Picasso's reported insistence that it was 'very easy to do a Miró' when the latter was mooted for the interior friezes.

Then it's time to head over to the Born for an afternoon at the

Museu Picasso (p76), currently in the middle of expansion. A converted old orphanage on C/Flassaders will open on to Plaça Jaume Sabartés, named after Picasso's lifelong Barcelona friend and personal secretary. This addition will also create a pedestrian thoroughfare and a new back patio, which will be named after Raimon Noguera, another good Barcelona friend of Picasso's.

Refresh with a coffee and snack in the luxurious museum café. It's an airy space with stone arches and squishy sofas serving up light dishes such as brie panini, rosemary focaccia, or scallop and grapefruit salad from a menu with good-resolution titles like Today I Feel Like a Sandwich, or Today I Will Take Care of Myself With a Delicious Salad.

Finish off with a stroll down C/Princesa to the Ciutadella park. Just down Passeig Picasso from the entrance stands Antoni Tàpies' 1981 centenary monument, *Homage to Picasso*. Commissioned by the Ajuntament, the water-covered glass cube and its contents quickly fell prey to the depredations of mould and graffiti, though the sculpture was renovated by Pere Casanovas for the Year of Picasso 2006. The sculpture within the cube is an assemblage of Modernista period furniture, cut through by white iron beams and draped cloth. This reflects the importance of industry and the working-class rebellion against wealthy Catalan society during Picasso's time in Barcelona. Quotations by the artist himself decorate the bottom of the sculpture, notably one stressing the social function of art, a motto which Tàpies took for his own: 'A painting is not intended to decorate a drawing room but is instead a weapon of attack and defence against the enemy.'

Route with a view

Once the bedrock of a feared bastion of suppression by a brutal faraway government, then a vast area of pleasure gardens for the idle rich and, more recently, the stage for the fabulously successful 1992 Olympics, the hill of Montjuïc has played many roles over the centuries. Nowadays, its formidable castle is being converted into the Centre for Peace, and access has been improved so that all citizens can make the most of its well-tended parks and treasury of museums and sculptures.

The possible routes are numerous, but following this one you can stroll around many of its attractions in an hour or two. If you plan to step into any of the museums, however, we'd allow a full day. Bear in mind, too, that eating options are limited up here, and carry water in summer.

Start at the lower entrance to the Poble Sec metro station and head up C/Badas to the gardens of the **Teatre Grec**, then take the gateway to the right of the amphitheatre. From here, head up to the **Fundació Miró** via the **Escales del Generalife**, a series of trickling fountains, flanked by stone steps, olive trees and benches, named after the water gardens of Granada's Alhambra palace. Instead of taking the steps, however, turn right into the **Jardins Laribal**, designed – like the Escales – by French landscape architect Jean-Claude Nicolas Forestier at the start of the last century. Ahead lie the **Colla de l'Arròs** rose gardens, at their best in late spring. From here, a long pergola leads up to the **Font del Gat** (Fountain of the Cat), a clearing on the slope with the rather modest fountain itself and a small restaurant – the perfect lunch stop if you've decided to spend an hour or two at the nearby Miró.

With your back to the restaurant follow the path east towards the Miró and you'll arrive at a clearing, in the middle of which is Josep Viladomat's bronze **Noia de la Trena** (Girl with a Plait). Straight ahead is the stone **Repòs**, also by Viladomat, a scaled-up version of a Manolo Hugué figure, undertaken when Hugué was too ill to finish the commission.

Turn right on to the Avda Miramar where, opposite the Miró museum, you'll find a flight of steps which lead up and around to the **Tres Pins nursery**, where grow the city's plants. From here the Avda Miramar runs seaward, past the **Plaça Dante Alighieri**. In front of Dante, and in contrast to his stern salute, stands Josep Llimona's curvaceous and coquettish **Bellesa** (Beauty).

At the end of this road is the Miramar area, fronted by formal gardens, the station for the cablecar over the port, and slightly south and below it, the **Costa i Llobera** cactus gardens. Backtracking, a road leads behind the hotel up the hill towards the castle, passing the Joan Brossa gardens en route. These were created on the site of the old fairground, and some of the stone statues from the time (such as Charlie Chaplin) are still in place. Just outside the gardens is the **Sardana**, a representation of the Catalan national dance. Cross the road here to walk up via the fountains and ceramic mosaics of the **Mirador de l'Alcalde**. From here the **Camí del Mar**, with great views out to sea, runs alongside the **castle** and, after five minutes or so, eventually to the **Mirador del Migdia**, one of the few places in Barcelona from which you can watch the sun set. There is a picnic area or, if you're lucky, La Caseta de Migdia, a wonderful outdoor café, might be open.

From here a path runs around the landward side of the castle – follow this until you reach the **cablecar** station and take the steps down on the left. Follow as straight a path as you can, cutting across various flights of steps, and turn right on the road at the bottom, which then curves round to the left. Here you'll arrive at an entrance to the **Jardins Mossèn Cinto**. The gardens are dedicated to the poet Jacint Verdaguer and specialise in bulbous plants (such as daffodils, hyacinths – *jacint* in Catalan – and tulips) and various types of waterlilies, with a series of terraced ponds running down the hillside to a small lake.

Exiting from the lower side of these gardens, turn left to catch the funicular down the hill to Avda Paral·lel and the metro.

Fundació Miró p47

Can Paixano

Rags to riches

In Barcelona for a couple of days? From Thursday night to Saturday evening, see how both halves live, with a bit of Barcelona on the cheap followed by a decadent splurge.

If you get to town in time, head to the **Picasso Museum** (p76) for 6pm. Every Thursday, at this hour, there are guided tours in English for no extra charge. After this, return to C/Princesa and turn right until you see C/Allada-Vermell on the left: up here is a good spot for a bargain alfresco pre-dinner drink, at **Casa Paco** (p79). The house mojitos are very big and very strong and won't break the bank. Over the road, the tiny and chaotic (in a good way) sister establishment, **Pizza Paco** (no.11, mobile 670 338 992) serves up good cheap pizzas, loud music and party attitude at its rickety tables.

When you're fed and watered, head back on to C/Princesa and bear left to C/Comerç. Turn right

and walk all the way to the end to catch a free film at **Sessió Contínua** (p103) held every Thursday at 9pm alongside the Estació de França train station, but note you need to send them an email in advance.

Turn left out of here and go down Avda Marquès de l'Argentera until you hit **Sala Monasterio** (p102) under the arcades of the Passeig Isabel II. This underground bar holds free blues jam sessions every Thursday night. When the wee hours start to get big again, cross over the road to dive bar, **Flor del Norte** (Passeig Colom 10, 93 315 26 59) for the cheapest after-hours drinks in the old town.

Friday morning will probably be a late starter (the really hardy may want to plough on through), so breakfast on the hair of the dog with a cheap-as-chips champagne breakfast in the same area, at **Can Paixano** (p98), where a coupe of house cava costs just 80¢ or you can get two sausage sandwiches and a whole bottle of cava for under €10. Just try to ignore the fact that you're standing ankle-deep in sawdust and used napkins.

For a great-value coffee chaser with a view, it's a mere hop over Ronda del Litoral to the **Museu d'Història de Catalunya** (p104). Take the lift up to the top floor (there's no need to buy a ticket) to the little-known **Miranda del Museu** roof café (p105) and stroll out on to the vast terrace for sweeping city views.

Then it's time for some complimentary culture. From Passeig Joan de Borbó take the 157 bus all the way to Plaça Espanya and then walk up Avda Reina Maria Cristina and turn right on to Avda Marquès de Comillas to reach the **CaixaForum** (p110). This impressive Modernista masterpiece has free entry and three excellent art and photography exhibition spaces that regularly host the most high-profile displays in the city.

Head back to the top of Avda Reina Maria Cristina and carry on straight down Avda Rius i Taulet to the end, right and then left on C/França Xica and its continuation C/Annibal until you see the Plaça Sortidor down on the left. Grab one of the terrace tables at the colourful **La Soleá** (p119), a charming Poble Sec restaurant which serves up an excellent lunch menu for under €7.

After lunch, walk down C/Blasco de Garay to Avda Paral·lel, turn left and catch the green metro line uptown to Diagonal. Walk downhill one block to Gaudí's **La Pedrera** (p128). Although visitors must pay (and queue interminably) to see the roof and apartment, entrance to the excellent art exhibitions run by the Caixa de Catalunya on the first floor is free and you can still appreciate the wonderful interiors

Palau Dalmases

of the building. Backtrack two blocks up Passeig de Gràcia and turn right on Avda Diagonal for a block to visit Puig i Cadafalch's Modernista masterpiece, the **Palau Baró de Quadras**. Entrance is free and the building is no less wonderful on the inside, with the added bonus that it houses the **Casa Àsia** (p121) cultural foundation, which lays on high-quality, free exhibitions. Continue along Avda Diagonal and take the third right down C/Girona for a spot of bargain shopping at the many discount outlets lining this street, including the ever popular **Mango Outlet** (C/Girona 37, 93 412 29 35), with last season's pieces at a fraction of the price.

Head back to your hotel or apartment to get gussied up and prepare for the splurging part of the holiday to begin. Again this begins on C/Montcada in the Born, for pre-dinner cocktails and opera arias at **Espai Barroc** (no.20, 93 310 06 73)

located in the 17th-century Palau
Dalmases. The dour old doorman
is unabashedly snotty about
turning away anyone who doesn't
look like they own their own yacht,
so dress accordingly. Entrance is
€10. Then work up an appetite with
a ten-minute stroll across Avda
Marquès de l'Argentera and over
to the Barceloneta district, walking
all the way down Passeig Joan de
Borbó to the bottom of the marina
to the cable-car tower. Take the lift
80 metres up to the **Torre d'Alta
Mar** (no.88, 93 221 00 07, www.
torredealtamar.com), a schmick
restaurant with unbeatable
panoramic views over Barcelona
and the Med. To dance it all off
afterwards, take a ten-minute walk
along the beachfront to **CDLC**
(p107) for a pose-off with local
celebs, models and footballers.

On Saturday morning, rise above
the hoi polloi by heading uptown
to the swanky neighbourhood of
Pedralbes, where shiny SUVs
gleam alongside enormous
mansions. Take the green metro
line to Palau Reial, which brings
you to the lower edge of the
manicured pleasure gardens of
the **Palau Reial de Pedralbes**
(p156). Stroll past the pampered
palms and around the small lake
to the palace, built in the 1920s
and briefly the royal residence
in Barcelona. Head inside to visit
the three quiet museums now
accumulated under the name of the
Museu de les Arts Aplicades
(p156): the Museu de les Arts
Decoratives, with furniture,
tapestries and jewellery dating
from the Middle Ages; the Museu
de Ceràmica with a collection of
Spanish ceramics including works
by Picasso and Miró; and the Museu
Tèxtil, a clothing museum recently
transplanted here from the Born.

Before the construction of the
palace, this land formed part of

the Güell estate. Eusebi Güell
was Gaudí's main patron and
commissioned him to design the
gatehouses and entrance. For a
more exclusive Gaudí experience
than the tourist-thronged Park
Güell, walk back down through
the gardens of the Palau Reial, left
on Avda Diagonal and left again
up Avda Pedralbes and look for
the ornately decorated mosaic
turrets. Although the houses are
only accessible by guided tour (in
English at 10.15am and 12.15pm
Monday to Friday), passers-by
can still admire the exteriors and
Gaudí's famous wrought-iron gate
in the form of a snarling dragon.

From here, cross over Avda
Pedralbes and, facing down the hill,
take the first turning on the left to
have lunch at **Neichel** (C/Beltrán
i Rózpide 1-5, 93 203 84 08, www.
neichel.es), a French restaurant that
is one of the favourite domains of
the Catalan moneyed classes.

After what is sure to be an epic
lunch, stagger back out on the Avda
Pedralbes and catch either the no.63
or the no.78 bus right up to the top
of the avenue to see the 14th-century
Gothic convent of **Monestir de
Pedralbes** (p156). Walk up the
Baixada del Monestir past the lovely
rose gardens to enter the nunnery
and view a breathtaking three-
storey cloister, along with well-
preserved kitchens and refectory.

Head back down the Baixada
del Monestir and turn left on to
the Plaça Pedralbes to catch the
no.22 bus for the long ride down
to the centre. Get off where it turns
off Avda Diagonal on to Passeig
de Gràcia to splash some cash at
the myriad designer shops. Finish
off by walking one block east to
C/Pau Claris, and up over Avda
Diagonal where it's time to show
off your shopping bags and enjoy
some classy tapas and a vermouth
at **Bar Mut** (p129).

ITINERARIES

Barcelona by Area

La Rambla

Barri Gòtic
& La Rambla

Barri Gòtic

There are few more atmospheric places in the world than this wonderfully preserved medieval quarter. The centrepiece, of course, is the **cathedral**, but nearby an equally grand cluster of buildings from the Middle Ages has as its heart the **Plaça del Rei**, where you'll find the former royal palace (**Palau Reial Major**). The complex houses the **Museu d'Història de la Ciutat** and some of Barcelona's most historically significant buildings: the **chapel of Santa Àgata** and the 16th-century watchtower (**Mirador del Rei Martí**). Parts of the palace are believed to date back to the tenth

century, and there have been many additions to it since, notably the 14th-century Saló del Tinell, a medieval banqueting hall. It is here that Ferdinand and Isabella are said to have received Columbus on his return from America.

For the last 2,000 years, however, the heart of the city has been Plaça Sant Jaume, where the main Roman axes used to cross. The **Temple of Augustus** stood where these streets met, and four of its columns can still be seen in C/Pietat. The square now contains the stolid neo-classical façade of the municipal government (**Ajuntament**) and the Renaissance seat of the Catalan regional government (**Palau de la Generalitat**), opposite each other.

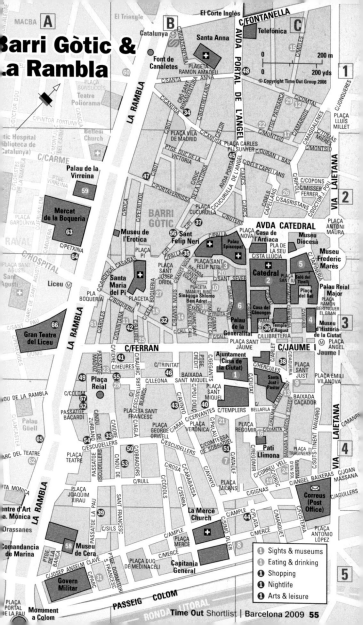

Sights & museums

Ajuntament (City Hall)

Plaça Sant Jaume (93 402 70 00/special visits 93 402 73 64/www.bcn.cat). Metro Jaume I or Liceu. **Open** *Office* 8.30am-2.30pm Mon-Fri. *Visits* 10am-1pm Sun. **Admission** free. **Map** p55 C3 ❶

The centrepiece and oldest part of the Casa de la Ciutat is the dignified 15th-century Saló de Cent, which is flanked by the semicircular Saló de la Reina Regent and the Saló de Cròniques, spectacularly painted with murals by Josep Maria Sert. On Sundays there are guided tours every 20 minutes.

Cathedral

Pla de la Seu (93 342 82 60/www.catedralbcn.org). Metro Jaume I. **Open** *Visita turística* 1.30-4.30pm daily. *Church* 8am-12.45pm, 5-7.30pm Mon-Fri; 8am-12.45pm, 5-6pm Sat; 8-9am, 5-6pm Sun. *Cloister* 9am-12.30pm, 5-7pm daily. *Museum* 10am-1pm, 5.15-7pm daily. **Admission** *Visita turística* €5. *Church* free. *Museum* €1. *Lift to roof* €2. *Choir* €2. No credit cards. **Map** p55 C3 ❷

The building is predominantly Gothic, save for the Romanesque chapel of Santa Llúcia to the right of the main façade. The cathedral museum, in the 17th-century chapter house, has paintings and sculptures, including works by the Gothic masters Jaume Huguet, Bernat Martorell and Bartolomé Bermejo. Santa Eulàlia, patron saint of Barcelona, lies in the dramatically lit crypt in an alabaster tomb carved with scenes from her martyrdom. To one side, there's a lift to the roof; take it for a magnificent view of the Old City. The *visita turística* ticket includes the cloister, museum, lift to roof and choir.

Museu del Calçat (Shoe Museum)

Plaça Sant Felip Neri 5 (93 301 45 33). Metro Jaume I. **Open** 11am-2pm Tue-Sun. **Admission** €2.50; free under-11s. No credit cards. **Map** p55 B2 ❸

One of only three such collections in the world, this tiny footwear museum details the cobbler's craft from Roman sandals through to the, er, glories of 1970s platform boots. Embroidered slippers from the Arabic world, 17th-century musketeers' boots and delicately hand-painted 18th-century party shoes are all highlights.

Museu d'Història de la Ciutat

Plaça del Rei 1 (93 315 11 11/www.museuhistoria.bcn.cat). Metro Jaume I. **Open** *June-Sept* 10am-8pm Tue-Sat; 10am-3pm Sun. *Oct-May* 10am-2pm, 4-7pm Tue-Sat; 10am-3pm Sun. *Guided tours* by appointment. **Admission** *Permanent exhibitions* €5; €2.50 reductions; free under-16s. *Temporary exhibitions* varies. *Both* free 4-8pm 1st Sat of mth. No credit cards. **Map** p55 C3 ❹

Stretching from the Plaça del Rei to the cathedral are 4,000sq m of subterranean Roman excavations, including streets, villas and storage vats for oil and wine, which were discovered by accident in the late 1920s, when a whole swathe of the Gothic Quarter was upended to make way for the central avenue of Via Laietana. The whole underground labyrinth can be visited as part of the City History Museum. The admission fee also gives you access to the Santa Àgata chapel and the Saló del Tinell, at least when there's no temporary exhibition. This majestic room (1370) began life as the seat of the Catalan parliament and was converted in the 18th century into a heavy Baroque church, which was dismantled in 1934. Tickets for the museum are also valid for the monastery at Pedralbes (p156).

Museu Frederic Marès

Plaça Sant Iu 5-6 (93 310 58 00/www.museumares.bcn.cat). Metro Jaume I. **Open** 10am-7pm Tue-Sat; 10am-3pm Sun. **Admission** €3; €1.50 reductions; free under-16s. Free 3-7pm Wed, 1st Sun of mth. **Guided tours** noon Sun. No credit cards. **Map** p55 C3 ❺

One of the city's most varied and charming museums, where the kaleido-

Museu Frederic Marès

scope of objects reflects sculptor and collector Frederic Marès' wide-ranging interests and his indulgently tolerated kleptomania as he 'borrowed' many items from his wealthy friends. The ground floor contains an array of Romanesque crucifixes, virgins and saints, while the first floor takes sculpture up to the 20th century. The basement contains remains from ecclesiastical buildings dating back to Roman times: on the second floor is the 'Gentlemen's Room', stuffed with walking sticks, smoking equipment and opera glasses, while the charming 'Ladies' Room' has fans, sewing scissors, nutcrackers and perfume flasks. **Event highlights** Porte-bouquets: 19th-century miniature flower vases (until 5 Oct 2008).

Palau de la Generalitat

Plaça Sant Jaume (93 402 46 17/ www.gencat.net/generalitat). Metro Jaume I. **Guided tours** every 30mins 10.30am-1.30pm 2nd & 4th Sun of mth;

also 9am-1pm, 4.30-7pm Sat, Sun by appointment. **Admission** free. **Map** p55 C3 ⑥
Like the Ajuntament, the Generalitat has a Gothic side entrance on C/Bisbe, with a beautiful relief of St George (Sant Jordi), patron saint of Catalonia, made by Pere Johan in 1418. Inside, the finest features are the first-floor Pati de Tarongers ('Orange Tree Patio') and the magnificent 15th-century chapel.

Eating & drinking

Bar Bodega Teo

C/Ataulf 18 (93 315 11 59). Metro Drassanes or Jaume I. **Open** 9am-4pm, 5pm-2am Mon-Thur; 9am-4pm, 5pm-3am Fri, Sat. **Bar**. **Map** p55 B4 ⑦
An old *bodega* by day, with wine stored in huge oak barrels. At night young foreigners and *barcelonins* sip Moscow Mules amid the varied decor – fairy lights, futuristic insect lamps, a backlit panel of an expressive Mandarin duck and a blaze of stargazer lilies on the bar.

No joke

Have you heard the one about the Catalan stand-up? No? No one else has either. In a land where comics are known only as 'monologuers', stand-up is dead on its feet.

American hellraiser Rachel Arieff (www.rachelarieff.com) has delivered a kick to the nuts of the staid comedy scene with her Gothic vaudeville wardrobe, sailor's tongue and don't-care attitude. Branding herself an 'extreme cabaret star and train-wreck comedian', her hugely successful **Anti-Karaoke** night (www.antikaraoke.com) involves rock, comedy and crowd-surfing and runs every Monday at Sidecar (p69), while for those who understand Spanish, there's her monthly show *Como ser feliz todo el tiempo* at the Café Teatre Llantiol (C/Riereta 7, Raval, 93 329 90 09, www.llantiol.com).

Other residents have raised a laugh by importing comedians from abroad. Stephen Garland launched the **Giggling Guiri** comedy club (mobile 610 317 656, www.comedyinspain.com) – *guiri* being slang for foreigner – while Steve Barry's **Guinness Laughter Lounge** (mobile 627 185 038, www.gloungebcn. com) started out with up-and-coming circuit comedians performing in pubs, but now books established top-liners at La Riereta theatre (C/Reina Amàlia 3, Raval, 93 442 98 44, www.lariereta.es). Aspiring hecklers should note that it is substantially cheaper to see stand-up comics when they are performing abroad.

Bar Celta

C/Mercè 16 (93 315 00 06). Metro Drassanes. **Open** noon-midnight Tue-Sun. **€**. **Tapas**. Map p55 C5 ❽

A bright and noisy Galician tapas bar, Bar Celta specialises in food from the region, such as *lacón con grelos* (boiled gammon with turnip tops) and good seafood – try the *navajas* (razor clams) or the *pulpo* (octopus) – and crisp Albariño wine served in traditional white ceramic bowls.

Cafè de l'Acadèmia

C/Lledó 1 (93 319 82 53). Metro Jaume I. **Open** 9am-noon, 1.30-4.30pm, 8.45-11.30pm Mon-Fri. Closed 3wks Aug. **€€€**. **Catalan**. Map p55 C3 ❾

Enjoy a power breakfast among the suits from the nearby town hall, bask in the sunshine over lunch at one of the tables outside on the evocative little Plaça Sant Just, or take a date for an alfresco candlelit dinner. The creative Catalan classics on offer include home-made pasta (try the shrimp and garlic), guineafowl with a tiny tarte tatin and lots of duck.

Čaj Chai

C/Sant Domènec del Call 12 (mobile 610 334 712). Metro Jaume I. **Open** 3-10pm daily. No credit cards. **Tearoom**. Map p55 B3 ❿

One for serious drinkers of the brown stuff, Čaj Chai is based on a Prague tea-room. Serenity reigns and First Flush Darjeeling is approached with the reverence usually afforded to a Château d'Yquem. A range of leaves come with tasting notes giving suggestions for maximum enjoyment.

Can Culleretes

C/Quintana 5 (93 317 30 22). Metro Liceu. **Open** 1.30-4pm, 9-11pm Tue-Sat; 1.30-4pm Sun. Closed July. **€€**. **Catalan**. Map p55 B3 ⓫

The rambling dining rooms at the 'house of teaspoons' have been packing in the customers since 1786, and show no signs of slowing. The secret to the place's longevity is straightforward enough: honest, hearty cooking and decent wine at the lowest possible

Palau de la Generalitat p57

prices. Expect sticky boar stew, pork with prunes and dates, goose with apples, partridge escabeche and superbly fresh seafood.

Cervecería Taller de Tapas

C/Comtal 28 (93 481 62 33/ www.tallerdetapas.com). Metro Catalunya or Urquinaona. **Open** 8.30am-midnight Mon-Thur; 8.30am-1am Fri, Sat; noon-midnight Sun. **Beer/tapas**. Map p55 C1 ⑫

A new venture from the people behind Taller de Tapas (p63), and still serving tapas, but this time with an emphasis on beers from around the world. The list provides a refreshing alternative to Estrella, with Argentinian Quilmes, Brazilian Brahma (this one, admittedly, via Luton), Bass Pale Ale, Leffe and Hoegaarden, among others.

Ginger

C/Palma de Sant Just 1 (93 310 53 09). Metro Jaume I. **Open** 7pm-2.30am Tue-Thur; 7pm-3am Fri, Sat. Closed 2wks Aug. **€€**. **Tapas/cocktails**. Map p55 C4 ⑬

Ginger manages to be all things to all punters: swish cocktail bar; purveyor of fine tapas and excellent wines, and,

above all, a superbly relaxing place to chat and listen to music. Be warned, it's no secret among the expat crowd.

La Granja

C/Banys Nous 4 (93 302 69 75). Metro Liceu. **Open** *June-Sept* 9.30am-2pm, 4-9pm Mon-Fri; 9.30am-2pm, 5-9pm Sat; 5-10pm Sun. *Oct-May* 9.30am-2.30pm, 5-9pm Mon-Sat; 5-10pm Sun. **€**. No credit cards. **Tearoom**. Map p55 B3 ⑭

There are a number of these old *granjes* (milk bars, often specialising in hot chocolate) around town, but this is one of the loveliest, with handsome antique fittings and its very own section of Roman wall at the back. You can stand your spoon in the chocolate, and it won't be to all tastes.

Machiroku

C/Moles 21 (93 412 60 82). Metro Catalunya. **Open** 1.30-3.30pm, 8.30-11.30pm Mon-Fri; 8.30-11.30pm Sat. **€€**. **Japanese**. Map p55 C1 ⑮

A cosy, modest space decorated with Japanese wall hangings and prints. Service is charming and friendly, and the various set menus at lunchtime offer good value, featuring rice and miso soup and then a choice of sushi,

Bar Bodega Teo p57

teriyaki, *yakinuku* (chargrilled beef) or a bento box with vegetable and prawn tempura. There's a good wine list.

Matsuri

Plaça Regomir 1 (93 268 15 35). Metro Jaume I. **Open** 1.30-3.30pm, 8.30-11.30pm Mon-Fri; 8.30pm-midnight Sat. €€. **Asian.** Map p55 C4 ⑯

The trickling fountain, wooden carvings and wall-hung candles are saved from Asian cliché by the occidental lounge soundtrack. Reasonably priced tom yam soup, sushi, pad thai and other South-east Asian favourites top the list, while less predictable choices include a zingy mango and prawn salad, and a rich, earthy red curry with chicken and aubergine.

Mercè Vins

C/Amargós 1 (93 302 60 56). Metro Catalunya. **Open** 8am-5pm Mon-Fri. €. **Catalan.** Map p55 C2 ⑰

With its green beams, buttercup walls and fresh flowers, few places are as cosy as Mercè Vins. The standard of cooking varies a bit, but occasionally a pumpkin soup or inventive salad might appear, before sausages with garlicky sautéed potatoes. Dessert regulars are flat, sweet coca bread with a glass of muscatel, chocolate flan or figgy pudding.

Mesón Jesús

C/Cecs de la Boqueria 4 (93 317 46 98). Metro Jaume I or Liceu. **Open** 1-4pm, 8-11pm Mon-Fri. Closed Aug-early Sept. €€. **Spanish.** Map p55 B3 ⑱

The feel is authentic Castilian, with gingham tablecloths, oak barrels, cartwheels and pitchforks hung around the walls, while the waitresses are incessantly cheerful. The dishes are reliably good and inexpensive to boot – try the sautéed green beans with ham to start, and then follow it with superb grilled prawns or a tasty fish stew.

Milk

C/Gignas 21 (93 268 09 22/www. milkbarcelona.com). Metro Jaume I. **Open** 6.30pm-3am Mon-Sat; noon-3am Sun. €€. **Fusion/cocktails.** Map p55 C4 ⑲

Milk's candlelit, low-key baroque look, charming service and loungey music make it an ideal location for that first date. Cocktails are a speciality, as is good solid home-made bistro grub, ranging from Caesar salad to fish and chips. A decent brunch is served on Sundays too.

Neri Restaurante

C/Sant Sever 5 (93 304 06 55/www. hotelneri.com). Metro Jaume I. **Open** 1.30-3.30pm, 8.30-11pm daily. €€€€. **Catalan.** Map p55 B3 ⑳

Chef Jordi Ruiz cooks with a quiet assurance in tune with the Gothic arches and crushed velvet of his dining room, creating a perfect, tiny lamb Wellington to start; later there are cannelloni stuffed with wild mushrooms, or a fillet of hake on creamed parsnip with apricots and haricot beans.

Peimong

C/Templers 6-10 (93 318 28 73). Metro Jaume I. **Open** 1-4pm, 8-11.30pm Tue-Sat; 1-4pm Sun. Closed mid Aug-Sept. €€. **Peruvian.** Map p55 B4 ㉑

Peimong wins no prizes for design, but makes up for its rather unforgiving and overlit interior with some tasty South American dishes. Start with stuffed corn tamales, and then move on to ceviche, *pato en aji* (duck with a spicy sauce and rice) or the satisfying *lomo saltado* – pork fried with onions, tomatoes and coriander.

Els Quatre Gats

C/Montsió 3 (93 302 41 40/www. 4gats.com). Metro Catalunya. **Open** *Restaurant* 1pm-1am daily. *Café* 8am-2am daily. €€€. **Bar/Catalan.** Map p55 C1 ㉒

This Modernista classic, which was frequented by Picasso and other luminaries of the period, nowadays caters mainly to tourists. The inevitable consequences include higher prices, so-so food and, worst of all, the house musicians. The place is still dazzling in its design, however, so avoid the worst excesses of touristification and come at lunchtime for a €12.70 *menú*, sparing yourself 'Bésame Mucho' in the process.

Dig this

Museu Marítim

To the constant chagrin of the construction industry and Barcelona's town planners, it can be impossible to lay foundations for so much as a lamp post in Barcelona without unearthing ruins of some description. Building sites all over the city are testament to the historical riches that lie beneath the surface, and can remain chained up for months while archaeologists duke it out with impatient property developers.

Work on the Born's Santa Caterina market slowed to a crawl when ruins of the 13th-century Convent de Santa Caterina were discovered, and ground to a halt when a Roman necropolis was found below that. Plans for the nearby Antic Mercat del Born's transformation into a library were also frustrated when medieval remains were discovered. After much debate the plans shifted to a nearby site where, even more recently, remains of the 18th-century citadel have been found. The project remains in limbo.

Small wonder, then, that the city has become so fascinated with archaeology. So much so that it has now become a selling point in the eyes of the tourist board. With this in mind it has created the **Arqueoticket**, a €17-pass allowing entry to the five museums with archaeological collections.

These range from the **Museu d'Història de la Ciutat** (p56), which itself had a chance beginning when building work uncovered 4,000sq m of Roman remains, to the archaeological wonders – including mummified cats and a 5,000-year-old bed – in the **Museu Egipci de Barcelona** (p127). The ticket also allows entry to the pre-Columbian collections of the **Museu Barbier-Mueller** (p73), pieces dating back to the Palaeolithic period at the **Museu d'Arqueologia de Catalunya** (p113) and the wonderful **Museu Marítim** (p104). Alternatively you can keep an eye out for the latest finds, coming soon to a Barcelona building site.

Les Quinze Nits

Plaça Reial 6 (93 317 30 75). Metro Liceu. **Open** 1-3.45pm, 8.30-11.30pm daily. **€€. Catalan. Map** p55 A3 ㉓

Top of many tourists' dining agenda, with a queue stretching halfway across the Plaça Reial, the Quinze Nits manages all this with distinctly so-so food. The secret? Combining fast-food speed and prices with striking spaces, smart table linen and soft lighting. Diners get to feel special, eat local dishes and come away with nary a dent in their wallets. Order simply and a reasonable meal can still be had.

Other locations La Fonda, C/Escudellers 10 (93 301 75 15).

El Salón

C/Hostal d'en Sol 6-8 (93 315 21 59). Metro Jaume I. **Open** 1.30-4pm; 8.30-11.30pm Mon-Sat. **€€. Mediterranean. Map** p55 C4 ㉔

El Salón's faintly bohemian style, its reasonable prices, and tables outside in the shadow of a Roman wall make it one of the nicer places to eat in the Barri Gòtic. Dishes are simple but well executed – creamed carrot soup, lamb brochettes, tuna with ginger and brown rice, botifarra and beans, and ice-cream made with Galician Arzoa-Ulloa cheese to finish.

Schilling

C/Ferran 23 (93 317 67 87). Metro Liceu. **Open** *Sept-July* 10am-3am Mon-Sat; noon-2.30am Sun. *Aug* 5pm-3am daily. **Café. Map** p55 B3 ㉕

Schilling's airy, smart interior and position smack in the centre of the Old City make it Barcelona's meeting place par excellence (not to mention the city's number one spot for budding travel writers to scribble in their journals), but the aloofness of the staff can become tiresome.

Shunka

C/Sagristans 5 (93 412 49 91). Metro Jaume I. **Open** 1.30-3.30pm, 8.30-11.30pm Tue-Fri; 2-4pm, 8.30-11.30pm Sat, Sun. Closed Aug and ten days at Christmas. **€€€. Japanese. Map** p55 C2 ㉖

Shunka is one of the better Japanese restaurants in town, and it is a favourite dining haunt of Catalan superchef Ferran Adrià. Reserve for the best seats in the house at the counter and watch the chefs create decent-sized portions of prawn and vegetable tempura, superb maki rolls and extremely good nigiri-zushi.

Taller de Tapas

Plaça Sant Josep Oriol 9 (93 301 80 20). Metro Liceu. **Open** noon-midnight Mon-Thur, Sun; noon-1am Fri, Sat. **€€. Tapas. Map** p55 B3 ㉗

At their best, the various branches of Taller de Tapas (see also Cerveceria de Tapas, p59) form an easy, tourist-friendly, multilingual environment in which to try a great range of tapas from razor clams to locally picked wild mushrooms, but the huge success of the operation means that the quality of service can be a bit of a lottery.

Taxidermista

Plaça Reial 8 (93 412 45 36). Metro Liceu. **Open** 1.30-4pm, 8.30pm-12.30am Tue-Sun. Closed 3wks Jan. **€€€. Mediterranean. Map** p55 B4 ㉘

When this place was a taxidermist's shop, Dalí famously ordered 200,000 ants, a tiger, a lion and a rhinoceros. Nowadays, those who leave here stuffed are generally tourists, though this has not affected standards, which remain reasonably high. À la carte offerings include foie gras with quince jelly and a sherry reduction; langoustine ravioli with seafood sauce; steak tartare; and some slightly misjudged fusion elements, such as wok-fried spaghetti with vegetables. The lunch *menú* is an excellent option, with two- or three-course deals.

Tokyo

C/Comtal 20 (93 317 61 80). Metro Catalunya. **Open** 1.30-4pm, 8-11pm Mon-Sat. Closed Aug. **€€€. Japanese. Map** p55 C1 ㉙

Don't believe it if you're told there's no *menú*; there is, and it's certainly the best way to eat here. A zingy little salad is followed by a mountain of

prawn and vegetable tempura, and a platter of maki rolls, nigiri and a bowl of miso soup. It's a simple, cosy space, with a reassuring Japanese presence. À la carte, the speciality is *edomae* (hand-rolled nigiri-zushi), but the meat and vegetable sukiyaki cooked at your table is also good.

La Vinateria del Call

C/Sant Domènec del Call 9 (93 302 60 92). Metro Jaume I or Liceu. **Open** 8.30pm-1am Mon-Sat; 8.30pm-midnight Sun. **€€. Tapas. Map** p55 ③⓪

La Vinateria's narrow entrance, furnished with dark wood and dusty bottles, has something of the Dickensian tavern about it, but once you're inside there's a varied music selection, from flamenco to rai, and lively multilingual staff. The wine list and range of hams and cheeses are outstanding; try the *cecina de ciervo* (wafer-thin slices of cured venison) and finish with home-made fig ice-cream.

Xeroga

C/Parc 1 (93 412 62 75). Metro Drassanes. **Open** 1-4pm, 8pm-midnight daily. **€€. Chilean. Map** p55 A5 ③①

A Chilean restaurant with a good-natured South American vibe, Xeroga has walls that are hung with bright oil paintings, a gold-stitched sombrero and a cracked and burnished guitar. On offer are various empanadas: *pino* is the classic option (meat, olives, egg and raisin), ceviche, *mariscal* (shellfish and hake in a fish broth) and a mighty *bife a lo pobre* (a proper trucker's breakfast of thin steak, two fried eggs and a stack of chips).

Shopping

Almacenes del Pilar

C/Boqueria 43 (93 317 79 84/www. almacenesdelpilar.com). Metro Liceu. **Open** 9.30am-2pm, 4-8pm Mon-Sat. Closed 2wks Aug. **Map** p55 B3 ③②

At Almacenes del Pilar there's an extensive array of fabrics and accessories for traditional Spanish costumes, displayed in a shambolic interior that dates back to 1886. As you make your way through the bolts of material, you'll find richly hued brocades, lace mantillas and the high combs over which they are worn, along

Els Quatre Gats p61

with fringed, hand-embroidered pure silk *mantones de manila* (shawls) and colourful wooden fans.

Art Escudellers

C/Escudellers 23-25 (93 412 68 01/ www.escudellers-art.com). Metro Drassanes. **Open** 11am-11pm daily. **Map** p55 B4 ③③

An extravaganza of clay and glassware, which is mostly handmade by Spanish artists and labelled by region. Decorative and practical items include sturdy kitchenware, ceramics and Gaudi-themed coffee cups.

Le Boudoir

C/Canuda 21 (93 302 52 81/www. leboudoir.net). Metro Catalunya. **Open** *Sept-July* 10am-8.30pm Mon-Fri; 10.30am-9pm Sat. *Aug* 11am-9pm Mon-Sat. **Map** p55 B1 ③④

Sensuality abounds in Barcelona's classy answer to Agent Provocateur. Sexy lingerie comes with designer labels (and prices to match), the swimwear is certainly not for shrinking violets and fluffy kitten-heeled mules have not been made with practicality chiefly in mind.

Caelum

C/Palla 8 (93 302 69 93). Metro Liceu. **Open** 5-8.30pm Mon; 10.30am-8.30pm Tue-Thur; 10.30am-midnight Fri, Sat; 11.30am-9pm Sun. Closed 2wks Aug. **Map** p55 B2 ③⑤

Spain's nuns and monks, even or perhaps especially those shut away in enclosed orders, have a naughty sideline in traditional sweets, including candied saints' bones, sugared egg yolks and drinkable goodies such as eucalyptus and orange liqueur, all of which are beautifully packaged. There's also a taster café downstairs, which is on the site of some medieval Jewish thermal baths.

Cereria Subirá

Baixada de Llibreteria 7 (93 315 26 06). Metro Jaume I. **Open** *Jan-July, Sept-Nov* 9am-1.30pm, 4-7.30pm Mon-Fri; 9am-1.30pm Sat. *Aug* 9am-1.30pm, 4-7.30pm Mon-Fri. *Dec* 9am-1.30pm, 4-7.30pm Mon-Sat. **Map** p55 C3 ③⑥

The interior, which dates back to 1761, is extraordinary, with grand swirling mint-green, gilt-adorned balustrades and torch-wielding maidens, but the

Taxidermista p63

range of candles is also impressive. The varieties include simple votive candles, scented and novelty wax creations, and tapered classics.

Drap

C/Pi 14 (93 318 14 87/www.ample 24.com/drap). Metro Liceu. **Open** 9.30am-1.30pm, 4.30-8.30pm Mon-Fri; 10am-1.30pm, 5-8.30pm Sat. **Map** p55 B2 ③⑦

The enthusiastic staff at Drap are happy to show you the astonishingly artistic Lilliputian wares on offer: tiny versions of everything to fully furnish the world's best-equipped dolls' houses: from mini saucepans bubbling on mini ovens to miniature dogs in tiny dog baskets.

Formatgeria La Seu

C/Daguería 16 (93 412 65 48/ www.formatgerialaseu.com). Metro Jaume I. **Open** 10am-2pm, 5-8pm Tue-Fri; 10am-3.30pm, 5-8pm Sat. Closed Aug. No credit cards. **Map** p55 C3 ③⑧

Formatgeria La Seu stocks a delectable range of Spanish farmhouse olive oils and cheeses, among them a fierce *tou dels til·lers* and a blackcurranty *picón* from Cantabria. On Saturdays, from noon to 3.30pm, there is a sit-down cheese tasting for €5.85, but you can wash down three cheeses with a glass of wine any time for €2.50.

La Gauche Divine

Passatge de la Pau 7 (93 301 61 25/ www.lagauchedivine.com). Metro Drassanes. **Open** 5-8.30pm Mon; 11am-2.30pm, 5-8.30pm Tue-Sat. **Map** p55 A5 ③⑨

Tucked away in the sidestreets running off C/Ample, La Gauche Divine enlivens the clothes shopping experience with art exhibitions, video projections and DJ sets. It has a laid-back friendly vibe that belies the serious quality of its collection, which includes elegant tailoring from Ailanto, and complex, ambitiously constructed pieces from the young and talented Txell Miras.

Gotham

C/Cervantes 7 (93 412 46 47/www. gotham-bcn.com). Metro Jaume I. **Open** Sept-June 11am-2pm, 5-8pm Mon-Fri; 11am-2pm Sat. July, Aug 11am-2pm, 5-8pm Mon-Fri. Closed 2wks end Aug. **Map** p55 B4 ④⓪

Fabulous 1950s ashtrays in avocado green, some bubble TV sets, teak sideboards, coat stands that look like molecular models, seats from the space shuttle in *2001: A Space Odyssey…* Take a trip down nostalgia lane with Gotham's classic retro furniture from the 1930s, '50s, '60s and '70s in warm cartoon colours.

Herboristeria del Rei

C/Vidre 1 (93 318 05 12). Metro Liceu.
Open 10am-2pm, 5-8pm Tue-Sat.
Closed 1-2wks Aug. **Map** p55 B3 ④①
Designed by a theatre set designer in
the 1860s, the shop's intricate wooden
shelving hides myriad herbs and infu-
sions, ointments and unguents for
health and beauty. Its more up-to-date
stock includes vegetarian foods, organic olive oils and mueslis.

El Ingenio

*C/Rauric 6 (93 317 71 38/www.
el-ingenio.com). Metro Liceu.* **Open**
10am-1.30pm, 4.15-8pm Mon-Fri; 11am-
2pm, 5-8.30pm Sat. **Map** p55 B3 ④②
At once enchanting and disturbing, El
Ingenio's handcrafted toys, tricks and
costumes are reminders of an all-but-
lost pre-digital world where people
made their own entertainment. Its cabinets are full of practical jokes and curious toys, while its fascinating workshop
produces the oversized heads and garish costumes used in Barcelona's traditional festivities during carnival and
the Mercè festival in September.

Loft Avignon

*C/Avinyó 22 (93 301 24 20). Metro
Jaume I or Liceu.* **Open** 10.30am-
8.30pm Mon-Sat. **Map** p55 B4 ④③
A smörgåsbord of top international
designers is on the menu at this purveyor of high-end informal fashion for
men and women. Think Diesel Style
Lab, Indian Rose, Vivienne Westwood
and Ungaro, with a gentle sprinkling
of Bikkemberg.
Other locations C/Boters 8 (93 301
37 95); C/Boters 15 (93 412 59 10).

Papabubble

*C/Ample 28 (93 268 86 25/www.
papabubble.com). Metro Barceloneta
or Drassanes.* **Open** 10am-2pm,
4-8.30pm Tue-Fri; 10am-8.30pm
Sat; 11am-7.30pm Sun. Closed Aug.
Map p55 C5 ④④
Crowds of children are lured by the sug-
ary wafts floating into the street at
sweet-making time. You can watch the
Aussie owners create their kaleidos-
copic humbugs before your eyes in
flavours both usual (orange, mint) and
unusual (lavender, passion fruit).
Confuse your teeth with a candy tooth-
brush. The adults are served by a recent
venture into obscene lolly territory.

Planelles Donat

*Avda Portal de l'Àngel 7 (93 317 29
26). Metro Catalunya.* **Open** 10am-
10pm Mon-Sat. Closed Jan-Mar &
2wks Oct. **Map** p55 B2 ④⑤
Turrón is Catalonia's traditional sweet
treat eaten at Christmas. It comes in
two types: the nougat-like *turrón de
Alicante* and grainy *turrón de Jijona*,
which is rather like marzipan. You can
try these, along with dusty *polvorones*
(crumbly marzipan-like sweets), ice-
cream and refreshing *horchata* (tiger
nut milk) here and at its nearby ice-
cream parlour (Portal de l'Àngel 25).

Tribu

*C/Avinyó 12 (93 318 65 10). Metro
Jaume I or Liceu.* **Open** 11am-2.30pm,
4.30-8.30pm Mon-Fri; 11am-8.30pm Sat.
Map p55 B3 ④⑥
One of the countless clued-up fashion
platforms in town, providing international and homegrown casual labels
such as Jocomomola, Nolita, Diesel and
Freesoul. Don't miss the designer trainers at the back.

Women's Secret

*C/Portaferrissa 7-9 (93 318 92 42/
www.womensecret.com). Metro
Liceu.* **Open** 10am-9pm Mon-Sat.
Map p55 B2 ④⑦
What's the secret? It seems to be that
women would rather wear underwear
that's cute, colourful and comfortable
than fussy, itchy bits of black nylon
string. There are some sexy pieces
here, but mostly it's versatile strap
bras, cool cotton Japanesey wrap-
around PJs and a funky line of skimpy
shorts, miniskirts and vest tops in car-
toonish stylings.

Zara

*Avda Portal de l'Àngel 32-34 (93
301 08 98/www.zara.com). Metro
Catalunya.* **Open** 10am-9pm Mon-Sat.
Map p55 C1 ④⑧

Zara's recipe for success has won over the world, but items are cheaper on its home turf. Well-executed, affordable copies of catwalk styles appear on the rails in a fashion heartbeat. The women's section is the front-runner, but the men's and children's sections cover good ground too. The introduction of the 'Zara Home' department has also been a success.

Nightlife

Barcelona Pipa Club

Plaça Reial 3, pral (93 302 47 32/ www.bpipaclub.com). Metro Liceu. **Open** 11pm-3am daily. **Admission** free. No credit cards. **Map** p55 A3 ❹

Once up some stairs and through a door, the chaos of the Plaça Reial below could not seem further away. Indeed, it feels less Barcelona, more Baker Street boozer c1900. Dusty wood, heavy curtains and cabinets full of antique pipes preserve a sedate atmosphere and, when it's not sectioned off for members' use, a small pool table sees a fair bit of action.

Fonfone

C/Escudellers 24 (93 317 14 24/www. fonfone.com). Metro Drassanes or Liceu. **Open** 11pm-2.30am Mon-Thur, Sun; 11pm-3am Fri, Sat. **Admission** free. **Map** p55 B4 ❺

A refreshingly spacious bar on a seedy backstreet, Fonfone stands out by virtue of its green-and-orange glowing decor. It pulls a mixed crowd of locals and lost tourists of a studenty bent. Pop, electronica, house and breakbeats attempt to distract the punters from their conversation.

Harlem Jazz Club

C/Comtessa de Sobradiel 8 (93 310 07 55). Metro Jaume I. **Open** 8pm-4am Tue-Thur, Sun; 8pm-5am Fri, Sat. *Gigs* 10.30pm, midnight Tue-Thur, Sun; 11.30pm, 1am Fri, Sat. Closed 2wks Aug. **Admission** free Mon-Thur; €7 (incl 1 drink) Fri-Sun. No credit cards. **Map** p55 B4 ❺

For a time, the gig looked over for this Barcelona institution, but it's managed

to come back bigger and stronger than ever, remodelled and, as a nod to the times, with a DJ booth. Live music is still what it does best, and it's a regular hangout for scruffy musicians, serious music buffs and students. Jazz, klezmer and flamenco fusion all get a run in a venue that holds no musical prejudices whatsoever.

Jamboree

Plaça Reial 17 (93 319 17 89/www. masimas.com). Metro Liceu. **Open** *Gigs* 8-11pm daily. *Club* 12.30pm-5.30am daily. **Admission** €6-€9. **Map** p55 A4 ❺

Every night Jamboree hosts jazz, Latin or blues gigs by mainly Spanish groups; when they're over, the beards wander off and the beatbox comes out. On Mondays, particularly, the outrageously popular What the Fuck (WTF) jazz jam session is crammed with a young and local crowd waiting for the funk/hip hop night that follows. Note: you have to pay separately for the club.

La Macarena

C/Nou de Sant Francesc 5 (no phone/ www.macarenaclub.com). Metro Drassanes. **Open** 11.30pm-4.30am

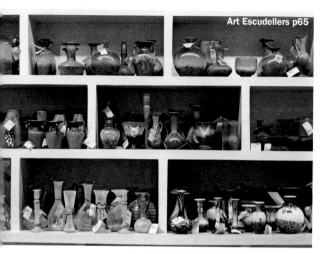

Art Escudellers p65

Mon-Thur, Sun; 11.30pm-5.30am Fri, Sat. **Admission** free before 1.30am; €5 afterwards. No credit cards.
Map p55 B4 ❸

Not a centre for embarrassing synchronised arm movements performed to cheesy pop tunes, but a completely soundproofed cosy little dance space/bar with a kicking sound system that will pound away electro, minimal and house beats until the early hours. Guest DJs Brett Johnson and Vincenzo have shared the decks with local talent, usually a day before or after a bigger gig elsewhere.

New York

C/Escudellers 5 (93 318 87 30).
Metro Drassanes or Liceu. **Open** midnight-5am Thur-Sat. **Admission** (incl 1 drink) €5 with flyer and before 2am, €10 without. No credit cards.
Map p55 A4 ❺

After a facelift and a change of management, this ancient former brothel-turned-rock-club is now happily indulging Spain's unlikely obsession for Depeche Mode and other newly trendy '80s sounds, alongside floppy-haired party fare from the likes of Franz Ferdinand, The Strokes et al. A long hallway bar leads on to the main dancefloor, where fairground figures leer from the stage and wallflowers gaze from the mezzanine.

Sidecar Factory Club

Plaça Reial 7 (93 302 15 86/www.
sidecarfactoryclub.com). Metro Liceu.
Open 6pm-4am Tue-Thur, Sun; 6pm-6am Fri, Sat. **Admission** (incl 1 drink) €7. *Gigs* €5-€15. No credit cards.
Map p55 B3 ❺

Sidecar still has all the ballsy attitude of the spit 'n' sawdust rock club that it once was and, while the gigs and weekend's rock-pop extravaganza continue to pack in the local indie kids and Interrailers, the programming has thankfully diversified considerably to include breakbeat on Wednesdays and Brazilian tunes on Tuesdays. Look out, too, for the Anti-Karaoke nights on Mondays (see box p58).

Arts & leisure

Cine Maldá

C/Pi 5 (93 481 37 04/www.
cinemalda.com). Metro Liceu.
No credit cards. **Map** p55 ❺

BARCELONA BY AREA

In 2007 the much-lamented rep cinema, Cine Maldá, reopened its doors on a Bollywood trip. This means that, alongside nearly new indie films (last season's David Lynch and so on), there will be subcontinental movies of all stripes, and those that straddle the east/west divide like *Monsoon Wedding* and *East is East*.

Los Tarantos

Plaça Reial 17 (93 319 27 89/www. masimas.com). Metro Liceu. **Open** *Flamenco show* 8.30-11.30pm daily. **Admission** €6. **Map** p55 A4 **⑤⑦**
This flamenco *tablao* has presented many top stars over the years. It now caters mainly to the tourist trade, but avoids the fripperies of some coach-party venues. Now under new ownership, prices have gone down, but the performers are less experienced. After 11.30pm Los Tarantos and Jamboree (p68) combine, but you have to pay again to join the jamboree.

La Rambla

This mile-long boulevard is one of the most famous promenades in the world. The identikit souvenir shops, pickpockets and surging crowds of tourists have driven away many of the locals who used to come here to play chess or have political debates, but despite a fall in fortunes, it remains the first port of call for visitors to the city. The human statues, fortune-tellers, card sharps, puppeteers, dancers and musicians might be infuriating to anyone late for work, but for those with a seat at a pavement café, it's not far short of pure theatre.

La Rambla is divided into five parts. First comes the **Font de Canaletes** drinking fountain; if you drink from it, goes the legend, you'll return to Barcelona. Here, too, is where Barça fans converge in order to celebrate their team's triumphs. Next comes perhaps the best-loved section of the boulevard,

known as **Rambla de les Flors** for its line of magnificent flower stalls, open into the night. To the right is the **Palau de la Virreina** exhibition and cultural information centre, and the superb Boqueria market. A little further is the **Pla de l'Os** (or Pla de la Boqueria), the centrepoint of the Rambla, with a pavement **mosaic** created in 1976 by Joan Miró. On the left, where more streets run off into the Barri Gòtic, is the **Bruno Quadros** building (1883), with umbrellas on the wall and a single Chinese dragon protruding over the street.

The lower half of the Rambla is more restrained, flowing between the sober façade of the **Liceu** opera house and the more *fin-de-siècle* **Cafè de l'Opera**. On the right is C/Nou de la Rambla (where you'll find Gaudí's neo-Gothic **Palau Güell**); the broad promenade then widens into the **Rambla de Santa Mònica**, long a prostitutes' haunt.

Drap p66

Sights & museums

Museu de Cera

Ptge de la Banca 7 (93 317 26 49/ www.museocerabcn.com). Metro Drassanes. **Open** *Mid July-mid Sept* 10am-10pm daily. *Mid Sept-mid July* 10am-1.30pm, 4-7.30pm Mon-Fri; 11am-2pm, 4.30-8.30pm Sat, Sun. **Admission** €7.50; €4.50 children; free under-5s. No credit cards. **Map** p55 A5 ⑤⑧

This is a wax museum that belongs to the so-bad-it's-good school of entertainment. Expect the savvy Playstation generation to be notably underwhelmed by clumsy renderings of Gaudi and Lady Di jumbled in with Frankenstein, neanderthals and ET (mysteriously perched atop the Millennium Falcon).

Palau de la Virreina

La Rambla 99 (93 301 77 75/www.bcn. cat/cultura). Metro Liceu. **Open** 11am-2pm, 4-8.30pm Tue-Fri; 11am-8.30pm Sat; 11am-3pm Sun. **Admission** €3.50; €1.75 reductions; free under-16s. No credit cards. **Map** p55 A2 ⑤⑨

The Virreina houses the city's cultural department, and has lots of information on events and shows, but also boasts strong programming in its two distinct exhibition spaces. Upstairs is dedicated to one-off exhibitions, with the downstairs gallery focused on historical and contemporary photography.

Event highlights Photos Joan Fontcuberta, 1973-2007 (6 Nov 2008-8 Feb 2009); 'Working documents' the relationship between art and society (20 Nov 2008-8 Feb 2009).

Eating & drinking

Boadas

C/Tallers 1 (93 318 95 92). Metro Catalunya. **Open** *Sept-June* noon-2am Mon-Thur; noon-3am Fri, Sat. *July, Aug* noon-3pm, 6pm-2am Mon-Thur; noon-3pm, 6pm-3am Fri, Sat. No credit cards. **Cocktail bar**. **Map** p55 B1 ⑥⓪

Set up in 1933 by Miguel Boadas, born to Catalan parents in Havana (where he became the first barman at the legendary La Floridita), this classic cocktail bar has changed little since Ernest Hemingway used to come here. In a move to deter the hordes of rubbernecking tourists, there is now an exacting dress code.

Café de l'Opera

La Rambla 74 (93 317 75 85). Metro Liceu. **Open** 8.30am-2.30am Mon-Thur, Sun; 8.30am-3am Fri-Sat. No credit cards. **Café**. **Map** p55 A3 ⑥①

Cast-iron pillars, etched mirrors and bucolic murals create an air of fading grandeur now incongruous among the fast-food joints and souvenir shops. A reasonable selection of tapas is served by attentive bow-tied waiters. Given the atmosphere (and the quality of the competition), there's no better place for a coffee on La Rambla.

Kiosko de la Cazalla

C/Arc del Teatre (93 301 50 56). Metro Drassanes. **Open** 10am-2am Tue, Wed, Sun; 10am-3am Thur-Sat. No credit cards. **Bar**. **Map** p55 A4 ⑥②

Recently reopened after seven years boarded up, this emblematic hole-in-the-wall bar set in to the arch at the entrance of C/Arc del Teatre was for most of the last century a firm favourite of bullfighters and flamenco dancers, prostitutes and sailors. Little has changed since it first raised its hatch in 1912, and the tipple of choice is still the *cazalla*, an aniseedy firewater to warm the cockles.

Shopping

La Boqueria
La Rambla 89 (93 318 25 84/www. boqueria.info). Metro Liceu. **Open** 8am-8.30pm Mon-Sat. **Map** p55 A2 ⑥

Barcelona's most central food market outstrips all the rest. Visitors and residents alike never tire of wandering the hectic, colourful aisles and ogling the gory spectacle of tripe and sheep heads, the flailing pincers of live crabs and crayfish, bins of nuts, tubs of aromatic olives, and sacks of herbs and spices. Packed under an impressive vaulted glass and iron structure, the succession of stalls – each one brimming with local produce – provides a cacophony of buying and selling. Don't miss Llorenç Petràs's woodland stall of mushrooms and insect goodies, at the back. If it all makes you hungry, there are some great places to eat incomparably fresh food, if you can hack the noise and are prepared to pull up a stool at a frenzied bar.

However, be sure to steer clear of the conspicuous stalls near the front, as their neatly stacked picture-perfect piles of fruit, mounds of sweets, candied fruit and nuts, and ready-to-eat fruit salads are designed to ensnare tourists and have the prices to match. The Barcelona authorities seem to have cottoned on to the market's potential as a tourist attraction and are capitalising on it with a range of Boqueria merchandise, available from a stall near the entrance.

Escribà
La Rambla 83 (93 301 60 27/www. escriba.es). Metro Liceu. **Open** 8.30am-9pm daily. **Map** p55 A3 ⑥

Antoni Escribà, who was known as the 'Mozart of Chocolate', died in 2004, but happily his legacy lives on. His team produces jaw-dropping confectionary creations for the Easter displays, from a hulking chocolate Grand Canyon to a life-size model of Michelangelo's *David*.

Nightlife

Club Fellini
La Rambla 27 (93 272 49 80/www. clubfellini.com). Metro Liceu. **Open** *Winter* midnight-5am Thur-Sat. *Summer* midnight-5am Mon-Sat. **Admission** €15. No credit cards. **Map** p55 A4 ⑥

Due to its location on the Rambla, Fellini has had to work pretty hard to earn kudos with Barcelona's more discerning club-goers. However, thanks to some determined flyering and imaginative programming, it's managed to establish itself as pretty much the most talked-about new club in town. The monthly polysexual Puticlub parties are relatively mixed and lots of fun, and the last Thursday of the month is the Mond Club, with everyone from The Glimmers to Freelance Hellraiser playing dancey rock and rocky dance for a muso crowd.

Arts & leisure

Gran Teatre del Liceu
La Rambla 51-59 (93 485 99 13/tickets 902 53 33 35/www.liceubarcelona.com). Metro Liceu. Closed 2wks Aug. **Map** p55 A3 ⑥

The Liceu has gone from strength to strength of late, steadily increasing the number of performances but still often selling out. The flames that swept away an outdated, rickety structure a decade ago cleared the decks for a fine new opera house. By comparison with the restrained façade, the 2,340-seat auditorium is an impressively elegant, classical affair of red plush, gold leaf and ornate carvings, but the mod cons include seat-back subtitles in various languages that complement the Catalan surtitles above the stage.

Arlequi Mascares p83

Born & Sant Pere

Despite frantic efforts at gentrification elsewhere in the city, the Born is Barcelona's rags-to-riches success story, and is rife with glitzy homeware stores and designer boutiques. The food stores clustered around the old market have become fashionable bars and restaurants, full of the designers and photographers who now populate the area. Not quite as impeccably groomed, but catching up fast, is the neighbouring district of Sant Pere. With its daring, Gaudiesque **Santa Caterina market** and freshly designed central avenue, it is gradually regaining some of the glory that it enjoyed during the Golden Age, when it was a favourite residential area of the city's merchant elite.

South of here, one of the truly unmissable streets of old Barcelona, the **Carrer Montcada**, leads into the handsome **Passeig del Born**. C/Montcada is lined with medieval merchants' mansions, the greatest of which house museums. Both districts together, demarcated to the east by the **Parc de la Ciutadella** and to the west by Via Laietana, are still sometimes referred to as La Ribera ('the waterfront'), a name that recalls the time before permanent quays were built, when the shore reached much further inland and the area was contained within a 13th-century wall.

Sights & museums

Museu Barbier-Mueller d'Art Precolombí

C/Montcada 12-14, Born (93 310 45 16/www.barbier-mueller.ch). Metro Jaume I. **Open** 11am-7pm Tue-Fri;

Museu de la Xocolata

10am-7pm Sat; 10am-3pm Sun.
Admission €3; €1.50 reductions;
free under-16s. Free 1st Sun of mth.
Map p75 B4 ❶

Located in the 15th-century Palau Nadal, this world-class collection of pre-Columbian art includes changing selections of masks, textiles, jewellery and sculpture, with pieces dating from as far back as the second millennium BC and running up to the early 16th century (showing just how loosely the term 'pre-Columbian' can be used). The holdings focus solely on the Americas, representing most of the styles that can be found among the ancient cultures of Meso-America, Central America, Andean America and the Amazon region.

Event highlights The Tainos culture in pre-Columbian Caribbean (until Oct 2008).

Museu de Ciències Naturals de la Ciutadella

Passeig Picasso, Parc de la Ciutadella, Born (93 319 69 12/www.bcn.cat/ museuciencies). Metro Arc de Triomf.
Open 10am-6.30pm Tue-Sat; 10am-2.30pm Sun. **Admission** *All temporary exhibitions & Jardí Botànic* €5; €3.50 reductions. *Museums only* €3.50; €2 reductions. *Temporary exhibitions* €3.50; €2 reductions. Free under-12s, 1st Sun of mth. No credit cards.
Map p75 C3 ❷

The Natural History Museum now comprises the zoology and geology museums in the Parc de la Ciutadella. Both suffer from old-school presentation: dusty glass cases that are filled with moth-eaten stuffed animals and serried rows of rocks. However, the zoology museum is redeemed by its location in the Castell dels Tres Dragons, which was built under the aegis of Domènech i Montaner as the café-restaurant for the 1888 Exhibition. The geology part of the museum is for aficionados only, with a dry display of minerals, painstakingly classified, alongside explanations of geological phenomena found in Catalonia. More interesting is the selection from the museum's collection of 300,000 fossils, many found locally. A combined ticket also grants you entrance to the Jardí Botànic (p111) on Montjuïc.

Event highlights 'Murder in the Museum': the science of solving crimes (until Oct 2008).

Museu de la Xocolata

C/Comerç 36, Sant Pere (93 268 78 78/www.museudelaxocolata.cat). Metro Arc de Triomf or Jaume I. **Open** 10am-7pm Mon, Wed-Sat; 10am-3pm Sun. **Admission** €3.90; €3.30 reductions; free under-7s. **Map** p75 C3 ❸

The best-smelling museum in town draws chocaholics of all ages to its collection of *mones* (chocolate sculptures) made by Barcelona's master *pastissers* for the annual Easter competition. The *mones* range from multicoloured models of Gaudí's Casa Batlló to extravagant scenes of Don Quixote tilting at windmills. Inevitably, this is not a collection that ages well: photos have replaced most of the older sculptures, and those that are not in glass cases bear the ravages of hands-on appreciation from the museum's smaller visitors.

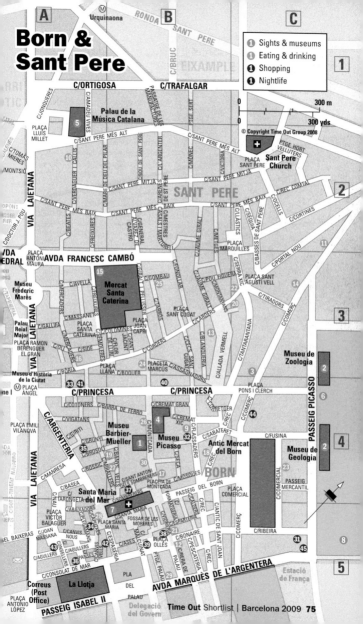

Born & Sant Pere

A Urquinaona **B** RONDA SANT PERE

C

- ① Sights & museums
- ① Eating & drinking
- ① Shopping
- ① Nightlife

1

C/BRUC
EIXAMPLE

300 m
300 yds
© Copyright Time Out Group 2008

C/ORTIGOSA   C/TRAFALGAR

PLAÇA LLUÍS MILLET
5 Palau de la Música Catalana

C/SANT PERE MÉS ALT

C/TOMÀS MIERES
/MONTSIÓ

C/SANT PERE MÉS ALT

PLAÇA SANT PERE
Sant Pere Church

PTGE. HORT VELLUTERS

2

10

C/VERDAGUER I CALLÍS
C/MARE DE DEU DEL PILAR

SANT PERE

C/SANT PERE MITJA

C/SANT PERE MÉS BAIX

C/SANT PERE MÉS BAIX

C/REC COMTAL

C/CURTINES

VIA LAIETANA

C/REATES
C/BREWERS

C/JAUME GIRALT

PLAÇA ANTONI MAURA

AVDA FRANCESC CAMBÓ

PLAÇA SANT AGUSTÍ VELL

11

Museu Frederic Marès

C/COMERCIANTS
C/AVELLA
C/MASSANET

15 Mercat Santa Caterina

C/GOMBAU
25

C/TIRADORS

PLAÇA SANT

14

Palau Reial Major
PLAÇA RAMON BERENGUER EL GRAN

C/GALLIFA
PLAÇA SANTA CATERINA
C/COLOMINES
16

PLAÇA JOAN CAPRÍ

PLAÇA SANT CUGAT

C/BLANQUERIA

C/TANTARANTANA

Museu de Zoologia **2**

Museu d'Història de la Ciutat
PLAÇA ÀNGEL

33 41
C/BÒRIA

PLAÇA LLANA

24
PLAÇETA MARCUS

3
PLAÇA PONS I CLERCH

6

C/PRINCESA   C/PRINCESA

40

C/COTONERS
C/BARRA DE FERRO
C/VIGATANS

C/CREMAT GRAN

C/REGOMIR

C/SABATERET

44

PASSEIG PICASSO

2

4

PLAÇA EMILI VILANOVA

C/ESPIRIT
C/GRUNYI

4 Museu Picasso

C/CREMAT XIC
9

C/FLASSADERS

C/FUSINA

Museu de Geologia **2**

C/ARGENTERIA

C/BROSOLI
19
C/SOMBRERERS

C/SECA

18

Antic Mercat del Born

35
1 Museu Barbier-Mueller
C/MONTCADA

32

C/SANT ANTONI

30
C/ROSSIC

PLAÇA DE MONTCADA

17

BORN

23

PASSEIG MERCANTIL

C/MANRESA
C/BASEA

C/CANVIS VELLS

PASSEIG DEL BORN

C/COMERCIAL

PLAÇA COMERCIAL

C/ANTIC DE SANT JOAN

7 Santa Maria del Mar

C/TARONGETA
C/ABAIXADORS
7
PLAÇA SANTA MARIA

C/CANVIS NOUS
37
FOSSAR DE LES MORERES

C/ESPARTERIA
C/VIDRIERIA

C/BONAIRE
38
C/OLLES
27

C/COMERÇ

C/RIBEIRA

31
45

8

PLAÇA VICTOR BALAGUER

C/AGULLERS
C/CANVIS NOUS
42
C/ESPASERIA

PTGE. PALAU
C/MALCUINAT

PTGE. PALAU
C/PALAU

5

EL BAIXERS

C/CONSOLAT DE MAR

Correus (Post Office)

La Llotja

La Llotja

PLA DEL PALAU

Delegació del Govern

AVDA MARQUÈS DE L'ARGENTERA

Estació de França

PLAÇA ANTONIO LÓPEZ

PASSEIG ISABEL II

Museu Picasso

from 1917. The pièce de résistance, however, is the complete series of 57 canvases based on Velázquez's famous *Las Meninas*, donated by Picasso himself, and now stretching through three rooms. The display later ends with a wonderful collection of ceramics that was donated by Picasso's widow. Temporary exhibitions are held under the magnificent coffered ceiling of the Palau Finestres.

Event highlights The concept of transformation in Picasso's art (Nov 2008-Feb 2009).

Palau de la Música Catalana

C/Sant Francesc de Paula 2, Sant Pere (93 295 72 00/www.palaumusica.org). Metro Urquinaona. **Open** *Box office* 10am-9pm Mon-Sat. *Guided tours* 10am-3.30pm daily (until 6pm Aug). **Admission** €9; €8 reductions. No credit cards (under €20). **Map** p75 A2 ❺

Possibly the most extreme expression of Modernista architecture ever built, the façade of Domènech i Montaner's concert hall, with its bare brick, busts and mosaic friezes representing Catalan musical traditions and composers, is impressive enough, but is surpassed by the building's staggering interior. Making up for its famously poor acoustics, decoration erupts everywhere: the ceiling centrepiece is of multicoloured stained glass; 18 half-mosaic, half-relief figures representing the musical muses appear out of the back of the stage; and on one side, massive Wagnerian valkyries ride out to accompany a bust of Beethoven. By the 1980s, the Palau was bursting under the pressure of the musical activity going on inside it, and as part of a 20-year renovation project, the ugly church next door was demolished to make way for the extension of the façade, a subterranean concert hall and a new entrance.

There are guided tours every 30 minutes or so, in either English, Catalan or Spanish. If you do have the chance, though, it's better to see the hall by catching a concert.

Museu Picasso

C/Montcada 15-23, Born (93 256 30 00/www.museupicasso.bcn.cat). Metro Jaume I. **Open** (last ticket 30mins before closing) 10am-8pm Tue-Sun. **Admission** *Permanent collection only* €6; €4 reductions. *With temporary exhibition* €8.50; €5.50 reductions; free under-16s. Free (museum only) 1st Sun of mth. **Map** p75 B4 ❹

The Picasso Museum takes up a row of medieval mansions, with the main entrance now at the Palau Meca, and the exit at the Palau Aguilar. By no means an overview of the artist's work, it is a record of the vital formative years that the young Picasso spent nearby at La Llotja art school (where his father taught), and later hanging out with Catalonia's fin-de-siècle avant-garde.

The presentation of Picasso's development from 1890 to 1904, from deft pre-adolescent portraits to sketchy landscapes to the intense innovations of his Blue Period, is seamless and unbeatable; the collection then leaps to a gallery of mature Cubist paintings

Palau de la Música Catalana

Parc de la Ciutadella

Passeig Picasso, Born (no phone).
Metro Arc de Triomf. **Open**
9am-sunset daily. **Map** p75 C4 ⑥
Named after the hated Bourbon citadel
– the largest in Europe – that occupied
this site from 1716 to 1869, this elegant
park contains a host of attractions,
including the city zoo, the Natural
History Museum, a boating lake and
more than 30 pieces of imaginative
statuary. The giant mammoth statue
at the far side of the boating lake is a
huge hit with kids, as is the trio of
prancing deer by the zoo dedicated to
Walt Disney. In the north-east corner
is the *Cascade*, an ornamental fountain
topped with Aurora's chariot, on which
a young Gaudí worked as assistant to
Josep Fontseré, the architect of the
park. Not to be missed are Fontseré's
slatted wooden Umbracle (literally,
'shade house'), which provides a pocket of tropical forest within the city, and
the elegant Hivernacle ('winter garden')
designed by Josep Amargós in 1884, an
excellent example of the iron and glass

architecture of the Eiffel Tower period.
Outside, on the Passeig Picasso, is
Antoni Tàpies's *A Picasso*, which is a
giant Cubist monument to the artist.

Santa Maria del Mar

*Plaça de Santa Maria, Born (93 310
23 90). Metro Jaume I.* **Open** 9am-
1.30pm, 4.30-8pm Mon-Sat; 10am-
1.30pm, 4.30-8pm Sun. **Admission**
free. **Map** p75 B5 ⑦
Possibly the most perfect surviving
example of the Catalan Gothic style,
this graceful basilica stands out for its
characteristic horizontal lines, large
bare surfaces, square buttresses and
flat-topped octagonal towers. Its
superb unity of style is down to the fact
that it was built relatively quickly, with
construction taking just 55 years (1329-
1384). Named after Mary in her role as
patroness of sailors, it was built on the
site of a small church known as Santa
Maria del Arenys (sand), for its position close to the sea. In the broad, single-
nave interior, two rows of perfectly
proportioned columns soar up to fan

Parc de la Ciutadella p77

farmyard zoo, pony rides, plenty of picnic areas and a brand-new adventure playground. If all that walking is too much, there's a mini-train, or you can rent electric cars from the C/Wellington entrance. Bear in mind that on hot days many of the animals are sleeping.

Eating & drinking

La Báscula

C/Flassaders 30, Born (93 319 98 66). Metro Jaume I. **Open** 7-11.30pm Wed-Fri; 1-11.30pm Sat. No credit cards. **€**. **Vegetarian**. Map p75 B4 ❾

Under threat from the demolition demons at City Hall (sign the petition near the till), this former chocolate factory is a real find, with excellent vegetarian food and a deceptively large dining room situated out back. An impressively encyclopaedic list of drinks runs from chai to Glühwein, taking in cocktails, milkshakes, smoothies and iced tea, and the pasta and cakes are as good as you'll find anywhere.

El Bitxo

C/Verdaguer i Callís 9, Sant Pere (93 268 17 08). Metro Urquinaona. **Open** 1-4pm, 7pm-midnight Mon-Thur, Sun; 1-4pm, 7pm-1am Fri, Sat. No credit cards. **€**. **Tapas**. Map p75 A2 ❿

A small, lively tapas bar, specialising in excellent cheese and charcuterie from the small Catalan village of Oix. Kick off the evening with a 'Power Vermut' (which is made of red vermouth, Picon, gin and Angostura Bitters) and end it with a bottle of the gutsy house red.

Bocamel

C/Comerç 8, Sant Pere (93 268 72 44/www.bocamel.com). Metro Arc de Triomf. **Open** 8.30am-8.30pm Mon-Fri; 8.30am-3pm, 5-8.30pm Sat; 8.30am-3pm Sun. **Café**. Map p75 C3 ⓫

It's the mouthwatering, home-made chocolate bonbons, Sachertorte, petits fours and brownies that bring most customers through the door, but Bocamel is also worth knowing about for its breakfast pastries and a short but sweet lunch menu. Needless to say, it's a good idea to hold out for pudding.

vaults, creating an atmosphere of space around the light-flooded altar. There's also superb stained glass, especially the great 15th-century rose window above the main door. The original window, built only slightly earlier, fell down during an earthquake, killing 25 people and injuring dozens more.

Event highlights Handel's *Messiah* (Christmas 2008 & 2009); Mozart's *Requiem* (Easter 2009).

Zoo de Barcelona

Parc de la Ciutadella, Born (93 225 67 80/www.zoobarcelona.com). Metro Barceloneta or Ciutadella-Vila Olímpica. **Open** Nov-Feb 10am-5pm daily. Mar, Oct 10am-6pm daily. Apr-Sept 10am-7pm daily. **Admission** €15.40; €9.30 3-12s; free under-3s. Map p75 C5 ❽

The live dolphin shows (hourly at weekends) are the big draw, but other favourites include the hippos, sea lions, elephants and wide-open monkey houses, although there's barely enough room to move in some of the enclosures. Child-friendly features include a

Cal Pep

Plaça de les Olles 8, Born (93 310 79 61/www.calpep.com). Metro Barceloneta or Plaça Àngel. **Open** 8-11.45pm Mon; 1.30-4pm, 8-11.45pm Tue-Sat. Closed Aug. €€€. **Seafood.** **Map** p75 B5 ⑫

Cal Pep is always packed so if you want a berth on the coveted seats at the front, get here early. There is a cosy dining room at the back, but it would be something of a shame to go through and miss the show behind the bar. Neophytes are steered towards the *trifásico*, which is a mélange of fried whitebait, squid rings and shrimp. Other favourites are the exquisite little *tallarines* (wedge clams), and botifarra sausage with beans.

Casa Paco

C/Allada Vermell 10, Sant Pere (no phone/www.casapaco.org). Metro Arc de Triomf or Jaume I. **Open** *Apr-Sept* 9am-2am Mon-Thur, Sun; 9am-3am Fri, Sat. *Oct-Mar* 6pm-2am Tue-Thur, Sun; 6pm-3am Fri, Sat. No credit cards. **Bar.** **Map** p75 B3 ⑬

It may sound like an old man's bar, it may look like an old man's bar, but this scruffy yet amiable hole-in-the-wall has been the underground hit of recent years, thanks largely to some sharp DJ programming. Other contributing and crucial factors include a sprawling terrace and the biggest V&Ts in the known world.

Comerç 24

C/Comerç 24, Sant Pere (93 319 21 02/www.comerc24.com). Metro Arc de Triomf. **Open** 1.30-3.30pm, 8.30-11pm Mon-Sat. €€€€. **Modern tapas.** **Map** p75 C3 ⑭

An urbane and sexy restaurant, where celeb chef Carles Abellan defines the new-wave tapas movement. Most of the selection of playful creations changes seasonally, but the signature dishes include a 'Kinder egg' (lined with truffle); tuna sashimi and seaweed on a wafer-thin pizza crust; a densely flavoured fish suquet; or a fun, truffled-edged take on the *bikini* (a cheese and ham toastie).

Turning the tables

Council crackdowns on noise pollution and opening hours mean that times are tough in Barcelona clubland, and owners are coping by shooting for mainstream appeal, with a resulting citywide aural monotony (tech-house, anyone?). Eclecticism isn't dead, but it's gone underground – kept alive by a handful of local promoters who recognise that while there's a thirst for four-on-the-floor beats, many want more from their music: more variety, more unpredictability, more disco-punk booty-bass with a dash of '60s soul.

Get your calendars out: on the second Saturday of every other month, the Boiler Club brings resident and international guest DJs to **Sala Jazzroom** (C/Vallmajor 33, Sarrià, 93 319 17 89, www.masimas.com/jazzroom) to play vintage soul and rare funk records 'til dawn.

Every now and then the aptly-named Contraflow Party – check its MySpace page www.myspace.com/contra flowparty – spreads the Ninja Tune gospel through performances by label DJs and live acts, and locals with a taste for worldlier rhythms, while every Sunday the recently transplanted Sunday Joint takes over the **Local Bar** (C/Ases 7, Born, 93 319 13 57), where Roger C digs into reggae, afrobeat, blues and funk, and comes up with all the records you've never heard before and can no longer live without.

BARCELONA BY AREA

Mundial Bar

nel and orange salad but can verge on the fussy – as in the *escalivada* (roast veg) with fried filo and a goat's cheese foam. Lemon mousse with Pop Rocks makes for a zingy finish.

Euskal Etxea

Placeta Montcada 1-3, Born (93 310 21 85). Metro Jaume I. **Open** *Bar* 7pm-midnight Mon; noon-4pm, 7pm-midnight Tue-Sat. *Restaurant* 8.30-11.30pm Mon; 1.30-4pm, 8.30-11.30pm Tue-Sat. Closed 1wk Dec/Jan. **€**. **Tapas**. **Map** p75 B4 ⑰

A Basque cultural centre and *pintxo* bar, where you can help yourself to chicken tempura with saffron mayonnaise, dainty *jamón serrano* croissants, melted provolone with mango and crispy ham, or a mini-brochette of pork. Make sure you hang on to the toothpicks spearing each one: they'll counted and charged for at the end.

Gimlet

C/Rec 24, Born (93 310 10 27). Metro Jaume I. **Open** 10pm-3am daily. No credit cards. **Cocktails**. **Map** p75 B4 ⑱

On a quiet night, this subdued little wood-panelled cocktail bar has something of an Edward Hopper feel, where the long mahogany counter has been burnished by the same well-clad elbows and patrolled by the same laconic barman for many years. At weekends a younger crowd steps in behind – and at – the bar, and it does lose a little of its classic appeal.

Itztli

C/Mirallers 7, Born (93 319 68 75/www.itztli.es). Metro Jaume I. **Open** noon-11pm Tue-Sun. **€**. **Mexican**. **Map** p75 B4 ⑲

Fortify yourself in the interminable queue for the Picasso Museum with a takeaway chicken burrito from this nearby Mexican snack bar. Keenly priced around the €3.50 mark, burritos or tacos come with beef, chilli con carne or veg. Also on offer are quesadillas, wraps, nachos and salads, and there's a good range of Mexican beers, tinned goods and fiery chilli sauces for sale.

Cuines Santa Caterina

Mercat Santa Caterina, Avda Francesc Cambó, Sant Pere (93 268 99 18). Metro Jaume I. **€€€**. **Global**. **Map** p75 A3 ⑮

Prices have crept up a little and there's a slightly more lax attitude to quality control, but CSC still has its charms. The menu is nothing if not varied, with dishes from langoustine tempura to a baked spud with cheese and sausage. The rice, flour, crates of veg and so on arrayed along the vast windows, coupled with the olive wood furniture, give a pleasant Mediterranean feel.

Diez

NEW *C/Mercaders 10, Sant Pere (93 310 21 79). Metro Jaume I.* **Open** 8pm-1am daily. **€€€**. **Mediterranean**. **Map** p75 A3 ⑯

Low ceilings, Gothic arches, subtle lighting and handsome flower arrangements make eating in this former stables a cosy affair, perfect for a date. The menu is almost as enticing, with a creative edge that works in a roast fen-

Mosquito

C/Carders 46, Sant Pere (93 268 75 69/www.mosquitotapas.com). Metro Arc de Triomf or Jaume I. **Open** 1-4pm, 7pm-1am Tue-Thur, Sun; 1-4pm, 7pm-3am Fri, Sat. **€€**.
Asian tapas. Map p75 C3 ⑳
Don't be put off. The announced 'exotic tapas' are not another lame attempt to sex up fried calamares by way of tower presentation and yucca chips, but tiny versions of good to excellent dishes from the subcontinent and elsewhere in Asia. The food ranges from chicken tikka to Chinese dumplings and there is now a dedicated sushi bar.

Mudanzas

C/Vidriería 15, Born (93 319 11 37). Metro Barceloneta or Jaume I. **Open** *Sept-July* 10am-2.30am Mon-Thur, Sun; 10am-3am Fri, Sat. *Aug* 5.30pm-2.30am Mon-Thur, Sun; 5.30pm-3am Fri, Sat.
Bar. Map p75 B5 ㉑
Eternally popular with all ages and nationalities, Mudanzas has a beguiling, old-fashioned look, with marble-topped tables, a black-and-white tiled floor and a jumble of well-thumbed newspapers. Be warned: it gets very smoky in the winter months, though some relief is to be had at the upstairs tables.

Mundial Bar

Plaça Sant Agustí Vell 1, Sant Pere (93 319 90 56). Metro Arc de Triomf or Jaume I. **Open** 1-4pm, 9pm-midnight Tue-Sat; noon-3.30pm Sun. Closed Aug. **€€€**. **Seafood**. Map p75 C3 ㉒
Recently given a rosy-pink lick of paint, the Mundial's cave-like interior is nothing if not cosy. It has become increasingly pricey of late but, while the mainstay is still no-frills platters of seafood, steaming piles of razor clams, shrimp, oysters, spider crabs and the like, there are now fancy desserts and a more extensive wine list.

La Paradeta

C/Comercial 7, Born (93 268 19 39). Metro Arc de Triomf or Jaume I. **Open** 8-11.30pm Tue-Fri; 1-4pm, 8pm-midnight Sat; 1-4pm Sun. **€€**. No credit cards.
Seafood. Map p75 C4 ㉓
Superb seafood, served refectory style. Choose from glistening mounds of clams, mussels, squid, spider crabs and whatever else the boats have brought in, let them know how you'd like it cooked (grilled, steamed or battered), pick a sauce (Marie Rose, spicy local *romesco*, *all i oli* or onion with tuna), buy a drink and wait for your number to be called. A great, cheap experience for anyone not too grand to clear their own plate.

Re-Pla

C/Montcada 2, Sant Pere (93 268 30 03). Metro Jaume I. **Open** 1.30-4pm, 8.30pm-midnight daily. **€€€**.
Global. Map p75 B3 ㉔
A casually hip but nonetheless welcoming restaurant serving Asian-Mediterranean fusion. The wildly varied menu might include anything from a sushi platter to ostrich with green asparagus, honey and grilled mango slices. Vegetarian options are clearly marked, and desserts are rich and creative. For once, the lighting is wonderfully romantic and the sleek artwork easy on the eye, though some may feel uncomfortable with the sort of waiters who pull up a chair while recounting the day's specials.

Rococó

C/Gombau 5-7, Sant Pere (93 269 16 58). Metro Jaume I. **Open** 9am-midnight Mon-Thur; 9am-1am Fri, Sat. **€€**. **Café**. Map p75 B3 ㉕
On the ground floor of a new and not especially characterful apartment block, Rococó manages to live up to its name thanks to an array of red velvet seating, along with flock wallpaper and gilt-edged paintings. The Vietnamese rolls and chocolate brownies are fun, but the real stars are the bocadillos on home-made ciabatta.

Tèxtil Cafè

C/Montcada 12, Born (93 268 25 98/www.textilcafe.com). Metro Jaume I. **Open** *Nov-Feb* 10am-8pm Tue, Wed; 10am-midnight Thur, Sun; 10am-1am Fri, Sat; *Mar-Oct* 10am-midnight Tue-Thur, Sun; 10am-2am Fri, Sat. **€€**.
Café. Map p75 B4 ㉖

BARCELONA BY AREA

Eastern promises

Wushu

Anecdotally, there was no good Asian food to be had in Barcelona until very recently. In the wealthy neighbourhoods a smattering of Japanese restaurants served respectable but pricey food to businessmen on expense accounts, but mere mortals struggled to find competent sushi and a decent curry. There was a handful of Indian and Chinese restaurants, but these were (and still are) rumoured to save the good stuff for their own people, and serve an anodyne version to everyone else.

This began to change in the 1990s, when the sudden influx of demanding tourists and rude financial health combined to bring about the opening of several Thai and Indonesian places. These, though, have had a tendency to push style over substance and no amount of trickling fountains and garlanded Buddhas can overcome congealed nasi goreng.

Suddenly, however, and perhaps thanks to Catalan wonderchef Ferran Adrià announcing that Chinese is the cuisine of the future, Asian restaurants are where the smart money is being invested. Indeed, Adrià's own former head chef is opening an Asian tapas bar, **Dos Palillos** (C/Elisabets 9, Raval, www. dospalillos.com) as part of the Casa Camper hotel (p169). The name plays with the word for 'toothpicks' (traditionally used to spear tapas) and 'chopsticks'.

Meanwhile Cambodian chef Ly Leap is set to open a new eaterie in a spectacular space – with a 720-sq m tropical garden – at C/Muntaner 82, in the Eixample.

The Tragaluz group are never slow to pick up on a trend, and are responsible for some of the hippest restaurants in town. Their latest venture is to be **La Xina**, a Chinese restaurant on C/Pintor Fortuny in the Raval, though, at the time of writing, and in common with all the restaurants mentioned here, they were foundering in bureaucracy and permits. For those too impatient to wait, we can recommend the excellent wok cooking at **Wushu** (p83) and daisy-fresh sushi at **Shunka** (p63).

Perfectly placed for visitors to the various C/Montcada museums, and with a graceful 14th-century courtyard, Têxtil Cafè is an elegant place in which to enjoy a coffee in the shade in summer or under gas heaters in winter. There are decent breakfast and lunch menus to boot. For music lovers, a DJ plays on Wednesday and Sunday evenings followed, on Sunday, by live jazz (for which there is a €5 supplement).

Va de Vi

C/Banys Vells 16, Born (93 319 29 00).
Metro Jaume I. **Open** 6pm-1am Mon-
Wed, Sun; 6pm-2am Thur; 6pm-3am
Fri, Sat. **Wine bar**. Map p75 B4 ㉗
Owned by a former sommelier, artist and sculptor, this Gothic-style wine bar lists over 1,000 wines, many by the *cata* (tasting measure). The usual Spanish selections are accompanied by wines from the New World and elsewhere.

La Vinya del Senyor

Plaça Santa Maria 5, Born (93 310
33 79). Metro Barceloneta or Jaume I.
Open noon-1am Mon-Thur; noon-2am
Fri, Sat; noon-midnight Sun. **Wine
bar/tapas**. Map p75 A5 ㉘
Another classic wine bar, this one with a well nigh unmatchable position right in front of the beautiful basilica of Santa Maria del Mar. With some high-quality tapas and so many excellent wines on its list (the selection changes every two weeks), it's a crime to do as most tourists do and take up those terrace tables just to take in the view.

Wushu

Avda Marquès de l'Argentera 2,
Born (93 310 73 13/www.wushu-
restaurant.com). Metro Barceloneta.
Open 1pm-midnight Tue-Sat; 1-4pm
Sun. **€€€**. **Pan-Asian**. Map p75 A3 ㉙
Wushu's enormous success in its short life has meant a 2008 move to bigger, sunnier premises. The formula is hard to beat: superb Asian wok cooking (pad thai, lo mein and the only laksa to be found in Barcelona) courtesy of Australian chef Bradley Ainsworth; charming service; scrumptious desserts, and a superb €9.90 set lunch.

El Xampanyet

C/Montcada 22, Born (93 319 70 03).
Metro Jaume I. **Open** noon-4pm, 7-
11.30pm Tue-Sat; noon-4pm Sun.
Closed Aug. **Bar**. Map p75 B4 ㉚
The eponymous poor man's champagne is actually a fruity and drinkable sparkling white wine, served here in old-fashioned coupes and best accompanied by the house tapa, a little plateful of delicious fresh anchovies from Cantábria. Run by the same family since the 1930s, El Xampanyet is lined with coloured tiles, barrels and antique curios, and has a handful of marble tables.

Shopping

Adolfo Domínguez

C/Ribera 16, Born (93 319 21 59/
www.adolfodominguez.com). Metro
Barceloneta. **Open** 11am-9pm Mon-Sat.
Map p75 C5 ㉛
Men's tailoring remains Domínguez's forte, with his elegantly cut suits and shirts. The women's line reciprocates with tame but immaculately refined outfits that are also aimed at the 30- to 45-year-old market. The more casual U de Adolfo Domínguez line courts the younger traditionalist, but doesn't quite attain the panache of its more grown-up precursor. This under-visited two-storey flagship store is supplemented by other locations around the city.

Almacen Marabi

C/Flassaders 30, Born (no phone/
www.almacenmarabi.com). Metro Jaume
I. **Open** noon-2.30pm, 5-8.30pm Tue-Fri;
5-8.30pm Sat. **No credit cards**.
Map p75 B4 ㉜
Mariela Marabi has created a felt fun-land with just a sewing machine and her imagination. Although she says she makes toys for adults, children will love her finger puppets and stuffed animals, and they'll be intrigued by her anatomically correct fabric dolls.

Arlequí Mascares

C/Princesa 7, Born (93 268 27 52/
www.arlequimask.com). Metro Jaume I.
Open 10.30am-8.30pm Mon-Sat;
10.30am-4.30pm Sun. Map p75 A4 ㉝

The walls at Arlequí Mascares drip with masks crafted from papier mâché and leather. Whether gilt-laden or done in feathered commedia dell'arte style, simple Greek tragicomedy versions or traditional Japanese or Catalan varieties, they make striking fancy dress or decorative staples. Other trinkets and toys include finger puppets and mirrors.

Bubó

C/Caputxes 10, Born (93 268 72 24/ www.bubo.ws). Metro Jaume I. **Open** 3-10pm Mon; 10am-10pm Tue, Wed, Sun; 10am-11pm Thur; 10am-1am Fri, Sat. **Map** p75 A5 **㉞**

The place for cakes. Be a hit at any dinner party with a box of Bubó's exquisitely sculpted petits fours, or make afternoon tea fashionable again with a tray of its colourful fruit sablés, raspberry and almond brandy snaps, or dreamily rich sachertorte.

Capricho de Muñeca

C/Brosoli 1, Born (93 319 58 91/ www.caprichodemuneca.com). Metro Liceu. **Open** 10am-9pm Mon-Sat. **Map** p75 A4 **㉟**

Soft leather handbags in cherry reds, chocolate browns and parma violet, are made by hand just up the stairs by designer Lisa Lempp. Belts and wallets complement the handbags.

Casa Antich SCP

C/Consolat del Mar 27-31, Born (93 310 43 91/www.casaantich.com). Metro Jaume I. **Open** 9am-8.30pm Mon-Fri; 9.30am-8.30pm Sat. **Map** p75 A5 **㊱**

Under the arches at the southern edge of the Born you'll find a luggage shop that in levels of service and size of stock recalls the golden age of travel. Here you can still purchase trunks for a steam across the Atlantic and ladies' vanity cases perfect for a sojourn on the Orient Express. But you'll also find cutting-edge bags from the likes of Samsonite and Mandarina Duck.

Casa Gispert

C/Sombrerers 23, Born (93 319 75 35/ www.casagispert.com). Metro Jaume I. **Open** *Jan-Sept* 9.30am-2pm, 4-7.30pm Tue-Fri; 10am-2pm, 5-8pm Sat. *Oct-Dec* 9.30am-2pm, 4-7.30pm Mon-Fri; 10am-2pm, 5-8pm Sat. **Map** p75 B4 **㊲**

Casa Gispert radiates a warmth that emanates from something more than its wood-fired nut and coffee roaster. The shop's Dickensian wooden cabinets and shelves groan with the finest and most fragrant nuts, spices, preserves, sauces, oils and, most importantly, huge, hand-made chocolate truffles. The pre-packaged kits for making various local specialities such as *panellets* (Hallowe'en bonbons) make great gifts.

Custo Barcelona

Plaça de les Olles 7, Born (93 268 78 93/www.custo-barcelona.com). Metro Jaume I. **Open** 10am-10pm Mon-Sat. **Map** p75 B5 **㊳**

The Catalan Dalmau brothers had to make it in LA before bringing their bright and brash T-shirts back home, but now the Custo look has spawned a thousand imitations. Custo's signature prints can be found on everything from coats to swimwear, but a T-shirt is still the most highly prized (and highly priced) souvenir for fashionistas.

Olive

NEW *Plaça de les Olles 2, Born (93 310 58 83). Metro Barceloneta.* **Open** 10am-9pm Mon-Sat. **Map** p75 B5 **㊴**

Buying from small-scale producers of olive oil-based delicacies in Provence, Tuscany and Spain, this successful French chain has ventured below the Pyrenees. As well as oils, fruit vinegars, compotes and other mouthwatering delights, it has gorgeously packaged soap, candles and cosmetics.

On Land

C/Princesa 25, Born (93 310 02 11/ www.on-land.com). Metro Jaume I. **Open** *Sept-July* 5-8.30pm Mon; 11am-3pm, 5-8.30pm Tue-Fri; 11am-8.30pm Sat. *Aug* 11am-3pm, 5-8.30pm Tue-Sat. **Map** p75 B4 **㊵**

On Land shows a refreshing lack of pretension, with simple decor and a hint of playfulness echoed in the fashions it stocks: local boy Josep Font's

Club Mix

The pared-down, post-industrial decor so beloved of this neighbourhood provides the perfect backdrop for bright and quirky shoes. Strange heels and toes are out in force this season, and after all those rubber wedgies and snub-nosed winkle-pickers from the likes of Helmut Lang, Fly, Fornarina and Irregular Choice, you can rest your weary pins on the giant chaise longue.

Vila Viniteca

C/Agullers 7, Born (93 268 32 27/ www.vilaviniteca.es). Metro Jaume I. **Open** *Sept-June* 8.30am-8.30pm Mon-Sat. *July, Aug* 8.30am-8.30pm Mon-Fri; 8.30am-2.30pm Sat. **Map** p75 A5 ㊸

This family-run business has built up a stock of over 6,000 wines and spirits since 1932. With everything from a 1953 Damoiseau rum, which costs as much as €500, through to €6 bottles of table wine, the selection is mostly Spanish and Catalan, but it also takes in some international favourites.

Nightlife

Club Mix

C/Comerç 21, Born (93 319 46 96/ www.clubmixbcn.com). Metro Jaume I. **Open** 8pm-3am daily. **Admission** free. **Map** p75 C4 ㊹

Opened in 2007, Mix is an urbane and classy DJ bar, serving cocktails and 'international tapas' to a grown-up crowd. As well as occasional live acts (most regularly, jazz on Wednesdays), DJs spin rare groove, neo-soul and the like from a deeply cool booth set high up in a copper-panelled wall.

Diobar

C/Marquès de L'Argentera 27, Born (93 221 19 39). Metro Barceloneta. **Open** 11pm-3am Thur-Sat. **Admission** (incl 1 drink) €8. **Map** p75 C5 ㊺

The latest underground hit has popped up in the most unlikely place – the basement of a Greek restaurant. Thursday through Saturday nights, this cosy, stone-walled space transforms into a temple of funk and soul, as the sofas and dancefloor host lounging urbanites and DJ Fred Spider hits the decks.

girly frocks are made for fun rather than flouncing, Petit Bateau's cute T-shirts are perfect for playing sailor girl, and Divinas Palabras' cartoony T-shirts put a smile on your face.

El Rei de la Màgia

C/Princesa 11, Born (93 319 39 20/ www.elreidelamagia.com). Metro Jaume I. **Open** *Sept-July* 10am-2pm, 5-8pm Mon-Fri; 11am-2pm Sat. *Aug* 11am-2pm, 5-8pm Mon-Fri. **Map** p75 A4 ㊹

Harry Potter syndrome has no doubt lured many a young visitor to the 'King of Magic'. Although it's a serious set-up that prepares stage-ready illusions for pros, it also welcomes the amateur magician, curious fan and prank-obsessed schoolboy, who may levitate with joy on seeing its fine range of fake turds, itching powder and the like.

U-Casas

C/Espaseria 4, Born (93 310 00 46/ www.casasclub.com). Metro Jaume I. **Open** 10.30am-9pm Mon-Thur; 10.30am-9.30pm Fri, Sat. **Map** p75 A5 ㊷

CCCB p88

Raval

Upper Raval

The Upper Raval is the city's gentrification success story, and though some may complain about the area losing its edgy appeal, there's no denying the amelioriation in the living standards and cultural life of its residents. The centre of the district is the Plaça dels Àngels, where the buildings that once formed the 16th-century Convent dels Àngels now house the **FAD** design institute; and a gigantic almshouse, the Casa de la Caritat, has been converted into a cultural complex housing the **MACBA** art museum and the **CCCB**. When the clean, high-culture MACBA opened in 1995, it appeared to embody everything the Raval was not, but it profoundly influenced what the Raval was to become.

Below here, C/Hospital and C/Carme meet at the Plaça Pedró, where the tiny Romanesque chapel (and ex-lepers' hospital) of Sant Llàtzer sits. From La Rambla, the area is accessed along either street or through the **Boqueria** market, itself the site of the Sant Josep monastery until the sale of church lands led to its destruction in the 1830s. Behind the Boqueria is the **Antic Hospital de la Santa Creu**, which took in the city's sick from the 15th century until 1926 (it now houses Catalonia's main library and the headquarters of the Institute of Catalan Studies); and **La Capella**, an attractive exhibition space. C/Carme is capped at the Rambla end by the 18th-century **Església de Betlem** (Bethlehem) with its serpentine pillars and geometrically patterned façade.

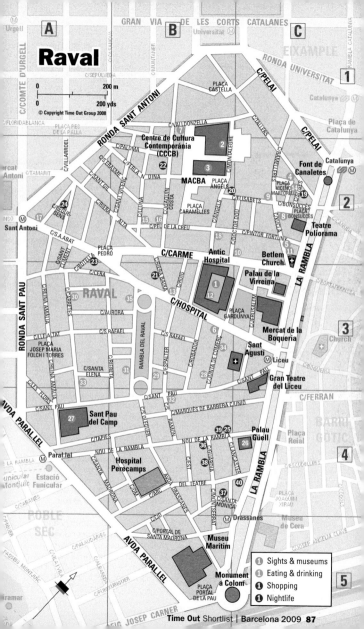

Raval

A   B   C

GRAN VIA DE LES CORTS CATALANES

Urgell

C/COMTE D'URGELL

C/FLORIDABLANCA

0   200 m
0   200 yds
© Copyright Time Out Group 2008

RONDA SANT ANTONI

Universitat

EIXAMPLE
RONDA UNIVERSITAT

C/PELAI

Plaça de
Catalunya

Catalunya

1

PLAÇA PES
DE LA PALLA

rcat
Antoni

C/TAMARIT

PLAÇA
CASTELLA

C/VALLDONZELLA

C/TALLERS

Font de
Canaletes

Catalunya

Centre de Cultura
Contemporánia
(CCCB) **22**

2

MACBA

PLAÇA
ÁNGELS **20**

C/ELISABETS

4
VICENÇ
MARTORELL **5**

9

C/BONSUCCES

8 PLAÇA
BONSUCCES

Teatre
Poliorama

2

Sant Antoni

17

C/RIERA
ALTA

24
C/REUS/
SENA

15 16
PLAÇA
DEL PEU DE LA CREU

18

PLAÇA
CARAMELLES

C/PINTOR FORTUNY

10

Betlem
Church

11

LA RAMBLA

PLAÇA
PEDRO

C/BOTELLA
23

C/CARME

Antic
Hospital

Palau de la
Virreina

RONDA SANT PAU

RAVAL **30**

C/AURORA

C/S. RAFAEL

RAMBLA DEL RAVAL

35

C/HOSPITAL

1
12

21
13

6

PLAÇA
GARDUNYA

Mercat de la
Boqueria

3

Church

C/JOSEP MARIA
FOLCH I TORRES

C/ELISA ELENA

31

33

29

34

28

Sant
Agustí

32

Liceu

Gran Teatre
del Liceu

C/FERRAN

BARRI
GÒTIC

AVDA PARALLEL

27

Sant Pau
del Camp

C/TAPIES

NOU DE LA RAMBLA

Hospital
Perecamps

39 25

36

38

26

Palau
Güell

40

Plaça
Reial

4

Paral·lel

Estació
Funicular

unicular
Montjuïc

37
C/SANTA
MÒNICA

Drassanes

Museu
de Cera

POBLE
SEC

Museu
Marítim

PLAÇA
JOAQUIM
XIRAU

iramar

AVDA PARALLEL

PLAÇA
PORTAL
DE LA PAU

Monument
a Colón

1 Sights & museums
1 Eating & drinking
1 Shopping
1 Nightlife

5

MACBA

Sights & museums

Antic Hospital de la Santa Creu & La Capella

C/Carme 47-C/Hospital 56 (Antic Hospital no phone/La Capella 93 442 71 71). Metro Liceu. **Open** *Antic Hospital* 9am-8pm Mon-Fri; 9am-2pm Sat. *La Capella* noon-2pm, 4-8pm Tue-Sat; 11am-2pm Sun. **Admission** free. **Map** p87 B3 ①

There was a hospital on this site as early as 1024, but in the 15th century it expanded to centralise all the city's hospitals and sanatoriums. By the 1920s it was hopelessly overstretched and its medical facilities moved uptown to the Hospital Sant Pau. One of the last patients was Gaudí, who died here in 1926; it was also here that Picasso painted one of his first important pictures, *Dead Woman* (1903).

The buildings artfully combine a 15th-century Gothic core with Baroque and neo-classical additions. They're now given over to cultural institutions, among them Catalonia's main library.

Highlights include a neo-classical lecture theatre complete with revolving marble dissection table, and the entrance hall of the Casa de Convalescència, tiled with lovely Baroque ceramic murals telling the story of Sant Pau (St Paul); one features an artery-squirting decapitation scene. La Capella, the hospital chapel, was rescued from a sad fate as a warehouse and sensitively converted to an exhibition space for contemporary art. The beautifully shady colonnaded courtyard is a popular spot for reading or eating lunch.

CCCB (Centre de Cultura Contemporània de Barcelona)

C/Montalegre 5 (93 306 41 00/www.cccb.org). Metro Catalunya. **Open** 11am-8pm Tue, Wed, Fri-Sun; 11am-10pm Thur. **Admission** *1 exhibition* €4.50; €3.40 reductions & Wed. *2 exhibitions* €6; €4.50 reductions & Wed. Free under-16s; 1st Wed of mth; 8-10pm Thur. **Map** p87 B2 ②

Spain's largest cultural centre was opened in 1994 at the huge Casa de la Caritat, built in 1802 on the site of a medieval monastery. The massive façade and part of the courtyard remain from the original building; the rest was rebuilt, all tilting glass and steel. As a centre for contemporary culture, the CCCB tends to pick up whatever falls through the cracks elsewhere: film cycles and multimedia presentations, and flamenco, literary, music and dance festivals.

Event highlights 'World Press Photo' (Nov-Dec 2008); 'Contemporary Chinese art' (Nov-Feb 2009); 'Bamako': contemporary African photography (Feb-May 2009); 'Visions of Catalonia': exploring ideas of a Catalan utopia (Feb-May 2009).

MACBA (Museu d'Art Contemporani de Barcelona)

Plaça dels Àngels 1 (93 412 08 10/ www.macba.es). Metro Catalunya. **Open** *June-Sept* 11am-8pm Mon, Wed; 11am-midnight Thur, Fri; 10am-8pm Sat; 10am-3pm Sun. *Oct-May* 11am-7.30pm Mon, Wed-Fri; 10am-8pm Sat; 10am-3pm Sun. **Admission** *All exhibitions* €7.50; €3-€6 reductions. *Permanent exhibition* €3; €2 reductions. *Temporary exhibitions* €4; €3 reductions. **Map** p87 B2 ③

No work of art inside the MACBA can quite live up to the wow factor of Richard Meier's cool iceberg of a museum. Even some of the best sculptures are on the outside: *La Ola* (The Wave), a curving bronze behemoth by Jorge Oteiza, and the monochrome mural *Barcelona*, by Eduardo Chillida. Inside, the shows are often heavily political in concept and occasionally radical to the point of inaccessibility. If you can't or won't see the socio-political implications of, say, a roomful of beach balls, the MACBA may leave you cold.

With a new director to be appointed in 2008, exhibits are subject to change, but for the present the earlier pieces are strong on artists such as Antonio Saura and Tàpies, who were members of the

Dau-al-Set, a group of radical writers and painters, influenced by Miró, who started the Catalan art movement after the apathy and stagnation of the post-Civil War years. Jean Dubuffet, and Basque sculptors Jorge Oteiza and Eduardo Chillida also feature. Works from the last 40 years are more global, with the likes of Joseph Beuys, Jean-Michel Basquiat, AR Penck and photographer Jeff Wall; the contemporary Spanish collection includes Catalan painting (Ferran Garcia Sevilla, Miquel Barceló) and sculpture (Sergi Aguilar, Susana Solano).

Event highlights A retrospective of Nancy Spero (until 5 Oct 2008); Photography as historical source and universal language (23 Oct 2008-6 Jan 2009).

Eating & drinking

Bar Kasparo

Plaça Vicenç Martorell 4 (93 302 20 72). Metro Catalunya. **Open** *May-Sept 9am-midnight daily. Oct-Apr 9am-11pm Tue-Sat. Closed mid Dec-mid Jan. No credit cards.* €€. **Café**. Map p87 C2 ④

In the running for the award of the favourite bar for Barcelona's parents – who often feel both beleaguered and neglected by business and municipality – Australian-run Bar Kasparo has outdoor seating (only) which overlooks a playground on an attractively quiet, traffic-free square. As well as sandwiches and tapas, there is a daily-changing selection of dishes from around the globe, plus soups and salads. Even better, the kitchen stays open all day too.

Bar Lobo

C/Pintor Fortuny 3 (93 481 53 46). **Open** *noon-midnight Mon-Wed, Sun; noon-2am Thur-Sat.* €€€. **Bar/Global**. Map p87 C2 ⑤

Bar Lobo is a starkly monochrome space, with high ceilings and punky artwork from celebrated graffiti artists. The watchword here is moody (not least among the too-cool-for-school waiting staff) but the bar comes alive with DJs and studied lounging on the mezzanine at night, and by day its terrace is a peaceful, sunny place for coffee or a light lunch.

Bar Mendizábal

C/Junta de Comerç 2 (no phone). Metro Liceu. **Open** *June-Oct* 10am-1am daily. *Nov-May* 10am-midnight daily. No credit cards. **Bar. Map** p87 B3 ⑥
An emblematic Raval bar, with its multi-coloured tiles featuring in many thousands of holiday snaps, Mendizábal has been around for decades but is really little more than a pavement stall. On offer are myriad fruit juices, bocadillos and, in winter, soup, served to tables across the road in the tiny square opposite.

Baraka

C/Valldonzella 25 (93 304 10 61). Metro Universitat. **Open** 11am-10.30pm Mon-Fri. **Café. Map** p87 B1 ⑦
At the back of a beautiful old building converted into a health-food shop is this cosy little bar, where everything, from the wine and the beer to the milk used in the fair-trade coffee, is organic and cheap – not a common combination elsewhere. And should anything ail you, staff will make up an appropriate medicinal tea from the shop's stock of more than 100 herbs.

Buenas Migas

Plaça Bonsuccés 6 (93 318 37 08). Metro Liceu. **Open** *June-Sept* 10am-midnight Mon-Thur, Sun; 10am-1am Fri, Sat. *Oct-May* 10am-11pm Mon-Thur, Sun; 10am-midnight Fri, Sat. €€. **Vegetarian. Map** p87 C2 ⑧
'Good Crumbs' (from a phrase meaning 'to get on with someone'), is a ferociously wholesome kind of place, all gingham and pine and chewy spinach tart. The speciality is tasty focaccia with various toppings, along with the usual high-fibre, low-fun cakes you expect to find in a vegetarian café. This branch has several tables outside.

Dos Trece

C/Carme 40 (93 301 73 06/www. dostrece.net). Metro Liceu. **Open** 1.30-4pm, 9pm-midnight Tue-Sun. €€. **Global. Map** p87 C2 ⑨
Another venue that has fallen victim to the council's crackdown on late-night music, Dos Trece had to ditch its DJs and jam sessions, and instead has turned its cosy basement space into another dining room – this one with cushions and candles suitable for post-prandial lounging. Apart from a little fusion confusion (ceviche with nachos, and all manner of things with yucca chips) the food's not half bad for the price, and includes one of the few decent burgers to be had in Barcelona.

Elisabets

C/Elisabets 2-4 (93 317 58 26). Metro Catalunya. **Open** 7am-11pm Mon-Sat. Closed 3wks Aug. €€. No credit cards. **Bar/Catalan. Map** p87 C2 ⑩
Elisabets maintains a sociable local feel, despite the recent gentrification of its street. Dinner (Fridays only) is actually a selection of tapas, and otherwise only the set lunch or myriad bocadillos are served. The lunch deal is terrific value, however, with osso buco, vegetable and chickpea stew, baked cod with garlic and parsley, and roast pork knuckle all making an appearance on the menu with gratifying regularity.

Granja M Viader

C/Xuclà 4-6 (93 318 34 86). Metro Liceu. **Open** 5-8.45pm Mon; 9am-1.45pm, 5-8.45pm Tue-Sat. Closed 3wks Aug. €€. **Tearoom. Map** p87 C2 ⑪
The chocolate milk drink Cacaolat was invented in this old *granja* in 1931, and is still on offer, along with strawberry and banana milkshakes, *orxata* (tiger nut milk) and hot chocolate. It's an evocative, charming place with century-old fittings and enamel adverts, but the waiters refuse to be hurried. Popular with Catalan families on the way back from picking up the children, and couples meeting after work.

El Jardi

C/Hospital 56 (93 329 15 50). Metro Liceu. **Open** 10am-11pm Mon-Sat. €€. **Café. Map** p87 B3 ⑫
A small terrace café in the dusty tree-lined grounds of the Antic Hospital (pxx), El Jardi provides a welcome spot of tranquillity just off La Rambla. Breakfast pastries and all the usual tapas are present and correct, along with pasta dishes, quiches and salads.

BARCELONA BY AREA

Voodoo chic

Spruce yourself up with a handmade little you, or liven up a loved one with a little them. Soft and smiling, Lolitas are 8-inch-high personalised rag dolls, made with love and enthusiasm by Barcelona-based designer Maria del Mar González.

Cute, quirky and occasionally sexy, Lolitas (male or female) are made in a workshop at the back of the shop: **Novedades** (C/Peu de la Creu 24, 93 329 16 36, www.lolitasbcn.com). They are based on a person's physical features, favourite clothing and character traits. They come in all ages and you can even order a celebrity dolly, just as Spanish *Marie Claire* did with their request for a mini Christina Ricci.

Maria del Mar began making Lolitas as gifts for her nephews five years ago and soon her friends were putting in orders. Since then the Lolitas empire has spread, with up to 50 of the little fellows flying out of the workshop every week.

She's up for a challenge and is happy to whip up anyone you like. The dolls even come with distinguishing props: a football or a handbag, say, a parachute or a pet. Personalised puppies are part of a new range and ready-made accessories include Lolitas bags, and T-shirts.

Simply fill in details of your friend's physical features, interests and mannerisms on the website and provide a good photo. It takes about six weeks for your Lolita to arrive and it costs around €100.

Juicy Jones

C/Hospital 74 (93 443 90 82). Metro Liceu. **Open** noon-11pm daily. **€€**. No credit cards. **Vegetarian**. **Map** p87 B3 ⑬

This is the most recent branch of this riotously colourful, vegan restaurant, oriented towards back-packers, with an endless and inventive list of juices, salads and filled baguettes. Staffed, it would seem, by slightly clueless language exchange students, its heart is in the right place, but it is not somewhere you can expect a speedy lunch. Bring a book.

Lili Deliss

Plaça Vicenç Martorell 2 (mobile 639 743 221). Metro Catalunya. **Open** 9.30am-7.30pm Mon-Sat. No credit cards. **Café**. **Map** p87 C2 ⑭

A respectable alternative when Bar Kasparo (p90) is full, this tiny French-run café also has tables in the shade overlooking the cheerful Plaça Vicenç Martorell. A short list of eating options includes filled baguettes, quiches, crêpes and home-made cakes. No alcohol.

Mam i Teca

C/Lluna 4 (93 441 33 35). Metro Sant Antoni. **Open** 1-4pm, 8.45pm-midnight Mon, Wed-Fri, Sun; 8.45pm-midnight Sat. Closed 2wks Aug. **€€**. **Tapas**. **Map** p87 B2 ⑮

Mam i Teca is a bright little tapas restaurant with only three tables, so it pays to reserve. All the usual tapas, from anchovies to cured meats, are rigorously sourced, and complemented by superb daily specials such as organic *botifarra*, pork confit and asparagus with shrimp. The bar (which is also open afternoons) is worth mentioning for its superior vodka and tonic.

Ravalo

Plaça Emili Vendrell 1 (93 442 01 00). Metro Sant Antoni. **Open** 6pm-1.30am Tue-Sun. **€€**. **Pizzeria**. **Map** p87 B2 ⑯

Perfect for fans of the thin and crispy variety pizza, Ravalo's table-dwarfing examples take some beating, thanks to flour, and a chef, imported from Naples. Most pizzas, like the Sienna, are furnished with the cornerstone toppings you'd expect – in this case mozzarella di bufala, speck, cherry tomatoes and rocket – but less familiar offerings include the pizza soufflé, which is filled with ham, mushrooms and an eggy mousse (better than it sounds, really). The terrace overlooking a quiet square is open year-round.

Sésamo

C/Sant Antoni Abat 52 (93 441 64 11).
Metro Sant Antoni. **Open** 1-3.30pm
Mon; 1-3.30pm, 8.30-11.30pm Wed-Sat;
8.30-11.30pm Sun. **€€**. **Vegetarian**.
Map p87 A2 ⑰

Another veggie restaurant that doesn't take itself too seriously (yoga ads, but no whale song), Sésamo offers a creative bunch of dishes in a cosy, buzzing back room. Salad with risotto and a drink is a bargain at €6.50, or try cucumber rolls stuffed with smoked tofu and mashed pine nuts, crunchy polenta with baked pumpkin, gorgonzola and radicchio, or the delicious spicy curry served in popadom baskets with dhal and wild rice.

Silenus

C/Àngels 8 (93 302 26 80). Metro
Liceu. **Open** 1.30-4pm, 8.30pm-11.30am
Mon-Thur; 1.30-4pm, 8.30pm-midnight
Fri, Sat. **€€€**. **Mediterranean**.
Map p87 B2 ⑱

Run by arty types for arty types, Silenus works hard on its air of scuffed elegance, with carefully chipped and stained walls on which the ghost of a clock is projected and the faded leaves of a book float up on high. The food, too, is artistically presented, and never more so than with the lunchtime tasting menu. This offers a tiny portion of everything on the menu, from French onion soup to a flavoursome haricot bean stew and entrecôte with mash.

Shopping

Discos Castelló

C/Tallers 3, 7, 9 & 79 (93 302 59
46/www.discoscastello.es). Metro
Catalunya. **Open** 10am-8.30pm
Mon-Sat. **Map** p87 C2 ⑲

Discos Castelló is a homegrown cluster of small music shops, each with a different speciality: no.3 is devoted to classical music and opera; the largest, no.7, covers pretty much everything; no.9 does hip hop, rock and alternative pop plus T-shirts and accessories; and no.79 is best for jazz, 1970s pop, ethnic music and electronica.

Giménez y Zuazo

C/Elisabets 20 (93 412 33 81/www.
boba.es). Metro Catalunya. **Open**
10.30am-3pm, 5-8.30pm Mon-Sat.
Map p87 B2 ⑳

This effortlessly cool designer duo has always been quirky. Previously, they've let themselves go when it comes to colour and print, although they have remained quite restrained with the silhouette of their women's clothing line. However, recently they seem to have thrown the A-line shape rule book out of the window and have started playing with layers and asymmetric cuts.

Le Swing

C/Riera Baixa 13 (93 324 84 02).
Metro Liceu. **Open** 10.30am-2.30pm,
4.30-8.30pm Mon-Sat. **Map** p87 B3 ㉑
Today's second-hand is known as 'vintage', and thrift is not on the agenda. Fervent worshippers of Pierre Cardin, YSL, Dior, Kenzo and other fashion deities scour all corners of the sartorial stratosphere and deliver their booty back to this little powder puff of a boutique. The odd Zara number and other mere mortal brands creep in as well.

Nightlife

Benidorm

C/Joaquín Costa 39 (no phone). Metro
Universitat. **Open** *Apr-mid Oct* 8pm-
2.30am Mon-Thur, Sun; 8pm-3am Fri,
Sat. *Mid Oct-Mar* 7pm-2.30am Mon-
Thur, Sun; 7pm-3am Fri, Sat. Closed
Aug. No credit cards. **Map** p87 B2 ㉒
This lively, smoky little place is a kitsch paradise of brothel-red walls, crystal lanterns and 1980s disco paraphernalia, boasting the world's smallest toilet, dancefloor and chill-out room.

Sant Pau del Camp

BARCELONA BY AREA

The sounds being absorbed by the seething mass of humanity that packs in here at weekends range from hip hop to 1970s funk and soul, although in the main they are variations on the same electronica theme. Because the crowds are so big, you should watch your wallet.

Big Bang

C/Botella 7 (93 443 28 13/www. bigbangbcn.net). Metro Sant Antoni. **Open** 9.30pm-2.30am Wed, Thur, Sun; 10.15pm-3am Fri, Sat. **Admission** *Bar* free. *Gigs* vary. **Map** p87 A3 ㉓
As well as rock gigs, this tiny, alluringly crusty bar hosts jam sessions and film nights. There's a somewhat cruddy football table overseen by straight-down-the-line bar staff. The place attracts all types, from local lowlife and perennial barflies to backpackers with a sense of adventure. It's a useful destination of last resort when everything else in the area has closed for the night – just bang on the shutters in order to be let in.

Jazz Sí Club

C/Requesens 2 (93 329 00 20/www. tallerdemusics.com). Metro Sant Antoni. **Open** 5pm-2.30am Mon-Thur, Sun; 5pm-3am Fri, Sat. No credit cards. **Map** p87 A2 ㉔
This tiny music school auditorium and bar is a space where students, teachers and music lovers can meet, perform and listen. Every night is dedicated to a different musical genre: there's trad jazz on Monday; pop, rock and blues jams on Tuesday; jazz sessions on Wednesday; Cuban music on Thursday; flamenco on Friday; and rock on Saturday and Sunday.

London Bar

C/Nou de la Rambla 34 (93 318 52 61). Metro Liceu. **Open** 7.30pm-3am Mon; 7.30pm-3.30am daily. **Admission** free. **Map** p87 B4 ㉕
The only thing familiar to Londoners will be the punters; otherwise, the Modernista woodwork and smoky, yellowing charm is 100% Barcelona. Problems with the Ajuntament put an end to the live music, but the owners promise the jazz, blues and rock will return soon.

Lower Raval

The **Barrio Chino** ('Barri Xino' in Catalan), as the lower half of the Raval is often known, is a nickname coined in the 1920s by a journalist comparing it to San Francisco's Chinatown, and referred to its underworld feel rather than to any Chinese population. The authorities have long been working on cleaning up the area. Whole blocks previously associated with prostitution or drugs have been demolished, a sports centre, a new police station and office blocks have been constructed, and some streets have been pedestrianised. But the most dramatic plan was to create a *'Raval obert al cel'* ('Raval open to the sky'), the most tangible result

Palau Güell

of which is the sweeping, palm-lined Rambla del Raval. This is now filling up nicely with new bars and restaurants, and boasts Botero's deliciously bulging **Gat** ('Cat') sculpture.

C/Nou de la Rambla, the area's main street, is home to Gaudí's first major project, the Palau Güell. Nearby, in C/Sant Pau, is a Modernista landmark, Domènech i Montaner's **Hotel España**, and at the end of the street sits the Romanesque tenth-century church of **Sant Pau del Camp**. Iberian remains dating to 200 BC have been found next to the edifice, marking it as one of the oldest parts of the city. At the lower end of the area were the Drassanes (shipyards), now home to the **Museu Marítim**. Along the Paral·lel side of this Gothic building is the only remaining large section of the city's 14th-century city wall.

Sights & museums

Palau Güell

C/Nou de la Rambla 3 (93 317 39 74/ www.palauguell.cat). Metro Drassanes or Liceu. **Open** 10am-2.30pm Tue-Sat. **Admission** free. **Map** p87 C4 ❷⁶
A fortress-like edifice shoehorned into a narrow six-storey sliver, the Palau Güell was Gaudí's first major commission, begun in 1886 for textile baron Eusebi Güell. After major structural renovation, it has partially reopened to the public, and is expected to fully reopen at the end of 2008. For the time being visitors can look around the subterranean stables, with an exotic canopy of stone palm fronds on the ceiling, and the ground floor. Here, the vestibule has ornate *mudéjar* carved ceilings from which the Güells could snoop on their arriving guests through the jalousie trellis-work; at the heart of the house lies the spectacular six-storey hall complete with musicians' galleries and topped by a dome covered in cobalt honeycomb tiles. The antidote to this dark and gloomy palace lies on its roof terrace, decorated with a rainbow forest of 20 mosaic-covered chimneys.

Sant Pau del Camp

C/Sant Pau 101 (93 441 00 01). Metro Paral·lel. **Open** *Visits* 10am-1.30pm; 5-8pm Mon-Fri. *Mass* 8pm Sat; noon Sun. **Admission** €2; €1 reductions; *Mass* free. No credit cards. **Map** p87 A4 ❷⁷
The name, St Paul in the Field, reflects a time when this was still countryside. This church goes back more than 1,000 years; the date carved on its most prestigious headstone – that of Count Guifré II Borell, son of Wilfred the Hairy and inheritor of all Barcelona and Girona – is AD 912. The façade includes sculptures of fantastical flora and fauna along with human grotesques. In the tiny cloister there are extraordinary Visigothic capitals and some triple-lobed arches. Restored after serving as a school in 1842, an army barracks from 1855 to 1890 and then as a bomb site during the Civil War, Sant Pau is now deservedly a national monument.

Biblioteca

C/Junta de Comerç 28 (93 412 62 21). Metro Liceu. **Open** 8-11.30pm Mon-Sat. Closed 2wks Aug. €€€.
Mediterranean. Map p87 B3 ㉕

A very Zen space with beige minimalist decor, Biblioteca is all about food. Food and books about food, that is. From Bocuse to Bourdain, they are all for sale, and their various influences collide in some occasionally sublime cooking. Beetroot gazpacho with live clams and quail's egg is a dense riot of flavour, and the endive salad with poached egg and romesco wafers is superb. Mains aren't quite as head-spinning, but are accomplished nevertheless.

Cafè de les Delicies

Rambla del Raval 47 (93 441 57 14). Metro Liceu. **Open** 6pm-2am Mon, Tue, Thur, Sun; 6pm-3am Fri, Sat. Closed 3wks Aug. €. No credit cards.
Café. Map p87 B3 ㉙

David Soul! Boney M! Olivia Newton-John! The functioning 1970s jukebox is reason enough to visit this cosy little bar, even without the excellent G&Ts, the chess, the variety of teas, the terrace and the shelves of books for browsing. A coveted alcove with a sofa, low armchairs and magazines is opened at busy times, or there is a quiet dining room at the back.

Las Fernández

C/Carretes 11 (93 443 20 43). Metro Paral·lel. **Open** 9pm-2am Tue-Sun. €€. **Spanish**. Map p87 A3 ㉚

An inviting entrance, coloured pillarbox red, is a beacon of cheer on one of Barcelona's more insalubrious streets. Inside, the three Fernández sisters have created a bright and unpretentious bar-restaurant that specialises in the wines, foods and dishes from their native León. Alongside regional specialities *cecina* (dried venison), gammon and sausages are lighter, Mediterranean dishes and generous salads; smoked salmon with mustard and dill, pasta filled with wild mushrooms, and sardines with a citrus escabeche.

Madame Jasmine

Rambla del Raval 22 (no phone). Metro Liceu. **Open** 10am-2.30am Tue-Fri, Sun; 10am-3am Fri, Sat. €. No credit cards.
Café. Map p87 B3 ㉛

Kitted out like a slightly bizarre and crumbling old theatre set, Madame Jasmine sports silver spray-painted geckos, oriental lamps and feather boas amid its beams and retro '70s tiling. Its generous salads and heaped bocadillos are named after historical Raval characters and local street names.

Marsella

C/Sant Pau 65 (93 442 72 63). Metro Liceu. **Open** 10pm-2.30am Mon-Thur; 10pm-3am Fri, Sat. No credit cards.
Bar. Map p87 B4 ㉜

Marsella was opened in 1820 by a native of Marseilles, who may have changed the course of Barcelona's artistic endeavour by introducing absinthe, still a mainstay of the bar's delights. Untapped 100-year-old bottles of the stuff sit in glass cabinets alongside old mirrors and William Morris curtains, probably covered in the same dust kicked up by Picasso and Gaudí.

Mesón David

C/Carretes 63 (93 441 59 34). Metro Paral·lel. **Open** 1-4.30pm, 8-11.45pm Mon, Tue, Thur-Sun. Closed Aug. €.
Spanish. Map p87 A3 ㉝

Rough and ready, noisy, chaotic and a lot of fun, Mesón David is also one of the cheapest restaurants in Barcelona. Be prepared to share a table. Mainly Galician dishes include *caldo gallego* (cabbage broth) or fish soup to start, followed by *lechazo* (a vast hunk of roast pork) or grilled calamares. Of the desserts, the almond *tarta de Santiago* battles for supremacy with fresh baby pineapple doused in Cointreau.

Organic

C/Junta de Comerç 11 (93 301 09 02). Metro Liceu. **Open** 12.30pm-midnight daily. €€. **Vegetarian**.
Map p87 B3 ㉞

The last word in refectory chic, Organic is better designed and lighter in spirit (its motto: 'Don't panic, it's organic!')

than the majority of the city's vegetarian restaurants. Options include an all-you-can-eat salad bar, a combined salad bar and main course, or the full whammy – salad, soup, main course and dessert. Beware the extras (such as drinks), which hitch up the prices.

La Verònica

Rambla del Raval 2-4 (93 329 33 03).
Metro Liceu. **Open** *Sept-July* noon-2am Tue-Sun. *Aug* 7pm-1am Tue-Sun. **€€**.
Pizzeria. Map p87 B3 C1 ⑤

La Verònica has moved from the Barri Gòtic to the newly cool Rambla del Raval. Its pizzas are properly crisp, thin and healthy, and come with such toppings as smoked salmon, or apple, gorgonzola and mozzarella. Salads include the Nabocondensor, a colourful, healthful tumble of parsnip, cucumber and apple, and there is a short but reliable wine list.

Shopping

Torres

C/Nou de la Rambla 25 (93 317 32 34/ www.vinosencasa.com). Metro Drassanes or Liceu. **Open** 9am-2pm, 4-9pm Mon-Sat. **Map** p87 B4 ㊱

After moving from its old and dusty grocery store across the road, Torres' shiny new shop is a bit out of place in the scruffy Lower Raval. It stocks an excellent range of Spanish wines (with a particularly good cava section) and black Mallorcan absinthe.

Nightlife

Bar Pastis

C/Santa Mònica 4 (93 318 79 80).
Metro Drassanes. **Open** 7.30pm-2am Tue-Thur, Sun; 7.30pm-3am Fri, Sat.
Map p87 B4 ㊲

This quintessentially Gallic bar once served pastis to visiting sailors and the denizens of the Barrio Chino underworld. It still has a louche Marseilles feel, floor-to-ceiling indecipherable oil paintings (by the original owner when drunk, apparently), Edith Piaf on the stereo, and latter-day troubadours on Tuesdays, Wednesdays and Sundays.

La Concha

C/Guàrdia 14 (93 302 41 18).
Metro Drassanes. **Open** 5pm-2.30am Mon-Thur, Sun; 5pm-3am Fri, Sat.
Admission free. No credit cards.
Map p87 B4 ㊳

Though it's not as gay as it used to be under its new management, the homo-to-hetero ratio of the crowd that packs La Concha every night to sip cocktails and dance to Moroccan pop, salsa and flamenco remains the highest for blocks. As does the camp factor, with Sara Montiel, queen of the Spanish silver screen, watching over her loyal subjects from hundreds of faded photographs.

Guru

C/Nou de la Rambla 22 (93 318 08 40/www.gurubarcelona.com).
Metro Liceu. **Open** 8pm-3am daily.
Admission free. No credit cards.
Map p87 B4 ㊴

Guru is set to become the sleekest addition yet to the newly hip Raval – even though, palm trees and mood lighting aside, its white padded walls do make it look unsettlingly like an asylum. As it has not yet achieved the exclusive status it's aiming for, Cosmo-sipping Parisiennes are still having to deal with gangs of tipsy Scousers hopping about to live salsa. For the moment, that is.

Moog

C/Arc del Teatre 3 (93 301 72 82/ www.masimas.com). Metro Drassanes.
Open midnight-5am daily.
Admission €9. **Map** p87 C4 ㊵

A night spent in Moog feels a little like going to a party on an aeroplane: it's long, narrow and completely enclosed, with full-blast air-conditioning and service that comes with a smile. Some fine techno and house keep everything ticking along just right though – Angel Molina, Laurent Garnier and Jeff Mills, among countless other notables, have all played here, with Wednesday nights being especially popular. Upstairs there's a tiny concession to those not feeling the bleeps – an even smaller dancefloor that plays R&B and 1970s tunes.

Bestial p107

Barceloneta & the Ports

Barceloneta

Despite many of its famously tiny apartments being converted into short-stay holiday flats, this working-class neighbourhood still has a local feel, and the narrow and chaotic streets hidden behind the restaurant-lined boulevard of Passeig Joan de Borbó form a real slice of old Barcelona.

Since the beach clean-up, Barceloneta has enjoyed a higher profile, and current redevelopment includes university housing and Enric Miralles's towering Gas Natural headquarters, which is covered in mirrored glass. In the heart of the neighbourhood is the new market designed by Josep Mias.

The area also has a staggering amount of sculpture, particularly around the Port Vell.

Eating & drinking

Can Paixano

C/Reina Cristina 7 (93 310 08 39/ www.canpaixano.com). Metro Barceloneta. **Open** 9am-10.30pm Mon-Sat. Closed 3wks Aug-Sept. No credit cards. **Bar**. **Map** p100 C2 ●
It's impossible to talk, get your order heard or move your elbows, yet the 'Champagne Bar', as it's invariably known, has a global following. It's always mobbed with Catalans and adventurous tourists making the most of dirt-cheap house cava and sausage bocadillos (you can't buy a bottle without a couple). A must.

Can Ramonet

C/Maquinista 17 (93 319 30 64). Metro Barceloneta. **Open** noon-midnight daily. Closed 2wks Jan, 2wks Aug. €€€. **Seafood**. Map p101 D3 ②

A classic among Barceloneta's seafood restaurants, this quaint, rose-coloured space with two quiet terraces is overlooked by tourists, being deep in the heart of the neighbourhood. Thus, it suffers none of the drop in standards of those paella joints on nearby Passeig Joan de Borbó. Spectacular displays of fresh seafood show what's on offer that day, but it's also worth sampling the velvety fish soup and the generous paellas.

Can Solé

C/Sant Carles 4 (93 221 50 12). Metro Barceloneta. **Open** 1.30-4pm, 8-11pm Tue-Thur; 1.30-4pm, 8.30-11pm Fri, Sat; 1.30-4pm Sun. Closed 2wks Aug. €€€. **Seafood**. Map p100 C4 ③

One of Barceloneta's most traditional seafood restaurants, where for over a century portly, jovial waiters have been charming moneyed regulars. Over the years many of these have added to the framed photos, sketches and paintings that line the walls. What continues to lure them is the freshest shellfish (share a plate of chipirones in onion and garlic, Cantabrian anchovies or red shrimp to start) and fillets of wild turbot, lobster stews and sticky paellas. Beware the steeply priced extras (coffee, cover).

La Cova Fumada

C/Baluard 56 (93 221 40 61). Metro Barceloneta. **Open** 9am-3pm Mon-Wed; 9am-3pm, 6-8.15pm Thur, Fri; 9am-1pm Sat. Closed Aug. €. No credit cards. **Tapas**. Map p100 C4 ④

This cramped bodega is the birthplace of the potato *bomba*, served with a fiery chilli sauce. Especially tasty are the chickpeas with *morcilla* sausage, roast artichokes and the marinated sardines. Its huge following of lunching workers means it's hard to get a table after 1pm.

Kaiku

Plaça del Mar 1 (93 221 90 82). Metro Barceloneta. **Open** 1-3.30pm Tue-Sun. €€€. **Seafood**. Map p100 C4 ⑤

With its simple look, missable façade and paper tablecloths, Kaiku looks a world apart from the upmarket seafood restaurants that pepper this *barrio*, but its dishes are in fact sophisticated takes on the seaside classics. At Kaiku a salad starter comes with shavings of foie gras or red fruit vinaigrette, and paella is given a rich and earthy spin with wild mushrooms. Book ahead, particularly for a terrace table looking out across the beach.

La Piadina

C/Meer 48 (mobile 660 806 172). Metro Barceloneta. **Open** 1-10pm Tue-Sun. €. No credit cards. **Italian**. Map p100 C4 ⑥

A *piadina* is a warmed Italian wrap, made using something like a pitta. Fillings here come in 30 permutations on the basic tomato, mozzarella, ham, rocket and mushroom theme. To find the place, turn inland at Rebecca Horn's tower of rusting cubes on the beach.

Set Portes

Passeig Isabel II 14 (93 319 30 33/ www.7portes.com). Metro Barceloneta. **Open** 1pm-1am daily. €€€. **Seafood**. Map p100 C2 ⑦

The eponymous seven doors open on to as many dining salons, all kitted out in elegant 19th-century decor. Regional dishes are served in enormous portions and include a stewy fish *zarzuela* with half a lobster, and a different paella daily (shellfish, for example, or with rabbit and snails). Reservations are only available for certain tables (two or even three days in advance is recommended); without one, get there early or expect a long wait outside.

Somorrostro

C/Sant Carles 11 (93 225 00 10/ www.restaurantesomorrostro.com). Metro Barceloneta. **Open** 7-11.30pm Mon, Thur-Sun. €€€. **Global**. Map p100 C4 ⑧

Named after the shanty town of Andalucian immigrants that once stood nearby on the beach, Somorrostro is a refreshingly non-fishy, non-traditional restaurant for these parts. Its bare-bricked walls and red and black decor

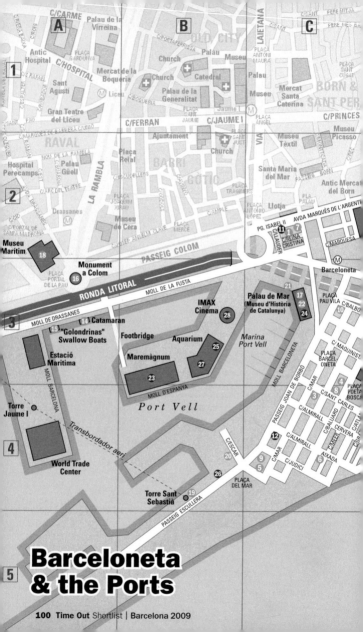

Barceloneta
& the Ports

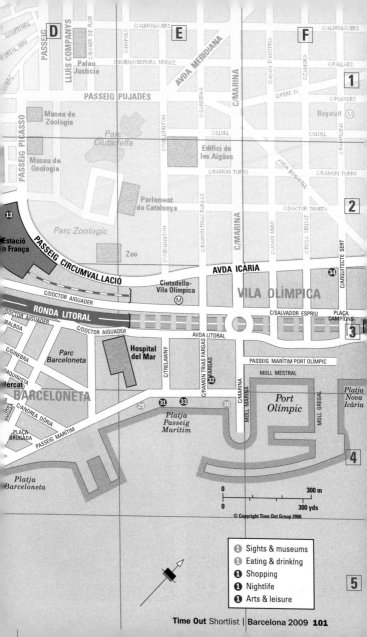

D

C/CORTINES

CORTES REIU

LLUIS COMPANYS

PASSEIG

PALAU Justicia

C/ROGER DE FLOR

C/CHAPOLS

C/BUENAVENTURA MUÑOZ

E

C/ALMOGÀVERS

AVDA MERIDIANA

C/MARINA

C/JOAN D'AUSTRIA

C/AUSTRIA

C/ZAMORA

F

C/ALMOGÀVERS

C/PALLARS

1

PASSEIG PUJADES

C/PERE IV

C/PUJADES

Bogatell Ⓜ

C/PAMPLONA

Museu de Zoologia

Parc Ciutadella

C/WELLINGTON

C/CARDENA

C/LLULL

C/LLULL

PASSEIG PICASSO

Museu de Geologia

Parlament de Catalunya

C/RAMON TRIAS FARGAS

C/RAMON TURRÓ

Edifici de les Aigües

C/RAMON TURRÓ

AVDA BOGATELL

C/DOCTOR TRUETA

2

C/MARINA

C/JOAN MIRÓ

C/ROSA SENSAT

C/ARQUITECTE SERT

Parc Zoologic

⑬

Estació de França

PASSEIG CIRCUMVAL.LACIÓ

Zoo

C/WELLINGTON

AVDA ICÀRIA

Ciutadella-Vila Olímpica Ⓜ

VILA OLÍMPICA

㉞

C/DOCTOR AIGUADER

RONDA LITORAL

C/SALVADOR ESPRIU

PLAÇA CAMPIONS

3

C/DOCTOR AIGUADER

C/DOCTOR AIGUADER

AVDA LITORAL

C/DOCTOR AIGUADER

BALBOA

C/GINEBRA

Parc Barceloneta

Hospital del Mar

PASSEIG MARÍTIM PORT OLÍMPIC

MOLL MESTRAL

C/MAQUINISTA

Mercat

BARCELONETA

C/ANDREA DÒRIA

PLAÇA BRUGADA

PASSEIG MARÍTIM

C/TRELAWNY

C/RAMON TRIAS FARGAS

㉜

㉙

㉛ ㉝

㉚

C/MARINA

C/MARINA

MOLL MARINA

Port Olímpic

MOLL GREGAL

Platja Nova Icària

4

Platja Passeig Marítim

Platja Barceloneta

0   300 m

0   300 yds

© Copyright Time Out Group 2008

5

Ⓘ Sights & museums
Ⓘ Eating & drinking
Ⓘ Shopping
Ⓘ Nightlife
Ⓘ Arts & leisure

attract a young, buzzy crowd, attended to by permanently confused waiters. The food ranges from cucumber, tomato and yoghurt soup to an unexpectedly successful tandoori duck magret.

El Suquet de l'Almirall

Passeig Joan de Borbó 65 (93 221 62 33). Metro Barceloneta. **Open** 1-4pm, 9-11pm Tue-Sat; 1-4pm Sun. Closed 2wks Aug. €€€. **Seafood**. Map p100 C4 ⑨

El Suquet remains a friendly family concern despite the smart decor and business lunchers. Fishy favourites range from *xató* salad to *arròs negre* and a variety of set menus, including the 'blind' selection of tapas, a huge taster menu and, most popular, the Pica-Pica, which includes roasted red peppers with anchovies, steamed cockles and clams, and a heap of *fideuà* with lobster.

El Vaso de Oro

C/Balboa 6 (93 319 30 98). Metro Barceloneta. **Open** 9am-midnight daily. Closed Sept. No credit cards. €€. **Tapas**. Map p100 C3 ⑩

The popularity of this long, narrow bar, styled like a cruise ship, tells you everything you need to know about the tapas. It also means that he who hesitates is lost when it comes to ordering. Elbow out a space and demand, loudly, *chorizitos*, *patatas bravas*, cubed steak (*solomillo*) or spicy tuna (*atún*).

Nightlife

Sala Monasterio

NEW *Passeig Isabel II 4 (mobile 609 780 405). Metro Barceloneta.* **Open** 9.30pm-2.30am Mon-Thur, Sun; 9.30pm-3am Fri, Sat. **Admission** varies. Map p100 C2 ⑪

The entrance to Sala Monasterio is easily missed; go in through the bar at street level and descend to this low-ceilinged, bare-brick cavern to hear all matter of jamming and live music coming through on a great sound system. On Monday there are singer-songwriters, rock jams on Tuesday, Wednesday sees Brazilian music, Thursday blues jams, and weekends vary.

Museu d'Història de Catalunya p104

Suite Royale

Passeig Joan de Borbó 54 (93 268 00 12). Metro Barceloneta. **Open** 10pm-3am daily. **Admission** free. **Map** p100 C4 ⓬

Barcelona night owls suffered when hotspot Café Royale closed, but the same crew have revamped the club in a new portside hotel. Jazz-funk DJ Fred Guzzo still has his swing, while the softly lit, retro bachelor pad decor of Café Royale has been reproduced in a tiny subterranean setting.

Arts & leisure

Sessió Continua

NEW *Sala de Cinema Auditori UPF, Estació de França, Passeig de la Circumval·lació 8 (93 265 64 62/ www.sessiocontinua.com). Metro Barceloneta.* **Open** 8.30pm Thur. **Admission** free. **Map** p75 C5 ⓭

Indie and cult films are shown every Thursday in this university auditorium at the side of the Estació de França. Entrance is free, but you need to put your name down on the Catalan-only website (click on 'Forum' and fill in your name and how many people) to be added to a list at the door.

Port Vell

Barcelona's first wharves were not built until the Middle Ages, when the city was on its way to being the dominant power in the western Mediterranean. The Drassanes Reials (Royal Shipyards) are among the world's finest surviving pieces of civilian Gothic architecture; they now house the **Museu Marítim** and bear witness to the strength of the Catalan navy as the city became the hub of trading routes between Africa and the rest of Europe. The city's power was dealt a blow when Christopher Columbus sailed west and found what he thought was the East; soon the Atlantic became the important trade route and Barcelona went into recession.

Despite putting the city out of business, Columbus was commemorated in 1888 with the **Monument a Colom**, a statue inspired by Nelson's Column, complete with eight majestic lions. Nearby is the **World Trade Center**, a ship-shaped construction built on a jetty and housing offices, a five-star hotel and a tower for the **Transbordador Aeri** cable car. The Moll d'Espanya wharf is an artificial island home to the **Maremàgnum** shopping mall, an **IMAX** cinema and **L'Aquàrium**. It's linked to land by the undulating Rambla de Mar footbridge.

Sights & museums

Catamaran Orsom

Portal de la Pau, Port de Barcelona (93 441 05 37/www.barcelona-orsom.com). Metro Drassanes. **Sailings** (approx 1hr 20mins) *Mar-Oct* noon-8pm 3-4 sailings daily. All sailings subject to weather conditions. **Tickets** €12-€14.50; €6-€9.50 reductions. No credit cards. **Map** p100 A3 ⓮

This 23-metre (75ft) catamaran – departing from the jetty by the Monument a Colom – chugs round the Nova Bocana harbour development, before unfurling its sails and peacefully gliding across the bay. There are 8pm jazz cruises from June to September or the catamaran can be chartered for private trips along the Costa Brava.

Las Golondrinas

Moll de Drassanes (93 442 31 06/ www.lasgolondrinas.com). Metro Drassanes. **Tickets** €5-€10.50; €2.50-€7.50 reductions; free under-4s. **Map** p100 A3 ⓯

For over 115 years the 'swallow boats' have chugged all around the harbour, giving passengers a bosun's-eye view of Barcelona's now rapidly changing seascape. The fleet is made up of three double-decker pleasure boats and two glass-bottomed catamarans, moored next to the Orsom catamaran. The boats leave around every 35 minutes for the shorter trip, and approximately every hour for the longer journey.

Monument a Colom

Plaça Portal de la Pau (93 302 52 24). Metro Drassanes. **Open** 9am-8pm daily. **Admission** €2.30; €1.50 reductions; free under-4s. No credit cards. **Map** p100 A3 ⑯
Where La Rambla meets the port you'll find the Columbus monument, which was designed for the 1888 Universal Exhibition. It's hard to believe from ground level, but Colom himself is actually 7m (23ft) high; his famous white barnet comes courtesy of the city pigeons. A tiny lift takes you up inside the column to a circular viewing bay for a panoramic view of city and port. The claustrophobic and acrophobic should stay away; the slight sway is particularly unnerving.

Museu d'Història de Catalunya

Plaça Pau Vila 3 (93 225 47 00/ www.mhcat.net). Metro Barceloneta. **Open** 10am-7pm Tue, Thur-Sat; 10am-8pm Wed; 10am-2.30pm Sun. **Admission** €3; €2.10 reductions; free under-7s. Free to all 1st Sun of mth. No credit cards. **Map** p100 C3 ⑰
Located in a lavishly converted 19th-century port warehouse, the Museum of Catalan History's compass runs from the Paleolithic era right up to Jordi Pujol's proclamation as President of the Generalitat in 1980. With very little in the way of original artefacts, it is more a virtual chronology of the region's past revealed through two floors of text, photos, film, animated models and reproductions of everything from a medieval shoemaker's shop to a 1960s bar. Hands-on activities such as trying to lift a knight's armour or irrigating lettuces with a Moorish water wheel add a little pzazz to the rather dry displays. Every section has a decent introduction in English, but the reception desk will also lend copies of the more detailed museum guide. Upstairs is a café with a terrace and an unbeatable view.

Event highlights International historical monument photography prize (Oct-Nov 2008); World War I photography (Dec 2008-Feb 2009); the relationship between Catalonia and Hungary in the 13th century (Mar-July 2009).

Museu Marítim

Avda Drassanes (93 342 99 29/ www.museumaritimbarcelona.com). Metro Drassanes. **Open** 10am-7pm daily. **Admission** €6.50; €3.25 reductions; free under-7s. *Temporary exhibitions* varies. *Combined ticket with Las Golondrinas (35 mins)* €9.20; €5.50-€7 reductions; free under-4s. **Map** p100 A2 ⑱
A full-scale replica of Don Juan de Austria's royal galley, from which he led the ships of the Holy League to victory against the invading Ottomans at Lepanto, is the mainstay of the collection at the Museu Marítim, complete with a ghostly crew of oarsmen projected on to the rowing banks. The original ship was built in these very same shipyards, one of the finest examples of civil Gothic architecture in Spain and a monument to Barcelona's importance in Mediterranean naval history. With the aid of an audio guide, the maps, nautical instruments, multimedia displays and models show how shipbuilding and navigation techniques have developed and evolved over the years. Admission also covers the *Santa Eulàlia* schooner docked in the Moll de la Fusta.

Transbordador Aeri

Torre de Sant Sebastià, Barceloneta (93 441 48 20). Metro Barceloneta. Also Torre de Jaume I, Port Vell, to Ctra Miramar, Montjuïc. Metro Drassanes. **Open** *Mid June-mid Sept* 11am-8pm daily. *Mid Sept-mid June* 10.45am-7pm daily. **Tickets** €9 single; €12.50 return; free under-6s. No credit cards. **Map** p100 B4 ⑲
These rather battered old cable cars run between the Sant Sebastià tower at the very far end of Passeig Joan de Borbó to the Jaume I tower in front of the World Trade Center; the final leg ends at the Miramar lookout point on Montjuïc.

Eating & drinking

Bar Colombo

*C/Escar 4 (93 225 02 00). Metro
Barceloneta.* **Open** noon-3am daily.
Closed 2wks Jan-Feb. No credit cards.
Bar. **Map** p100 B4 ㉑

Deckshoe yachties and chic moneyed
locals stroll by all day, apparently oblivious to this little bar and its sunny terrace overlooking the port. In fact,
nobody seems to notice it, which is odd
given its fantastic location and generous portions of *patatas bravas*. The only
drawback is the nerve-jangling techno
that fetches up on the sound system.

Luz de Gas – Port Vell

*Opposite the Palau de Mar, Moll
del Dipòsit (93 484 23 26). Metro
Barceloneta or Jaume I.* **Open** Apr-
Oct noon-3am daily. Closed Nov-Mar.
Bar. **Map** p100 C3 ㉑

It's cheesy, but this boat/bar also has
its romantic moments. By day, bask in
the sun with a beer on the upper deck,
or rest in the shade below. With nightfall, candles are brought out and, if you
can blot out the Lionel Richie, it's
everything a holiday bar should be.

La Miranda del Museu

*Museu d'Història de Catalunya, Plaça
Pau Vila 3 (93 225 50 07). Metro
Barceloneta.* **Open** 10am-7pm Tue;
10am-8pm Wed; 10am-7pm, 9-11pm
Thur-Sat; 10am-4pm Sun. **€€**. **Café**.
Map p100 C3 ㉒

Don't go spreading this about, but
there's a secret café with terrific views,
cheap and reasonable food and a vast
terrace, sitting right at the edge of the
marina, perched high above the humdrum tourist traps. Stroll into the
Catalan History Museum and take the
lift to the top floor. And, what's more,
you don't need a ticket.

Shopping

Maremàgnum

*Moll d'Espanya (93 225 81 00/
www.maremagnum.es). Metro
Drassanes.* **Open** 10am-10pm
daily. **Map** p100 B3 ㉓

After years of declining popularity, the
Maremàgnum shopping centre has
been spruced up, ditched most of the
bars and discos, and taken a step
upmarket with shops such as Xocoa
(for mouthwatering chocolate), Calvin
Klein and Parisian accessories from
boudoirish Lollipops. The high-street
staples are all present and correct –
Mango, H&M, Women's Secret and so
on – and the ground floor still focuses
on the family market with sweets,
clothes for children and a Barça shop.
There's also a Starbucks and a handful of tapas bars and restaurants.

Nightlife

Le Kasbah

*Plaça Pau Vilà (Palau del Mar) (93
238 07 22/www.ottozutz.com). Metro
Barceloneta.* **Open** 11pm-3am daily.
Admission free. **Map** p100 C3 ㉔

A white awning heralds the entrance
to this louche bar behind the Palau de
Mar. Inside, a North African harem

Museu Marítim

look seduces a young and up-for-it mix of tourists and students. As the night progresses so does the music, from chill-out early on to full-on boogie later.

Mondo

Edifici IMAX, Moll d'Espanya (93 221 39 11/www.mondobcn.com). Metro Barceloneta or Drassanes. **Open** 11.30pm-3am Wed-Sat. **Map** p100 B3 **25**

Arrive by yacht or by Jaguar – anything less might not get you so far. Upscale dining alongside amazing views of the port precede late-night caviar and champagne house parties with DJs from Hed Kandi and Hotel Costes.

Red Lounge Bar

NEW *Passeig Joan de Borbó 78 (93 221 31 93/www.redloungebcn.com). Metro Barceloneta.* **Open** 8pm-3am daily. **Admission** free. **Map** p100 B4 **26**

More good news for those that miss the legendary Café Royale (see Suite Royale p103) with this stylish new bar. DJ Fred Guzzo is also working the decks here, blending funk, latin and rare groove for a mix of music aficionados and glossy-haired uptown kids drawn to the high-class harem look.

Arts & leisure

L'Aquàrium

Moll d'Espanya (93 221 74 74/www. aquariumbcn.com). Metro Barceloneta or Drassanes. **Open** Oct-May 9.30am-9pm Mon-Fri; 9.30am-9.30pm Sat, Sun. *June, Sept* 9.30am-9.30pm daily. *July, Aug* 9.30am-11pm daily. **Admission** €16; €11-€12.50 reductions; free under-4s. **Map** p100 B3 **27**

The aquarium houses more than 450 species of Mediterranean marine life. Miniaquària is devoted to the smaller animals such as sea cucumbers and seahorses, but the main draw is the Oceanari, a giant shark-infested tank traversed via a glass tunnel. The upstairs section is devoted to children, with knobs-and-whistles style activities for pre-schoolers or Planet Aqua – an extraordinary, split-level circular space with Humboldt penguins and a walk-through model of a sperm whale.

IMAX Port Vell

Moll d'Espanya (93 225 11 11/ www.imaxportvell.com). Metro Barceloneta or Drassanes. **Tickets** €7-€10. **Map** p100 B3 **23**

A squat white hulk in the middle of the marina, the IMAX has yet to persuade many that it's anything more than a gimmick. The rather predictable programming covers fish, birds, ghosts and adventure sports.

Vila Olímpica

The land further up the coast was once an area of thriving industry, but by the 1980s it had fallen into disuse and presented the perfect blank sheet for a team of 30 prize-winning architects to design the Olympic Village, with quarters for 15,000 athletes, parks, a metro stop, four beaches and a leisure marina. The result is a spacious district but the lack of cafés and shops leaves it devoid of bustle.

Most social activity takes place in the seafront Port Olímpic, home to docked sailboats, restaurants, beaches, a large casino, and a waterfront strip of cheesy clubs and theme pubs. Wide empty boulevards lend themselves well to large-scale sculpture; landmark pieces include a jagged pergola on Avda Icària by Enric Miralles and Carme Pinós, in memory of ripped-up industrial railway tracks, and Antoni Llena's abstract *David i Goliat* in the Parc de les Cascades.

Eating & drinking

Agua

Passeig Marítim 30 (93 225 12 72/ www.aguadeltragaluz.com). Metro Barceloneta, then bus 45, 57, 59, 157. **Open** 1-3.45pm, 8-11.30pm Mon-Thur, Sun; 1-4.30pm, 8pm-12.30am Fri, Sat. €€€. **Mediterranean**. **Map** p101 E4 **29**

One of the freshest, most relaxed places to eat in the city, with a large terrace smack on the beach and an animated sunny interior. The menu itself rarely changes, but the regulars never seem to tire of the competently executed monkfish tail with tomato and onion, the risotto with partridge, and fresh pasta with juicy little prawns. Scrummy puddings include marron glacé mousse and a sour apple sorbet.

Bestial

C/Ramón Trias Fargas 2-4 (93 224 04 07). Metro Barceloneta. **Open** 1-3.45pm, 8-11.30pm Mon-Thur; 1-3.45pm, 8pm-12.30am Fri; 1-4.30pm, 8pm-12.30am Sat; 1-4.30pm, 8-11.30pm Sun. **€€€. Italian. Map** p101 E4 ③⓪

Its tiered wooden decking and ancient olive trees make Bestial a peerless spot for alfresco seaside dining. At weekends, coloured lights play over the tables as a DJ takes to the decks. The food is modern Italian: dainty little pizzas, rocket salads with parma ham and a lightly poached egg, tuna with black olive risotto and all the puddings you would expect to find.

Nightlife

Around the Port Olímpic, you'll find endless dance bars, seafood restaurants, fast-food outlets and mock-Irish pubs.

CDLC

Passeig Marítim 32 (93 224 04 70/ www.cdlcbarcelona.com). Metro Ciutadella-Vila Olímpica. **Open** 10pm-2.30am Mon-Wed; noon-3am Thur-Sun. **Admission** free. **Map** p101 E4 ③①

The Carpe Diem Lounge Club remains at the very forefront of Barcelona's splash-the-cash, see-and-be-seen celeb circuit – the white beds flanking the dancefloor, guarded by a clipboarded hostess, are perfect for showing everyone who's the daddy. Or, for those not celebrating record deals, funky house and a busy terrace provide an opportunity for mere mortals (and models) to mingle and discuss who's going to finance their next drink and how to get chatting to whichever member of the Barça team has just walked in.

Club Catwalk

C/Ramon Trias Fargas s/n (93 221 61 61/www.clubcatwalk.net). Metro Ciutadella-Vila Olímpica. **Open** midnight-5.30am Wed-Sun. **Admission** €15-€18. **Map** p101 E3 ③②

Maybe it's the name or maybe it's the location (slap bang under celeb-tastic Hotel Arts), but most of the Catwalk queue seems to think they're headed for the VIP room – that's crisp white collars and gold for the boys and short, short skirts for the girls. Inside it's suitably snazzy; upstairs there's R&B and hip hop, but the main house room is where most of the action is, with regular appearances from the likes of Erick Morillo and Roger Sánchez keeping the club's prestige firmly intact.

Shôko

Passeig Marítim 36 (93 225 92 03/ www.shoko.biz). Metro Ciutadella-Vila Olímpica. **Open** 11.30pm-3am daily. **Admission** free. **Map** p101 E4 ③③

Another semi-exclusive restaurant-club concept in the Port Olímpic. The tried and tested formula continues to go down a treat with Sarrià's pseudo-fashionistas – all Britney hats, spray-on jeans and little wiggles – as they strut their stuff on the dancefloor, gutted they couldn't get into the more exclusive CDLC. Meanwhile, outside on the terrace, civilised sets of chino-clad tourists recline on the comfy beds sipping cocktails.

Arts & leisure

Yelmo Icària Cineplex

C/Salvador Espriu 61, Vila Olímpica (information 93 221 75 85/tickets 902 22 09 22/www.yelmocineplex.es). Metro Ciutadella-Vila Olímpica. **Tickets** *Mon* €5.30. *Tue-Sun* €6.80; €5.30 before 3pm & reductions. No credit cards. **Map** p101 F3 ③④

The Icària has all the atmosphere of the empty shopping mall that surrounds it, but what it lacks in charm, it makes up for in choice, with 15 screens offering a commercial roster of mainstream films. Queues tend to be slow-moving; it's worth booking your seat online.

Fundació Joan Miró p110

Montjuïc & Poble Sec

Montjuïc's plentiful gardens and green spaces are greatly underused by local citizens; plans to convert it into the 'Central Park' of Barcelona have seen improved access and a raft of attractions from outdoor cinema to a new sports museum, but still the climb up the hill proves off-putting for many people. For many others the peace this bestows is its greatest attraction – as well as the variety of museums, there are lots of tranquil picnic spots, with spectacular views, and very few tourists, even in high season.

The mists of time obscure the etymology of Montjuïc, but an educated guess is that 'juïc' comes from the old Catalan word meaning Jewish. It was here that the medieval Jewish community buried their dead; some of the excavated headstones are now kept in the Museu Militar, inside the 17th-century Castell de Montjuïc. This was rebuilt in its current form after Philip V's troops broke the siege of Barcelona in 1714. From its vantage point overlooking the city, the central government was able to impose its will on the unruly populace until the death of Franco.

The most popular access to the park is still the long way from Plaça d'Espanya, with the climb eased by a sequence of open-air escalators. Where Avda Paral·lel meets Plaça d'Espanya you'll find Las Arenas, the old bullring. The

BARCELONA BY AREA

108 Time Out Shortlist | Barcelona 2009

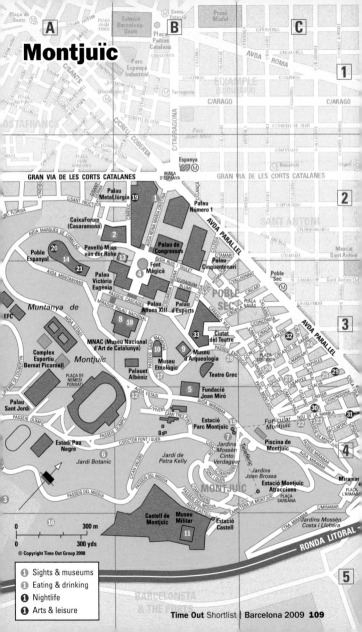

Montjuïc

last bull met its fate here in the 1970s and for decades the bullring lay derelict. The ubiquitous Lord Rogers is currently overseeing a mammoth transformation project, to be completed in 2010, which will turn the ring into a circular leisure complex while restoring the original neo-Mudéjar façade. The vision encompasses a 'piazza in the sky', a giant roof terrace that will allow for alfresco events and offer panoramic views over Barcelona.

Sights & museums

Bus Montjuïc Turístic

Torres Venecianas, Plaça d'Espanya (93 415 60 20). Metro Espanya. **Open** *Mid Sept-June 10am-9.20pm Sat, Sun. July-mid Sept 10am-9.20pm daily.* **Tickets** *Day pass €3; €2 reductions. No credit cards.* **Map** p109 B2 ❶

An open-top tourist bus. There are actually two routes: the blue line starts and ends here at Plaça Espanya, the red one at Portal de la Pau (p100 A3), near the Monument a Colom; they coincide at the Olympic stadium and the castle. Tickets are valid for both routes.

CaixaForum

Casaramona, Avda Marquès de Comillas 6-8 (93 476 86 00/www.fundacio.lacaixa.es). Metro Espanya. **Open** *10am-8pm daily.* **Admission** *free.* **Map** p109 A/B2 ❷

One of the masterpieces of industrial modernism, this former red-brick yarns and textiles factory was designed by Puig i Cadafalch in 1911. It spent most of the last century in a sorry state, acting briefly as a police barracks and then falling into dereliction. Fundació La Caixa, the charitable arm of Catalonia's largest savings bank, bought it and gave it a huge rebuild. The brick factory was supported while the ground below was excavated to house an entrance plaza by Arata Isozaki (who designed the Palau Sant Jordi on the other side of the hill), a Sol LeWitt mural, a 350-seat auditorium, bookshop and library. In addition to the smaller permanent contemporary art collection, upstairs there are three impressive spaces for temporary exhibitions – often among the most interesting in the city.

Cementiri del Sud-oest

C/Mare de Déu de Port 54-58 (93 484 17 00). Bus 38. **Open** *8am-6pm daily.* **Admission** *free.* **Map** p109 A4 ❸

This enormous necropolis, perched at the side of the motorway out of town, serves as a daily reminder to commuters of their own mortality. It has housed the city's dead since 1883, originally placing them in four sections: one for Catholics, one for Protestants, one for non-Christians and a fourth for unborn babies. It now stretches over the entire south-west corner of the mountain, with family tombs stacked up to six storeys high. Many, notably those belonging to the city's gypsy community, are a riot of colour.

Font Màgica de Montjuïc

Plaça Carles Buïgas 1 (93 316 10 00). Metro Espanya. **Fountain** *May-Sept 8-11.30pm Thur-Sun; music every 30mins 9.30pm-midnight. Oct-Apr 7-9pm Fri, Sat; music every 30mins 7-9pm.* **Map** p109 B3 ❹

Still using its original art deco waterworks, the 'magic fountain' works its wonders with the help of 3,600 pieces of tubing and 4,500 light bulbs. Summer evenings after nightfall see the multiple founts swell and dance to various hits ranging from Sting to the *1812 Overture*, showing off a kaleidoscope of pastel colours, while searchlights play in a giant fan pattern over the palace dome. Current drought conditions may mean that the fountain is turned off in summer 2008 until the situation improves.

Fundació Joan Miró

Parc de Montjuïc (93 443 94 70/www.bcn.fjmiro.es). Metro Paral·lel then Funicular de Montjuïc/bus 61. **Open** *July-Sept 10am-8pm Tue, Wed, Fri, Sat; 10am-9.30pm Thur; 10am-2.30pm Sun. Oct-June 10am-7pm Tue, Wed, Fri, Sat;*

Font Màgica de Montjuïc

10am-9.30pm Thur; 10am-2.30pm Sun. *Guided tours* 11.30pm Sat, Sun. **Admission** *All exhibitions* €7.50; €5 reductions. *Temporary exhibitions* €4; €3 reductions. Free under-14s.
Map p109 B4 ⑤

Josep Lluis Sert, who spent the years of the dictatorship as Dean of Architecture at Harvard University, designed one of the world's great museum buildings on his return. Approachable, light and airy, these white walls and arches house a collection of more than 225 paintings, 150 sculptures and all of Miró's graphic work, plus some 5,000 drawings. The permanent collection, highlighting Miró's trademark use of primary colours and simplified organic forms symbolising stars, the moon, birds and women, occupies the second half of the space. On the way to the sculpture gallery is Alexander Calder's lovely reconstructed *Mercury Fountain*, which was originally seen at the Spanish Republic's Pavilion at the 1937 Paris Fair. In other works, Miró is shown as a Cubist (*Street in Pedralbes*, 1917), Naïve (*Portrait of a Young Girl*, 1919) or Surrealist (*Man and Woman in Front of a Pile of Excrement*, 1935). The works downstairs were donated to the museum by 20th-century artists. In the upper galleries, large, black-outlined paintings from the final period precede a room of works with political themes.

Temporary shows vary wildly in content and quality, but at best can match the appeal of the permanent exhibition. The Espai 13 in the basement features young contemporary artists. Outside is a pleasant sculpture garden with fine work by some contemporary Catalan artists.

Jardí Botànic

C/Doctor Font i Quer (93 426 49 35/ www.jardibotanic.bcn.cat). Metro Espanya. **Open** *Apr-May, Sept* 10am-6pm Mon-Fri; 10am-8pm Sat, Sun. *June-Aug* 10am-8pm daily. *Oct-Mar* 10am-5pm daily. **Admission** €3; €1.50 reductions. Free under-16s & last Sun of mth. No credit cards.
Map p109 A4 ⑥

MNAC

The botanic garden was opened in 1999, with the idea of collecting plants from the seven global regions that share a western Mediterranean climate. The result is impressive. Everything about the futuristic design, from the angular concrete pathways to the raw sheet-steel banking, is the antithesis of the more naturalistic, Jekyll-inspired gardens of England. It is meticulously kept, with the added advantage of wonderful views across the city. There is a small space housing occasional temporary exhibitions and free audio guides to lead visitors through the gardens.

Jardins Mossèn Costa i Llobera

Ctra de Miramar 38. Metro Drassanes or Paral·lel. **Open** 10am-sunset daily. **Admission** free. **Map** p109 B4 **7**

The port side of Montjuïc is protected from the cold northerly wind, which creates a microclimate that is some two degrees warmer than the rest of the city. This has made it perfect for 800 species of the world's cacti. It is said to be the most complete collection of its type in Europe. Along with the botanical curiosities, there is a vast bronze of a young girl making lace.

MNAC (Museu Nacional d'Art de Catalunya)

Palau Nacional, Parc de Montjuïc (93 622 03 76/www.mnac.cat). Metro Espanya. **Open** 10am-7pm Tue-Sat; 10am-2.30pm Sun. **Admission** (valid 2 days) *Permanent exhibitions* €8.50; €6 reductions. *Temporary exhibitions* €3-€5. *Combined entrance with Poble Espanyol* (p114) €12. Free over-65s, under-15s and 1st Thur of mth. **Map** p109 B3 **8**

The National Museum of Catalan Art gives a dizzying overview of Catalan art from the 12th to the 20th centuries. In recent years, the museum has added a whole extra floor to absorb holdings of the Thyssen-Bornemisza collection previously kept in the convent in Pedralbes, along with Modernista work from the former Museum of Modern Art in Ciutadella park.

The highlight of the museum, however, is still the Romanesque collection, with 21 murals rescued from Pyrenean churches, including the tremendous *Crist de Taüll* from the 12th-century church of Sant Climent de Taüll.

The Gothic collection is also excellent and starts with some late 13th-century frescoes. There are carvings and paintings from local churches, including works of the Catalan masters of the Golden Age, Bernat Martorell and Jaume Huguet. The highlight of the Thyssen collection is Fra Angelico's *Madonna of Humility* (c1430s), while the Cambó bequest contains some stunning Old Masters – Titian, Rubens and El Greco. Also unmissable is the Modernista collection, which includes the original mural of *Ramon Casas and Pere Romeu on a Tandem* (1897), which decorated Els Quatre Gats. The rich collection of decorative arts includes furniture from Modernista houses such as the Casa Amatller and Gaudí's Casa Batlló.

Event highlights A retrospective of 20th century avant-garde sculptor Juli González (27 Oct 2008-Jan 2009); Drawings and paintings by turn of the century artist Eugenio Lucas (3 Nov 2008-Jan 2009); 'Coinage at War. Catalonia in Napoleonic Europe' (until May 2009).

Museu d'Arqueologia de Catalunya

Passeig de Santa Madrona 39-41 (93 423 21 49/93 423 56 01/www.mac.cat). Metro Poble Sec. **Open** 9.30am-7pm Tue-Sat; 10am-2.30pm Sun. **Admission** €3; €2.10 reductions; free under-16s. No credit cards. **Map** p109 B3 ⑨

The time frame for this archaeological collection starts with the Palaeolithic period, and there are relics of Greek, Punic, Roman and Visigoth colonisers, up to the early Middle Ages. A massive Roman sarcophagus is carved with scenes of the rape of Persephone, and an immense statue of Asklepios, the god of medicine, towers over one room. The display ends with the marvellous, jewel studded headpiece of a Visigoth king. One of the best-loved pieces is an alarmingly erect Priapus, found during building work in Sants in 1848 but kept under wraps 'for moral reasons' until 1986.

Museu Etnològic

Passeig de Santa Madrona s/n (93 424 68 07/www.museuetnologic.bcn.cat). Metro Poble Sec. **Open** *Late June-late Sept* noon-8pm Tue-Sat; 11am-3pm Sun. *Late Sept-late June* 10am-7pm Tue, Thur; 10am-2pm Wed, Fri-Sun. **Admission** €3; €1.50 reductions; free under-16s, over-65s & 1st Sun of mth. No credit cards. **Map** p109 B3 ⑩

Recently spruced up and expanded, the Ethnology Museum houses a vast collection of items, from Australian Aboriginal boomerangs to rugs and jewellery from Afghanistan, although by far the most comprehensive collections are from Catalonia. Of the displays upstairs, most outstanding are the Moroccan, Japanese and Philippine exhibits, though there are also some interesting pre-Columbian finds. Of the attempts to arrange the pieces in interesting ways, 'Taboo' turns out to be a limp look at nudity in different cultures; more successful is 'Sacred', a run through the world of religious rituals.

Museu Militar

Castell de Montjuïc, Ctra de Montjuïc 66 (93 329 86 13). Metro Paral·lel, then funicular & cable car. **Open** *Apr-Oct* 9.30am-7pm Tue-Fri; 9.30am-8pm Sat, Sun. *Nov-Mar* 9.30am-5pm Tue-Fri; 9.30am-7pm Sat, Sun. **Admission** €3; €1.50 reductions; free under-7s. No credit cards. **Map** p109 B5 ⑪

Appropriately housed in one wing of the old hilltop castle, the Military Museum is a grim slice of local history. The fortress was used to bombard rather than protect Barcelona in past conflicts, and as a prison and place of execution, the castle has strong repressive associations. The exhibits include armour, swords, lances, muskets, rifles and pistols. Other highlights include 23,000 lead soldiers representing a Spanish division of the 1920s. Oddly, a display of Jewish tombstones from the moun-tain's desecrated medieval cemetery is the only direct reminder of death within its walls. If the Spanish government cedes the castle to the city of Barcelona, there are plans to turn part of the building into a centre for peace studies.

Museu Olímpic i de l'Esport

Avda Estadi 60 (93 292 53 79). Bus 50, 55, 61. **Open** *Apr-Sept* 10am-6pm Mon, Wed-Sun. *Oct-Mar* 10am-1pm, 4-6pm Mon, Wed-Sun. **Admission** €8; €6 reductions; free under-5s. **Map** p109 B4 ⑫

Opened in 2007 in a new building across from the stadium, the Olympic and Sports Museum gives an overview of the Games (and indeed, all games) from Ancient Greece onwards. As well as photos and videos of great sporting moments and heroes, there are objects such as Ronaldinho's boots or Mika Häkkinen's Mercedes, along with a collection of opening ceremony costumes and Olympic torches. Perhaps more entertaining are the interactive displays, such as one that compares your effort at the long jump with that of the pros.

Pavelló Mies van der Rohe

Avda Marquès de Comillas (93 423 40 16/www.miesbcn.com). Metro Espanya. **Open** 10am-8pm daily. **Admission** €3.50; €2 reductions; free under-18s. No credit cards. **Map** p109 B2 ⑬

Mies van der Rohe built the Pavelló Alemany (German Pavilion) for the 1929 Exhibition not as a gallery, but as a simple reception space, sparsely furnished by his trademark 'Barcelona Chair'. The pavilion was a founding monument of modern rationalist architecture, with its flowing floor plan and revolutionary use of materials. Though the original was demolished after the Exhibition, a fine replica was built on the same site in 1986, the simplicity of its design setting off the warm tones of the marble and the expressive Georg Kolbe sculpture in the pond.

Poble Espanyol

Avda Marquès de Comillas (93 325 78 66/www.poble-espanyol.com). Metro Espanya. **Open** 9am-8pm Mon; 9am-

Park life

Parc Diagonal Mar

Until a century or so ago, parks were all but unknown in Barcelona. The Parc de la Ciutadella was the first, and was followed by some small gardens, while access to the city's green lungs of Tibidabo and Montjuïc was much improved.

As design fever swept Barcelona in the 1980s, however, most available public space was put in the hands of high-profile architects. This resulted in some truly unforgiving squares, such as the Plaça Països Catalans in Sants or the bare skateboarder piste outside the MACBA.

Despite the unenthusiastic welcome afforded to these urban experiments, recent attempts have followed a similar pattern. **Parc Diagonal Mar**, the work of Catalan architect Enric Miralles, opened in 2002, with each of its 35 acres having cost a million euros to create. There is water, though the public does not have access to it, and a lot of art,

though few trees. Its playground is imaginative but would be improved enormously by the addition of old-fashioned swings and slides. It's unwelcoming, and little used.

The **Parc Central del Poblenou** opened in spring 2008, and was designed by the French architect Jean Nouvel. Also highly designed, it includes giant plants, an island, a cratered lunar landscape and a perfumed garden. It has been criticised as 'exclusive', for sitting inside high concrete walls.

Perhaps in response to these criticisms, the council has created an open, simple and verdant park in the shape of the new **Parc de la Primavera** in Poble Sec. There is a large playground with swings, slides and a seesaw, while terraced paths run through land planted with trees, shrubs and rose bushes. It opened in 2008 and will take a while to bloom, but is nonetheless a welcome boost to the city's none-too-green parks.

2am Tue-Thur; 9am-4am Fri, Sat; 9am-midnight Sun. **Admission** €7.50; €4-€5.50 reductions; €15 family ticket; free under-7s. *Combined entrance with MNAC (p112)* €12. **Map** p109 A2 ⑭

Built for the 1929 Universal Exhibition, this mock Spanish village is a minimally cheesy architectural theme park with reproductions of traditional buildings from every region in Spain. The cylindrical towers at the entrance are copied from the walled city of Ávila and lead on to a typical Castilian main square from which visitors can explore a tiny whitewashed street from Arcos de la Frontera in Andalusia, then on to the 16th-century House of Chains from Toledo, and so on. There are numerous bars and restaurants, a flamenco *tablao* and more than 60 shops selling Spanish crafts. The Poble is unmistakably aimed at tourists, but it has been working to raise its cultural profile, with the Fundació Fran Daurel collection of contemporary art, hosting music festivals such as B-estival and the opening of a quality gallery of Iberian arts and crafts.

Telefèric de Montjuïc

Estació Funicular, Avda Miramar (93 441 48 20/www.tmb.net). Metro Paral·lel, then funicular. **Open** Oct-Mar 11am-6pm daily. Apr-June 11am-7pm daily. July-Sept 11am-8pm daily. **Admission** *Return* €12.50. *Single* €9. Free under-6s. **Map** p109 B4 ⑮

The rebuilt cable-car system, with brand new, eight-person cars that have disabled access, has reopened after two years of work. The prices have also been brought sharply up to date, which may put many off, despite the fantastic views over the city.

Eating & drinking

La Caseta del Migdia

Mirador de Migdia, Passeig del Migdia s/n (mobile 617 956 572/ www.lacaseta.org). Bus 55 or bus Parc de Montjuïc/funicular de Montjuïc, then 10min walk. Follow signs to Mirador de Montjuïc. **Open** June-Sept 8pm-2.30am Thur, Fri; 11am-2.30am

Sat; 11am-1am Sun. Oct-May 11am-midnight Sat, Sun. No credit cards. **Bar**. **Map** p109 A5 ⑯

Follow the Camí del Mar footpath around Montjuïc castle to find one of the few places in the city from which to watch the sun set. Entirely alfresco, high up in a clearing among the pines, this is a magical space, scattered with deckchairs, hammocks and candlelit tables. DJs spinning funk, rare groove and lounge alternate in surreal fashion with a faltering string quartet.

La Font del Gat

Passeig Santa Madrona 28 (93 289 04 04). Funicular Parc Montjuïc/bus 55. **Open** 1-4pm Tue-Sun. Closed 3 wks Aug. €€. **Catalan**. **Map** p109 B3 ⑰

A welcome watering hole perched high on Montjuïc between the Miró and Ethnological Museum. Most come for the set lunch: start with scrambled egg with Catalan sausage and peppers or a salad, follow with baked cod or chicken with pine nuts and basil, and finish with fruit or dessert. Tables outside attract a surcharge, but enjoy fantastic views.

Oleum

MNAC, Palau Nacional (93 289 06 79). Metro Espanya. **Open** 1-4pm Tue-Sun. €€€€. **Modern Mediterranean**. **Map** p109 B3 ⑱

That the MNAC's restaurant is to be considered a serious contender is indicated by two Antoni Tàpies canvases flanking the wonderful view across the city. Dishes run from scallops on squid ink noodles with lime foam to suckling pig with an onion tarte tatin. Despite some teething troubles (distracted service and a couple of deliquescent foams), in its first years of life, your average museum caff this is not.

Nightlife

Sala Instinto

NEW *C/México 7 (93 424 83 31/ www.salainstinto.com). Metro Espanya.* **Open** midnight-6am Wed-Sat; 9pm-4am Sun. **Admission** (incl 1 drink) €10. **Map** p109 B2 ⑲

Sessions in this packed, eclectic club run from soul and funk to world and

Pavelló Mies van der Rohe p114

house music, and the crowd varies accordingly: Thursday's is young and beer-swilling (hip hop on a work night); Friday's is dreadlocked (reggae and jungle); Saturday's is changeable (check the website – DJs vary). Not for glamour queens, and the shoes are as low-key as the vibe, but if the music makes the party, it's worth the trip.

La Terrrazza

Poble Espanyol, Avda Marquès de Comillas (93 272 49 80/www.la terrrazza.com). Metro Espanya. **Open** *May-mid Oct* midnight-6am Thur-Sat. **Admission** (incl 1 drink) €15 with flyer, €18 without. **Map** p109 A2 ⑳

Driven by resident DJ Sergio Patricio, the city's best-loved club packs them in on a huge outdoor space that moves to a tech-house beat. Compilation albums, international guest DJs and partner club Fellini on La Rambla make it one energetic enterprise. If you only go to one nightclub in Barcelona, or indeed Spain, make it this one. A long cold drink on a balmy night checking the eye-candy is hard to beat.

Arts & leisure

El Tablao de Carmen

Poble Espanyol, Avda Marquès de Comillas, Montjuïc (93 325 68 95/ www.tablaodecarmen.com). Metro Espanya. **Open** 7pm-midnight Tue-Sun. *Shows* 7.45pm, 10pm Tue-Sun. Closed 2wks Jan. **Admission** *Show & 1 drink* €34. *Show & dinner* €69. **Map** p109 A3 ㉑

This rather sanitised version of the traditional flamenco *tablao* sits in faux-Andalucían surroundings in the Poble Espanyol. You'll find both established stars and new young talent, displaying the various styles of flamenco singing, dancing and music. The emphasis is on panache rather than passion, so you might prefer your flamenco with a bit more spit and a little less polish. You must reserve in advance, which will allow you to enter the Poble Espanyol free after 7pm. There is a hall, seating some 170 people, and a rather lovely outside patio that can take 75. Set menus range from €69 to €94.

Poble Sec & Paral·lel

Poble Sec is a friendly, working-class area of quiet streets and leafy squares. Towards Paral·lel are some distinguished Modernista buildings, which local legend has maintained were built for *artistas* from the nude cabarets by their rich sugar daddies. At C/Tapioles 12 is a beautiful, narrow wooden Modernista door with particularly lovely writhing ironwork, while at C/Elkano 4 is **La Casa de les Rajoles**, which is known for its peculiar mosaic façade.

On the stretch of Avda Paral·lel opposite the city walls, three tall chimneys stand amid modern office blocks. They are all that remain of the Anglo-Canadian-owned power station known locally as *La Canadença* ('The Canadian'). This was the centre of the city's largest general strike, which took place in 1919. Beside the chimneys an open space has been created and dubbed the **Parc de les Tres Xemeneies** (Park of the Three Chimneys).

The name Avda Paral·lel derives from the fact that it coincides exactly with 41° 44' latitude north, one of Ildefons Cerdà's more eccentric conceits when he was planning this part of the city. The avenue was the prime centre of Barcelona nightlife in the first half of the 20th century, and was full of theatres, nightclubs and music halls, although these have almost all closed down now.

Sights & museums

Refugi 307
C/Nou de la Rambla 169 (93 256 21 22/www.museuhistoria.bcn.es). Metro Paral·lel. **Open** 11am-2pm Sat, Sun. **Admission** €3; free under-7s. No credit cards. **Map** p109 C4 ㉒

About 1,500 Barcelona civilians were killed during the vicious aerial bombings of the Civil War, a fact that the government long tried to suppress. As Poble Sec particularly suffered from these bombing raids, a large air-raid shelter was built partially into the mountain at the top of C/Nou de la Rambla; one of some 1,200 in the entire city. Now converted into a small museum, it is worth a visit.

Eating & drinking

Bar Seco
NEW *Passeig Montjuïc 74 (93 329 63 74). Metro Paral·lel.* **Open** 9am-1am Tue-Thur; 9am-2.30am Fri, Sat. €€. No credit cards. **Café.** **Map** p109 C4 ㉓

The 'Dry Bar' is anything but, and its ethically friendly choices range from local beers and organic wine to fairtrade Brazilian *cachaça*. Despite a quiet location, it has already gathered quite a following for the quality of its Italian-Spanish vegetarian dishes and tapas, its fresh milkshakes and a heavenly home-made chocolate and almond cake.

Poble Espanyol p114

La Bella Napoli

C/Margarit 14 (93 442 50 56). Metro Paral·lel. **Open** 8.30pm-midnight Tue; 1.30-4pm, 8.30pm-midnight Wed-Sun. **€€. Pizzeria.** Map p109 C3 ㉔
The once-legendary queues at La Bella Napoli are happily a thing of the past, thanks to a major renovation and the addition of a new and spacious bare-brick dining room. Welcoming Neapolitan waiters, in nifty red T-shirts to match the red gingham table-cloths, are able to talk you through the long, long list of antipasti and pasta dishes, but you can't go wrong with the crispy baked pizzas, such as the Sofia Loren, with provolone, basil, bresaola, cherry tomatoes, rocket and parmesan. Beer is Moretti and the wine list is all-Italian.

Quimet i Quimet

C/Poeta Cabanyes 25 (93 442 31 42). Metro Paral·lel. **Open** noon-4pm, 7-10.30pm Mon-Fri; noon-4pm Sat. Closed Aug. **€€. Tapas.** Map p109 C3 ㉕

Packed to the rafters with dusty bottles of wine, this miniscule bar makes up in tapas what it lacks in space. The speciality is preserved clams, cockles, mussels and so on, which are not to all tastes, but the *montaditos* (sculpted tapas served on bread) are spectacular. Try salmon sashimi with cream cheese, honey and soy, or cod, passata and black olive pâté.

La Soleá

Plaça del Sortidor 14 (93 441 01 24). Metro Poble Sec. **Open** noon-midnight Tue-Sat; noon-4pm Sun. **€€.** No credit cards. **Global.** Map p109 C3 ㉖
From the name to the sprawling terrace and the cheerful waiters to the orange and yellow decor, everything about La Soleá radiates sunshine. There's barely a continent that hasn't been visited on the menu, which holds houmous, tabouleh and goat's cheese salad alongside juicy burgers served with roquefort or mushrooms, smoky tandoori chicken, Mexican tacos, vegetable samosas and slabs of Argentine beef.

Tapioles 53

C/Tapioles 53 (93 329 22 38/www.tapioles53.com). Metro Paral·lel or Poble Sec. **Open** 9-11pm Tue-Sat. **€€€.** **Global.** Map p109 C3 ㉗
Eating at Tapioles 53 would be just like eating at a friend's house; if, that is, you happened to have friends who could cook this well and had as canny an eye for seductive lighting. It's the brainchild of Australian chef Sarah Stothart, who wanted to create a cosy atmosphere in which to serve accomplished but unpretentious food – fabulous home-made bread with wild mushroom soup; fresh pasta with baby broad beans and artichokes; boeuf bourgignon; rosewater rice pudding with pomegranate, or ginger and mascarpone cheesecake.

Xemei

Passeig de la Exposició 85 (93 553 51 40). Metro Poble Sec. **Open** 1.30-3.30pm, 9.30pm-midnight Mon, Wed-Sun. **€€€. Italian.** Map p109 B3 ㉘
Heartwarming Venetian country cooking, from home-made pasta to peppered

ribbons of liver and onions with fried polenta. The *cicchetti* are a great way to start: a plate of antipasti involving fresh anchovies, figs with pecorino and *sarda in saor* (sardines marinated in vinegar and onions), while peach crostata makes for an indulgent finish. When the weather allows, book a pavement table; the dining room can get cramped and noisy.

Nightlife

Barcelona Rouge

C/Poeta Cabanyes 21 (93 442 49 85). Metro Paral·lel. **Open** 11pm-4am Tue-Sat. **Admission** free. No credit cards. **Bar.** **Map** p109 C3 ㉙

A hidey-hole of a place, small enough to get packed even though it's little known, hard to get into and hard on the wallet. Once inside there's ambient music, good cocktails and battered sofas draped with foreign and local thirtysomethings – those with a bit of money and a bit of class who want to avoid the more obvious nightspots. Ring the buzzer to get in.

Maumau

C/Fontrodona 33 (93 441 80 15/ www.maumaunderground.com). Metro Paral·lel. **Open** 11pm-2.30am Thur; 11pm-3am Fri, Sat; 7pm-midnight Sun. **Admission** *Membership* €5. No credit cards. **Map** p109 C4 ㉚

Behind the anonymous grey door (ring the bell), first-timers to this likeable little chill-out club pay €5 to become members, though in practice it rarely charges out-of-towners. Inside, a large warehouse space is humanised with colourful projections, IKEA sofas and scatter cushions, and a friendly, laid-back crowd. DJ Wakanda schools us in the finer points of deep house, jazz, funk or whatever takes his fancy.

Sala Apolo

C/Nou de la Rambla 113 (93 441 40 01/www.sala-apolo.com). Metro Paral·lel. **Open** midnight-5am Wed, Thur; midnight-7am Fri, Sat; 10.30pm-3am Sun. **Admission** varies. No credit cards. **Map** p109 C4 ㉛

Who'd have thought one of the most popular clubs in this most stylish city would be a poorly lit 1940s dancehall. A new, more intimate space downstairs hosts relaxed gigs from up-and-coming talent, while upstairs features bigger acts. Afterwards, Wednesdays and Thursdays are an upbeat affair, with an international crowd of music buffs, from hipster geeks to hip hop gals, trekking across the Raval for funk and Latin grooves. And, ten years on, there are still epic queues for the weekend's bleepity-bleep techno extravaganza, Nitsa.

Tinta Roja

C/Creu dels Molers 17 (93 443 32 43/ www.tintaroja.net). Metro Poble Sec. **Open** *Bar* 8pm-2am Wed, Thur; 8pm-3am Fri, Sat; 7pm-1am Sun. *Shows* 10pm-midnight Wed-Sat. Closed 2wks Aug. **Admission** *Bar* free. *Shows* (incl 1 drink) €8-€10. No credit cards. **Map** p109 C3 ㉜

Push through the depths of the bar and you'll find yourself transported to a Buenos Aires bordello/theatre/circus/cabaret by the array of plush red velvet sofas, smoochy niches and an ancient ticket booth. It's an atmospheric place for a late-ish drink, and a distinctly different entertainment experience from Friday to Sunday when you'll get to take in live tango, jazz and flamenco in a small theatre at the back.

Arts & leisure

Mercat de les Flors

Plaça Margarida Xirgú, C/Lleida 59 (93 426 18 75/www.mercatflors.org). Metro Poble Sec. **Box office** 1hr before show. Advance tickets also from Palau de la Virreina. **Tickets** varies. No credit cards. **Map** p109 B3 ㉝

A huge converted flower market housing three performance spaces, the Mercat is one of the most innovative venues in town. Performances here experiment with formats and mix new technologies, pop culture and the arts. Film nights and DJ sessions also feature; events include June's Marató de l'Espectacle and the Festival Asia.

La Pedrera (Casa Milà) p127

Eixample

A late 19th-century extension ('*eixample*') to the city, this grid-like neighbourhood is home to some of Barcelona's most elegant buildings, its swankiest shops and some of its best-heeled residents. Its showpiece is the plush bisecting avenue of **Passeig de Gràcia**, with buildings by some of the finest Modernista architects. The period of construction coincided with Barcelona's financial golden age, and the city's bourgeoisie employed Gaudí, Puig i Cadafalch, Domènech i Montaner and the like to build them a series of increasingly daring townhouses in an orgy of avant-garde one-upmanship.

The result is extraordinary but can be tricky to negotiate on foot; the lack of open spaces and similarity of many streets can leave you somewhat confused. The city council, meanwhile, is attempting to make the area more liveable: in 1985 the ProEixample was set up to reclaim some of the courtyards proposed in the plans of the original design of the Eixample, drawn up by Ildefons Cerdà, so that everybody living in the area should be able to find an open space within 200 metres (650 feet) of their home. Two of the better examples are the fake beach and wide, shallow pool for children next to the **Torre de les Aigües** water tower (C/Roger de Llúria 56) and the patio at **Passatge Permanyer** (C/Pau Claris 120).

Sights & museums

Casa Àsia
Avda Diagonal 373 (93 238 73 37/ www.casaasia.es). Metro Diagonal. **Open** 10am-8pm Mon-Sat; 10am-2pm Sun. **Admission** free. **Map** p123 D2 ❶

Eixample

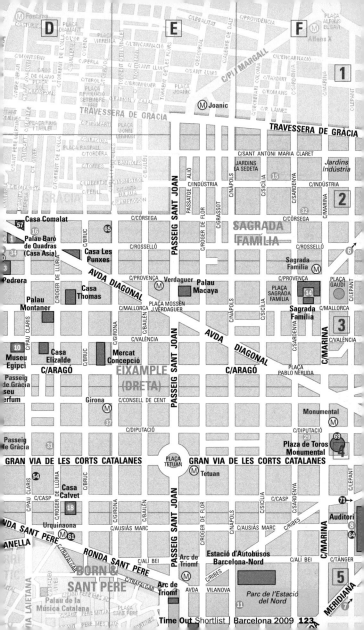

Casa Batlló

This much-needed Asian contribution to Barcelona's cultural scene is located in another of Modernista architect Puig i Cadafalch's creations, the Palau Baró de Quadras. The Casa Àsia cultural centre acts as both an exhibition space and ambassador for all things in Asia and the Asian Pacific. It also features an oriental café on the ground floor and an excellent multimedia library.
Event highlights 'Beijing East Village' contemporary Chinese art photographer Rong Rong (until Dec 2008).

Casa Batlló

Passeig de Gràcia 43 (93 216 03 06/ www.casabatllo.cat). Metro Passeig de Gràcia. **Open** 9am-8pm daily. **Admission** €16.50; €13.20 reductions; free under-7s.
Map p122 C3 ❷
For many people the Casa Batlló is the most telling example of Gaudí's pre-eminence over his Modernista contemporaries; the comparison is easy, since it sits in the same block as masterworks by his two closest rivals, Puig i Cadafalch and Domènech i Montaner.

Opinions differ on what the building's remarkable façade represents, with its polychrome shimmering walls, the sinister skeletal balconies and the humpbacked, scaly roof. Some maintain it shows the spirit of carnival, others insist it is a cove on the Costa Brava. The most popular theory, however, which takes into account the architect's patriotic feelings, is that it depicts Sant Jordi and the dragon. The idea is that the cross on top of the building is the knight's lance, the roof is the back of the beast, and the balconies below are the skulls and bones of its victims.

Exploring the interior (at a cost) offers the best opportunity of understanding how Gaudí, who is sometimes considered the lord of the bombastic and overblown, was really the master of tiny details. Witness the ingenious ventilation in the doors and the amazing natural light reflecting off the azure walls of the inner courtyard, or the way in which the brass window handles are curved to fit precisely the shape of a hand. An apartment within Casa Batlló is now open to the public, along with the roof terrace and attic: the whitewashed arched rooms of the top floor, which were originally used for washing and hanging clothes, are among the master's most atmospheric spaces.

Fundació Antoni Tàpies

C/Aragó 255 (93 487 03 15/www. fundaciotapies.org). Metro Passeig de Gràcia. **Open** 10am-8pm Tue-Sun. **Admission** €6; €4 reductions; free under-16s. **Map** p122 C3 ❸
Antoni Tàpies is Barcelona's most celebrated living artist. In 1984, he set up the Tàpies Foundation in the former publishing house of Muntaner i Simon, dedicating it to the study and appreciation of contemporary art. He then promptly crowned the building with a glorious tangle of aluminium piping and ragged metal netting (*Núvol i Cadira*, meaning 'cloud and chair'). This was a typically contentious act by an artist whose work, a selection of which remains on permanent display on the top floor of the gallery, has been

causing controversy ever since he burst on to the art scene in the 1960s. 'Give the organic its rights', he proclaimed, and devoted his time and work to making the seemingly insignificant significant, using such everyday materials as mud, string, rags and cardboard to build his rarely pretty but always striking works.

Fundación Francisco Godia

C/Diputació 250 (93 272 31 80/ www.fundacionfgodia.org). Metro Passeig de Gràcia. **Map** p123 D3 **❹**

Godia's first love was motor-racing: he was a Formula 1 driver for Maserati in the 1950s. His second, though, was art, which is how this private museum has come to house an interesting selection of medieval religious art, historic Spanish ceramics and modern painting. Highlights include Alejo de Vahía's medieval *Pietà* and a Baroque masterpiece by Luca Giordano, along with some outstanding Romanesque sculptures, and 19th-century oil paintings by Joaquín Sorolla and Ramon Casas. The modern collection has works by Miró, Julio González, Tàpies and Manolo Hugué. From October 2008, the Fundació will be housed in this new, vastly bigger space, which means that much more of the collection can be displayed at once, along with temporary exhibitions. Opening hours and admission prices are still to be confirmed.

Fundació Suñol

NEW *Passeig de Gràcia 98 (93 496 10 32/www.fundaciosunol.org). Metro Diagonal.* **Open** 4-8pm Mon-Wed, Fri, Sat. **Admission** €4; €2 reductions. No credit cards. **Map** p123 D2 **❺**

Opened in 2007, the foundation's two floors house the contemporary art collection of businessman Josep Suñol. There are 100 pieces, including painting, sculpture and photography, on show at a time, shuffled every six months (Jan and July) from an archive of 1,200 artworks. The collection includes historic artists of the avantgarde, predominantly Catalan and Spanish: Picasso, Miró, Gargallo, with international input from Giacometti, Man Ray and Andy Warhol. With superfluities removed, including labels, and chronology abandoned, works are arranged in careful, coherent compositions, by style, colour or even mood. Nivell Zero offers a large exhibition space to younger avant-garde artists.

Hospital de la Santa Creu i Sant Pau

C/Sant Antoni Maria Claret 167 (93 291 90 00/www.santpau.cat). Metro Hospital de Sant Pau. **Map** p123 F2 **❻**

Domènech i Montaner's 'garden city' of a hospital, a short walk from the madding crowds at the Sagrada Familia, is a collection of pavilions abundantly adorned with the medieval flourishes that characterise the architect's style. The hospital, now a UNESCO World Heritage Site, is composed of 18 pavilions and connected by an underground tunnel system. Domènech i Montaner built the hospital very much with its patients in mind, convinced that pleasant surroundings and aesthetic harmony were good for health. Unfortunately, the old buildings don't entirely suit the exigencies of modern medicine; patient care is being phased out and moved to a blocky, white monstrosity of a building on the north side of the hospital grounds. The public has free access to the grounds; guided tours (€5, call 93 256 25 04) are offered every morning.

Museu de Carrosses Fúnebres

C/Sancho de Avila 2 (93 484 17 10). Metro Marina. **Open** 10am-1pm, 4-6pm Mon-Fri; 10am-1pm Sat, Sun (weekends call to check). **Admission** free. **Map** p123 F5 **❼**

Finding this, the most obscure and macabre museum in Barcelona, hasn't got any easier over the years. You'll need to ask at the reception desk of the Ajuntament's funeral service and, eventually, a security guard will take you down the stairs to a perfectly silent and

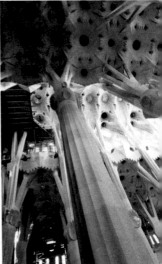

Sagrada Família

splendidly shuddersome basement housing the world's biggest collection of funeral carriages and hearses, dating from the 18th century through to the 1950s. There are ornate Baroque carriages and more functional Landaus and Berlins, and a rather wonderful silver Buick. The white carriages were designed for children and virgins, and there's a windowless black velour mourning carriage for the forlorn mistress, from which to mourn in secret. The vehicles are manned by ghoulish dummies dressed in period gear whose eyes follow you around the room, making you glad of that security guard.

Museu de la Música

L'Auditori, C/Padilla 155 (93 256 36 50/www.museumusica.bcn.cat). Metro Glòries. **Open** 11am-9pm Mon, Wed-Fri; 10am-7pm Sat, Sun. **Admission** €4; €3 reductions. **Map** p123 F5 ⑧

As part of the efforts to turn the Plaça de les Glòries into a cultural hub, the contents of the old Music Museum, which were under wraps for six years, have finally been rehoused in the Auditori concert hall. The idea behind the vast and glittering displays of instruments and fun interactive exhibits is not to provide a historical overview of the art, but to take a look at some of its defining moments.

Museu del Perfum

Passeig de Gràcia 39 (93 216 01 21/ www.museodelperfume.com). Metro Passeig de Gràcia. **Open** 10.30am-7.30pm Mon-Fri; 10.30am-1.30pm Sat. **Admission** €5; €3 reductions. **Map** p122 C4 ⑨

In the back room of the Regia perfumery sits this collection of nearly 5,000 scent bottles, cosmetic flasks and related objects. On display you'll find such familiar perfume brands as Dior and Guerlain in extremely rare bottles – among them a garish creation by Dalí made for Schiaparelli and a set of rather disturbing golliwog flasks for Vigny. The Museu del Perfum's most recent acquisitions include a collection of 19th-century perfume powder bottles and boxes.

Museu Egipci de Barcelona

C/València 284 (93 488 01 88/ www.fundclos.com). Metro Passeig de Gràcia. **Open** 10am-8pm Mon-Sat; 10am-2pm Sun. **Admission** *Museum* €7; €5 reductions; free under-5s. **Map** p123 D3 ⑩

Two floors of this museum showcase a well-chosen collection that spans some 3,000 years of Nile-drenched culture. Exhibits run from religious statuary, such as the massive baboon heads used to decorate temples, to everyday objects like copper mirrors and alabaster headrests. Outstanding pieces include the painstakingly matched fragments from the Sixth Dynasty Tomb of Iny, a bronze statuette of the goddess Isis breastfeeding her son Horus, and mummified cats, baby crocodiles and falcons.

Parc de l'Estació del Nord

C/Nàpols (no phone). Metro Arc de Triomf. **Open** 10am-sunset daily. **Admission** free. **Map** p123 F5 ⑪

This slightly shabby space is perked up by three pieces of land art in glazed blue ceramic by New York sculptor Beverley Pepper. Along with a pair of incongruous white stone entrance walls, *Espiral Arbrat* ('Tree Spiral') is a spiral bench set under the shade of lime-flower trees and *Cel Caigut* ('Fallen Sky') is a 7m-high (23ft) ridge rising from the grass, while the tilework recalls Gaudí's *trencadís* smashed-tile technique.

Parc Joan Miró (Parc de l'Escorxador)

C/Tarragona (no phone). Metro Tarragona or Espanya. **Open** 10am-sunset daily. **Map** p122 A3 ⑫

The demolition of the old slaughterhouse provided some much-needed urban parkland, although there's precious little greenery here. The rows of stubby palmera trees and grim cement lakes are dominated by a library and Miró's towering phallic sculpture *Dona i Ocell* ('Woman and Bird'). There are also a couple of excellent playgrounds.

La Pedrera (Casa Milà)

Passeig de Gràcia 92-C/Provença 261-265 (93 484 59 00/www.la pedreraeducacio.org). Metro Diagonal. **Open** *Mar-Oct* 9am-8pm daily; *Nov-Feb* 9am-6.30pm daily. **Admission** €8; €4.50 reductions; free under-12s. **Guided tours** (in English) 4pm Mon-Fri. **Map** p123 D3 ⑬

The last secular building designed by Antoni Gaudí, the Casa Milà (usually referred to as La Pedrera, 'the stone quarry') is a stupendous and daring feat of architecture, the culmination of the architect's experimental attempts to recreate natural forms with bricks and mortar. Its marine feel is complemented by Jujol's tangled balconies, doors of twisted kelp ribbon, sea-foamy ceilings and interior patios as blue as a mermaid's cave. Ridiculed when it was completed in 1912, it has become one of Barcelona's best-loved buildings, and is adored by architects for its extraordinary structure: it is supported entirely by pillars, without a single master wall, allowing the vast asymmetrical windows of the façade to invite in great swathes of natural light.

There are three exhibition spaces: the first-floor art gallery hosts free exhibitions of eminent artists; you can visit a reconstructed Modernista flat on the fourth floor; and the attic holds a museum dedicated to an insightful overview of Gaudí's career. Best of all is the chance to stroll on the roof of the building amid its *trencadís*-covered ventilation shafts: their heads are shaped like the helmets of medieval knights. Informative titbit-filled guided tours in English are run daily at 4pm.

Event highlights Russian constructivist artist Alexander Rodchenko (13 Oct 2008-6 Jan 2009).

Sagrada Família

C/Mallorca 401 (93 207 30 31/ www.sagradafamilia.org). Metro Sagrada Família. **Open** *Mar-Sept* 9am-8pm daily. *Oct-Feb* 9am-6pm daily. **Admission** €8; €5 reductions; €3 8-10 years; free under-8s. *Lift to spires* €2. No credit cards. **Map** p123 F3 ⑭

Small is beautiful

Tapaç24

'Tapas', says Michelin-starred chef Carles Abellan, 'are one Spanish thing I really like.' He's not talking about the Spain he lives in, he's talking about the other Spain, the non-Catalan one. This passionately felt divide is one of the reasons that tapas bars in Barcelona, where they exist at all, tend to be oriented towards tourists. They are simply not seen as Catalan enough.

Abellan set out to change all that a few years ago, with his übercool **Comerç 24** (p79). Often described by a fawning international press as an 'avant-garde tapas restaurant', in fact it serves *platillos*, small dishes of which the diner can order several. These are inspired by Abellan's time in the kitchens of El Bulli, under experimental chef Ferran Adrià, and bear little resemblance to the ham croquettes and *patatas bravas* to which he refers.

His newer venture, **Tapaç24** (p133) redresses the balance;

an old-school bar, it serves traditional tapas of excellent quality. Among the lentils with chorizo and cod croquettes, however, his fans will also find playful snacks more in keeping with his previous style. The McFoie Burger is an exercise in fast-food heaven, as is the Bikini – a small version of his signature take on the ham and cheese toastie.

Abellan is not the only El Bulli alumnus to attempt a revival of trad tapas in the city. Brother (and pastry chef) to Ferran Adrià, Albert, opened **Inopia** (p131) in 2007, and it's been rammed ever since. As with Tapaç24, the emphasis is on a revival of old techniques and recipes, using the very best ingredients. Its bright, old-school look has disappointed those expecting El Bulli-style culinary fireworks, but of the old classics (*patatas bravas*, Russian salad, croquettes and tripe) Inopia does them better than anywhere – even, perhaps, the other Spain.

The Temple Expiatori de la Sagrada Familia manages to be both Europe's most fascinating building site and Barcelona's most emblematic creation. In the 1930s, anarchists managed to destroy Gaudí's intricate plans and models for the building by setting fire to them, which means that the ongoing work is a matter of conjecture and considerable controversy; the putative finishing date of 2020 is, however, looking increasingly optimistic.

Gaudí, buried beneath the nave of the Sagrada Familia, dedicated more than 40 years of his life to the project, the last 14 exclusively, and the crypt, the apse and the nativity façade, all of which were completed in his lifetime, are the most beautiful elements of the church. The latter, facing C/Marina, looks at first glance as though some careless giant has poured candlewax over a Gothic cathedral, but closer inspection reveals that every protuberance is an intricate sculpture of flora, fauna or a human figure, combining to form an astonishingly moving stone tapestry depicting scenes from Christ's life. The other completed façade, the Passion, which faces C/Sardenya, is more austere, with vast diagonal columns in the shape of bones and haunting sculptures by Josep Maria Subirachs. Japanese sculptor Etsuro Sotoo has chosen to adhere more faithfully to Gaudí's intentions, and has fashioned six more modest musicians at the rear of the temple, as well as the exuberantly coloured bowls of fruit to the left of the nativity façade.

Eating & drinking

Alkimia

C/Indústria 79 (93 207 61 15). Metro Joanic or Sagrada Família. **Open** 1.30-3.30pm, 8.30-11pm Mon-Fri. Closed 2wks Aug. €€€€. **Catalan**. Map p123 F2 ⑮

It came as no surprise to the regulars at Alkimia when it was awarded a Michelin star (as a consequence of which, making a reservation is now all but essential). A great way to explore what the restaurant has to offer is to sample the gourmet menu, which offers four savoury courses, including complex dishes that play around with the Spanish classics – for instance, liquid *pa amb tomàquet* (bread with tomato) with *fuet* sausage, wild rice with crayfish, strips of tuna on a bed of foamed mustard – and a couple of desserts.

Bar Mut

C/Pau Claris 192 (93 217 43 38). Metro Diagonal. **Open** 8.30am-midnight Mon-Fri; 10.30am-midnight Sat; noon-5pm, 8.30pm-midnight Sun. €€€. **Tapas**. Map p123 D2 ⑯

There's more than a soupçon of the *16ème arrondissement* about this smart and traditional bar; well-heeled Catalans, BCBG to the core, chatter loudly and dine on excellent tapas – foie, wild sea bass and *espardenyes* (sea cucumbers). The wine selection is similarly upmarket and displayed so seductively behind glass that you may find yourself drinking and spending rather more than you bargained for.

La Bodegueta

Rambla de Catalunya 100 (93 215 48 94). Metro Diagonal. **Open** 8am-2am Mon-Sat; 6.30pm-1am Sun. Closed 2wks Aug. €€. No credit cards. **Tapas**. Map p122 C3 ⑰

Resolutely resisting the rise of the surrounding area, this former wine bodega is unreconstructed, dusty and welcoming, supplying students, businessmen and everyone in between with reasonably priced wine, vermouth on tap and prime-quality tapas amid the delicate patterns of tiling that's a century old. In summer, there are tables outside on the almost pedestrianised Rambla de Catalunya.

Casa Calvet

C/Casp 48 (93 412 40 12). Metro Urquinaona. **Open** 1-3.30pm, 8.30-11pm Mon-Sat. Closed 2wks Aug. €€€€. **Catalan**. Map p123 D4 ⑱

One of Gaudí's more understated buildings from the outside, Casa Calvet has an interior crammed full of glorious detail in the carpentry, stained glass and tiles. The food is up to par, with surprising combinations almost always hitting the mark: squab with puréed pumpkin, risotto of duck confit and truffle with yoghurt ice-cream, and smoked foie gras with mango sauce. The puddings are supremely good, particularly the pine nut tart with foamed crema catalana.

Cervesería Catalana

C/Mallorca 236 (93 216 03 68). Metro Passeig de Gràcia. **Open** *8am-1.30am Mon-Fri; 9am-1.30am Sat, Sun.* €€. **Tapas.** Map p122 C3 ⑲

The 'Catalan Beerhouse' lives up to its name with a winning selection of brews from around the world, but the real reason to come is the tapas. A vast array is yours for the pointing; only hot montaditos, such as bacon, cheese and dates, have to be ordered from the kitchen. Arrive early for a seat at the bar, even earlier for a pavement table.

Cinc Sentits

C/Aribau 58 (93 323 94 90/www. cincsentits.com). Metro Passeig de Gràcia or Universitat. **Open** *1.30-3.30pm Mon; 1.30-3.30pm, 8.30-11.15pm Tue-Sat. Closed 2wks Aug.* €€€€. **Modern Spanish.** Map p122 B3 ⑳

Run by Catalan-Canadian siblings, the 'Five Senses' is the most reasonably priced of Barcelona's top-end restaurants, and should be on everyone's dining agenda. Talented chef Jordi Artal shows respect for the classics (melt-in-the-mouth suckling pig with apple compôte; Catalan flat *coca* bread with foie gras and crispy leeks), while adding a personal touch in dishes such as lamb cutlets with a crust of porcini dust. To finish, try the artisanal Catalan cheese pairings or the 'five textures of lemon'. Reservations are generally essential at night; visit at lunch for a more peaceful experience.

Cremeria Toscana

C/Muntaner 161 (93 539 38 25). Metro Hospital Clínic. **Open** *1pm-midnight Tue-Thur; 1pm-1am Fri, Sat; noon-10pm Sun.* €. *No credit cards.* **Ice-cream.** Map p122 B2 ㉑

In this charming little ice-cream parlour, with its lovely, antique-strewn mezzanine, around 20 authentically Italian flavours are made daily, ranging from zingy mandarin to impossibly creamy coconut. '*I dopocena*' ('after dinner') are miniature gourmet sundaes, mixing parmesan and pear flavours; mascarpone and tiramisu; chocolate and pistachio; or liquorice and mint.

Dolso

C/València 227 (93 487 59 64). Metro Passeig de Gràcia. **Open** *9am-10.30pm Mon; 9am-11.30pm Tue-Thur; 9am-1am Fri; 11am-1am Sat.* €€. **Desserts.** Map p122 C3 ㉒

Heaven on earth for the sweet of tooth, Dolso is a 'pudding café' where even the retro-baroque wallpaper is the colour of chocolate. Desserts run from light (a gin and tonic rendered in clear jelly, lemon sorbet, candied peel and juniper berries) to wickedly indulgent (chocolate fondant with passion fruit sorbet and a sherry reduction). A short range of sandwiches and topped ciabatta keeps the spoilsports happy.

Dry Martini

C/Aribau 162-166 (93 217 50 72). FGC Provença. **Open** *Sept-July 1pm-2.30am Mon-Thur; 1pm-3am Fri; 6.30pm-3am Sat; 6pm-2.30am Sun. Aug 6.30pm-2.30am Mon-Thur, Sun; 6.30pm-3am Fri, Sat.* **Cocktail bar.** Map p122 B2 ㉓

A shrine to the eponymous cocktail, honoured in martini-related artwork and served in at least a hundred forms. All the trappings of a traditional cocktail bar are in place – the bow-tied staff, the leather banquettes, the drinking antiques and the wooden cabinets displaying a century's worth of bottles – but the stuffiness is absent: music owes more to trip hop than middle-aged crowd-pleasers, and the barmen welcome all comers.

Fast Good

NEW *C/Balmes 127 (93 452 23 74). Metro Diagonal.* **Open** *noon-midnight daily.* €€. **Café.** Map p122 C3 ㉔

See box p132.

Gaig

Hotel Cram, C/Aragó 214 (93 429 10 17/www.restaurantgaig.com). Metro Passeig de Gràcia. **Open** 9-11pm Mon; 1.30-3.30pm, 9-11pm Tue-Sat. Closed 1wk Easter, 3wks Aug. **€€€€**. **Modern Catalan**. Map p122 B3 ㉕

Sadly displaced from its 130-year home in Horta after structural problems, Gaig has lost none of its shine despite its anodyne new surroundings. Carles Gaig's cooking never fails to thrill, from the crayfish tempura amuse-gueule, served with a dip of creamed leek salted with a piece of pancetta, through to a shot-glass holding layers of tangy lemon syrup, crema catalana mousse and caramel ice-cream, topped with burnt sugar.

Gresca

NEW *C/Provença 230 (93 451 61 93/www.gresca.net). Metro Hospital Clínic.* **Open** 1.30-3.30pm, 8.30-10.30pm Mon-Fri; 8.30-10.30pm Sat. Closed 2wks Aug. **€€€€**. **Modern Spanish**. Map p122 C3 ㉖

A potentially great new restaurant let down by a dining room made clamorous by a steel floor. The lighting, too, is a bit spotty and unforgiving, but sympathetic, if harried, service and excellent food go some way towards smoothing what, with luck, are teething troubles. There is a classy wine list, sensibly organised by style, but the real highlights are dishes such as foamed egg on a bed of *jamón ibérico*, fennel and courgette, or puddings like the *coca* bread with roquefort and lychee and apple sorbet. One to watch.

Hanoi II

Avda Sarrià 37 (93 444 10 99). Metro Hospital Clínic. **Open** 12.30-4pm, 8.30pm-midnight Mon-Sat; 8.30pm-midnight Sun. **€€€**. **Vietnamese**. Map p122 A1 ㉗

This little sister of the frenetic original Hanoi on C/Enric Granados is a muted version, with low lighting, teak chairs and prints of Miró paintings. It's also considerably easier to get a table. The menu is the same, however, with duck or prawn nem rolls, chicken *musi* (chopped with water chestnuts and pine nuts and rolled in lettuce leaves) and beef *chempy* (with orange peel and vegetables, fried with honey).

Inopia

C/Tamarit 104 (93 424 52 31). Metro Poble Sec. **Open** 7pm-midnight Mon-Fri; 1-3.30pm, 7pm-midnight Sat. Closed Aug. **€€€**. **Tapas**. Map p122 A5 ㉘

See box p128.

Manairó

NEW *C/Diputació 424 (93 231 00 57/www.manairo.com). Metro Monumental.* **Open** 1.30-4pm, 8.30-11pm Tue-Sat. **€€€€**. **Modern Catalan**. Map p123 F4 ㉙

If you've ever been curious to try some of the more extreme experiences in postmodern haute cuisine (we're talking tripe and brains), Manairó is the place to start. Its divine tasting menu takes in small portions of Catalan specialities such as *cap i pota* (a stew of calves' heads and feet), and langoustine with *botifarra* sausage and cod tripe, and makes them so delicately that the most squeamish diner will be seduced. Other star turns include a 'false' anchovy – actually a long strip of marinated tuna dotted prettily with pearls of red vermouth.

Moo

C/Rosselló 265 (93 445 40 00/www.hotelomm.es). Metro Diagonal. **Open** 1.30-3.45pm, 8.30-10.45pm Mon-Sat. **€€€€**. **Modern European**. Map p123 D2 ㉚

Superbly inventive cooking is overseen by renowned Catalan chef Joan Roca and designed as 'half portions', the better to experience the full range, from sea bass with lemon grass to exquisite suckling pig with a sharp Granny Smith purée. Wines from a list of 500 are suggested for every course, and many dishes are even built around them: you can finish, for example, with 'Sauternes', the wine's bouquet perfectly rendered in mango ice-cream, saffron custard and grapefruit jelly.

A quick bite

Fast Good

The gastronomic world holds its breath whenever Catalan superchef Ferran Adrià announces his latest project, but there were more than a few raised toques and scratched heads when he declared a foray into the murky and often ugly world of fast food.

The result is the hugely successful (if woefully named) **Fast Good** (p130); a stylish hot pink and lime green chain of restaurants aiming to bring gourmet dining to people who are either short of money, short of time, or both. All share a common menu that, naturally, includes burgers (though of the sort that come garnished with mint and tarragon), along with panini, various ethnic takes on roast chicken and a sublime fry-up – eggs with *jamón ibérico* and chips fried in olive oil.

Where Adrià leads, other chefs will follow, and more quizzical eyebrows must have been raised when, in February 2008, Michelin-starred Catalan chef Sergi Arola described his own populist bid for the casual diner, **La Paninoteca D'E** (p133), as 'a new concept of "luxury fast food"'. Arola's shtick is the 'cocapizza' – a fusion of the Catalan *coca* (a flat, crispy, bread) and a traditional pizza.

In truth, what this amounts to is, well, a pizza. But oh, what a pizza! The toppings bring together the finest of ingredients, adding the odd delicacy brought in from afar and drizzling the whole thing with a rich and fruity olive oil. Along with the familiar, such as a Four Seasons involving mozzarella, artichokes, Portobello mushrooms, petals of *lacón* (Galician gammon) and black olives, there is the Caesar, or the Smoked Chicken (with egg and green tomatoes), or our favourite, the Roast Beef (with mozzarella, gherkins, rocket, tomato and Kalamata oil).

As to the fast food aspect, well, we waited 45 minutes for ours to arrive, but there was something about that we found curiously reassuring.

Noti

*C/Roger de Llúria 35 (93 342 66 73/
www.noti-universal.com). Metro Passeig
de Gràcia or Urquinaona.* **Open** 1.30-
4pm, 8.30pm-midnight Mon-Fri;
8.30pm-midnight Sat. €€€€.
Mediterranean. Map p123 D4 ③①

With a new chef at the helm, Noti has
lost the French influences in its menu
and now marks more familiar
Barcelona territory with Mediterranean
dishes revisited Asian style: the catch
of the day with peanut sauce; tuna with
a sauce of Chardonnay and wasabi;
duck with lotus root, and so on. The DJ
bar at the front is now a thing of the
past, but the look is still supremely cool,
with beaten copper panelling and
splashes of hot pink.

Ot

*C/Corsega 537 (93 435 80 48). Metro
Sagrada Família.* **Open** 1.30-3.30pm,
8.30-11pm Tue-Sat. Closed 3wks Aug.
€€€€. **Modern Mediterranean**.
Map p123 F2 ③②

It's the extras that make the Ot experience memorable: an olive-oil tasting to
start; a shot of cauliflower soup speckled with herring eggs as an amuse-
bouche; or the sweet and sour layers of
coconut and hibiscus flower foam with
the coffee. There is no à la carte menu,
just a couple of set-price deals, but
these are very safe hands in which to
leave yourself.

La Paninoteca Cremoni

*C/Rosselló 112 (93 451 03 79). Metro
Hospital Clínic.* **Open** 9.30am-5pm,
7.30pm-midnight Mon-Fri; 1.30-5pm,
8.30pm-midnight Sat. Closed 3wks Aug.
€€. **Panini**. Map p122 B2 ③③

Named after the 19th-century inventor
of the celebrated Italian sandwich, this
is a sunny spot, with a white-painted
rustic look that is enlivened by a huge
photograph of Siena. Neither the owners nor the ingredients can make much
claim to Italian provenance, but panini
such as the Siciliano – consisting of
olive bread, mozzarella, tomato,
aubergine and basil – do make a wonderful change from the seemingly endless *bocadillos de jamón*.

La Paninoteca D'E

NEW *C/Rosselló 242 (mobile 639 061
072). Metro Diagonal.* **Open** 9am-1am
Mon-Fri; 1pm-1am Sat, Sun. €€. **Café**.
Map p123 D2 ③④

See box p132.

Saüc

*Ptge Lluís Pellicer 12 (93 321 01 89).
Metro Hospital Clínic.* **Open** 1.30-
3.30pm; 8.30-10.30pm Tue-Sat. Closed
3wks Aug. €€€€. **Modern Catalan**.
Map p122 B2 ③⑤

Book early for one of the coveted tables
at Saüc ('Elderberry'), particularly for
lunch. The classy set lunch runs from
accomplished Catalan comfort food, in
the shape of spicy Mallorcan sausage
with potatoes and poached egg, to
more sophisticated fare such as cod
with apple aïoli, cherry tomatoes and
spinach. Excellent bread.

Tapaç24

*C/Diputació 269 (93 488 09 77/www.
carlesabellan.com). Metro Passeig de
Gràcia.* **Open** 8am-midnight Mon-Sat.
€€€. **Tapas**. Map p123 D4 ③⑥

See box p128.

Toc

*C/Girona 59 (93 488 11 48/www.
tocbcn.com). Metro Girona.* **Open** 1.30-
3.30pm, 8.30-10.45pm Mon-Fri; 8.30-
11.30pm Sat. €€€€. **Modern
Catalan**. Map p123 E4 ③⑦

Minimalist to the point of clinical, Toc
nonetheless offers a menu that is full of
heart and colour. Old Catalan favourites such as *esqueixada* (salt cod salad)
and *cap i pota* (calves' head stew) are
revived with pzazz alongside squab
and truffled pâté or chilled beetroot
gazpacho. Look out for the green-tea
fruitcake with pears in red wine to finish, and a well-thought-out wine list
that contains some excellent local bottles at low mark-ups.

Tragaluz

*Ptge de la Concepció 5 (93 487 01
96/www.grupotragaluz.com). Metro
Diagonal.* **Open** 1.30-4pm, 8.30pm-
midnight daily. €€€€.
Mediterranean. Map p122 C3 ③⑧

BARCELONA BY AREA

Tragaluz is the stylish flagship for an extraordinarily successful group of restaurants (which includes Agua, Bestial and Omm). Prices have risen a bit recently and the wine mark-up is hard to swallow, but there's no faulting tuna tataki with a cardamom wafer and a dollop of ratatouille-like pisto. Finish the meal with cherry consommé or a thin tart of white and dark chocolate.

Ty-Bihan

Ptge Lluís Pellicer 13 (93 410 90 02). Metro Hospital Clínic. **Open** 1.30-3.30pm Mon; 1.30-3.30pm, 8.30-11.30pm Tue-Fri; 8.30-11.30pm Sat. Closed Aug. **€€. Breton.** Map p122 B2 ㊴

Functioning both as crêperie and Breton cultural centre, Ty-Bihan has chosen a smart, spacious look over wheat sheaves and pitchforks. A long list of sweet and savoury *galettes* (crêpes made with buckwheat flour) are followed up with scrumptious little blinis smothered in strawberry jam and cream, and crêpes suzettes served in a pool of flaming Grand Marnier. The Petite menu will take care of *les enfants*, cider the grown-ups.

La Verema

C/Comte d'Urgell 88 (93 451 68 91). Metro Urgell. **Open** 1.30-4pm Mon; 1.30-4pm, 8.30-11pm Tue, Wed; 1.30-4pm, 8.30pm-midnight Fri, Sat. **€€.** Map p122 B4 ㊵

An unexpected little neighbourhood find, La Verema doesn't look much from the outside, but takes its food very seriously. Sit up at the bar to enjoy three oysters, a glass of cava (€7), and some tapas, or step down into a small dining room for a great-value *menú del día*. From the night-time à la carte menu, don't miss the artichoke hearts filled variously with wild mushrooms and quail's egg, goat's cheese and anchovy, or Iranian caviar.

Windsor

C/Còrsega 286 (93 415 84 83). Metro Diagonal. **Open** 1-4pm, 8.30-11pm Mon-Fri; 8.30-11pm Sat. Closed Aug. **€€€€. Modern Catalan.** Map p122 C2 ㊶

Let down by a smart but drab dining room and a preponderance of foreign businessmen, Windsor nevertheless serves some of the most creative food around. Start with an amuse-gueule of a tomato reduction with pistachio; warm up with wild mushroom cannelloni in truffle sauce or divine foie gras on thin slices of fruit cake; and peak with turbot and a citrus risotto or squab with a sauce of fortified wine.

Xix Bar

C/Rocafort 19 (93 423 43 14/www. xixbar.com). Metro Poble Sec. **Open** 9am-4.30pm, 6.30pm-1.30am Mon-Thur; 9am-4.30pm, 6.30pm-3am Fri, Sat. No credit cards. **Cocktail bar.** Map p122 A5 ㊷

Xix (pronounced 'chicks', and a play on the address, among other things) is a unconventional cocktail bar in the candlelit surroundings of an old tiled *granja* (milk bar). It's dead cosy but a little bit scruffy, which makes the list of 20 brands of gin all the more unexpected. Simple pasta dishes, salads and *bocadillos* are served during the day.

Shopping

Altaïr

Gran Via de les Corts Catalanes 616 (93 342 71 71/www.altair.es). Metro Universitat. **Open** 10am-2pm, 4.30-8.30pm Mon-Fri; 10am-3pm, 4-8.30pm Sat. Map p122 C4 ㊸

The largest travel bookshop in Europe, where you can pick up guides to free eating in Barcelona, tomes on geolinguistics, handbooks on successful outdoor sex and CDs of tribal music. Of course, all the less arcane publications are here too: maps for hikers, travel guidebooks, multilingual dictionaries, travel diaries and notebooks, and select equipment such as money belts and mosquito nets.

BY

NEW C/Muntaner 22 (93 451 89 83/ www.bybcn.es). Metro Universitat. **Open** 10.30am-8pm Mon-Sat. Map p122 B4 ㊹

See box p136.

Camper

*C/Pelai 13-37 (93 302 41 24/www.
camper.com). Metro Catalunya.* **Open**
10am-10pm Mon-Sat. **Map** p123 D3 ⑮
Mallorca-based eco-shoe company
Camper has sexed up its ladies' line
recently. Each year it seems to flirt
more with high heels (albeit rubbery,
wedgy ones) and girly straps. Of
course, it still has its round-toed and
clod-heeled classics, along with the
iconic bowling shoes, but it's worth
taking another look, particularly if
you've previously dismissed this lot.

Casa del Llibre

*C/Passeig de Gràcia 62 (93 272 34 80/
www.casadellibro.com). Metro Passeig
de Gràcia.* **Open** 9.30am-9.30pm Mon-
Sat. **Map** p123 D3 ⑯
Part of a well-established Spanish
chain, this general bookstore offers a
diverse assortment of titles, including
some English-language fiction. Glossy
Barcelona-themed coffee-table tomes
with good gift potential sit by the front
right-hand entrance.

El Corte Inglés

*Plaça Catalunya 14 (93 306 38 00/
www.elcorteingles.es). Metro Catalunya.*
Open 10am-10pm Mon-Sat.
Map p123 D5 ⑰
El Corte Inglés' flagship store is a dominant landmark in Plaça Catalunya. It
flies defiantly in the face of Barcelona's
retail traditions: the goods are easy to
return, and staff are helpful when you
want assistance, unobtrusive when
you don't. The Plaça Catalunya branch
is the place to go for cosmetics, clothes
and homewares. It also houses a well-
stocked but rather pricey supermarket
and gourmet food store, plus services
ranging from key cutting through to
currency exchange. The Portal de l'Àngel branch stocks music, books, sta-
tionery and sports gear from trainers
to training bikes.

FNAC

*El Triangle, Plaça Catalunya 4 (93 344
18 00/www.fnac.es). Metro Catalunya.*
Open 10am-10pm Mon-Sat.
Map p122 C5 ⑱

Altaïr

This French multimedia superstore
supplies information and entertainment in all the formats possible nowadays. The ground floor has a great
selection of magazines, along with a
small café, a ticket desk and a travel
agent. Above this there are two floors
of CDs, DVDs, software, hardware and
peripherals, hi-fis, cameras, MP3 players, home cinema systems and books
in various languages.

Mango

*Passeig de Gràcia 65 (93 215 75 30/
www.mango.es). Metro Passeig de
Gràcia.* **Open** 10am-9pm Mon-Sat.
Map p122 C3 ⑲
A small step up from Zara in quality
and price, Mango's womenswear is less
chameleon-like but still victim to the
catwalks. Strong points include tai-
lored trouser suits and skirts, knitwear
and stretchy tops. Unsold items end up
at the Mango Outlet (C/Girona 37, 93
412 29 35), which is packed with frenzied girls on a mission.
Other locations Passeig de Gràcia
8-10 (93 412 15 99).

Queer eye for the marrying guy

Saturated with gay restaurants, shops, clubs and hotels, the pink microcosm of the 'Gaixample' is probably one of the few places in the world where a couture wedding outfitters for gay grooms could survive. The first shop of its kind in Europe, **BY** (p134) opened in May 2007 – timed to coincide with Barcelona Bridal Week fashion show – and is already attracting clients from Spain and abroad with its suave yet quirky bespoke suits for the big day.

The shop is only possible because, since 2005, Spain has enjoyed the most liberal laws in Europe governing homosexual rights; same-sex couples are not only allowed to marry (rather than just form a 'civil partnership'), but also to adopt children. Even non-Spaniards may marry on Spanish territory if they are legally resident.

After an initial rush of weddings – over 4,500 gay couples tied the knot in the first year after the law was passed – the Ministry of Justice estimates that around 2,000 gay couples marry each year in Spain.

Naturally, in Barcelona the same-sex marriage law soon translated to a new fashion opportunity. BY's couture wedding suits are squarely aimed at the slim of hip and the fat of wallet and cost from around €2,500 to over €15,000. To make them extra special, the linings can be personalised with initials, poems or even photos. Owner Santiago Porrero claims that suits can be just as varied and original as a bridal dress and that the secret is all in the details: wool inlaid with 22-carat gold; one piece jacket and waistcoat combinations; tasselled cummerbunds; leather gloves; satin epaulettes; two-tone lapels and collars, along with wedding bands and cufflinks from Mallorcan jeweller Helena Rohner. And none of it pink.

Vinçon

Passeig de Gràcia 96 (93 215 60 50/
www.vincon.com). Metro Diagonal.
Open 10am-8.30pm Mon-Sat. **Map**
p123 D2 ⑩

Vinçon is one of the vital organs that
keeps Barcelona's reputation as a city
of cutting-edge design alive. The building itself is a monument to the history
of local design: its furniture showroom,
located upstairs, is surrounded by
Modernista glory (and you get a peek
at Gaudí's La Pedrera); downstairs in
the kitchen, bathroom, garden and various other departments, everything is
super-stylish. As you'd expect, there is
no shortage of design classics, ranging
from a Bonet armchair to the so-called
'perfect' corkscrew.

Other locations Tinc Çon, C/Rosselló
246 (93 215 60 50).

Nightlife

Antilla BCN Latin Club

C/Aragó 141 (93 451 45 64/www.
antillasalsa.com). Metro Urgell. **Open**
11pm-3.30am Mon-Wed, Sun; 11pm-
4.30am Fri, Sat. Gigs around 1am.
Admission (incl 1 drink) €10. No
credit cards. **Map** p122 A3 ⑤

The Antilla prides itself on being a
'Caribbean cultural centre', but its true
calling lies in being the self-proclaimed
best *salsoteca* in town, offering dance
classes (including acrobatic salsa and
Afro-Cuban styles) and a solid programme of live music, which covers all
Latin flavours from son to merengue
and Latin jazz.

Arena

Classic & Madre *C/Diputació 233.*
Map p122 C4 ⑤

VIP & Dandy *Gran Via de les Corts*
Catalanes 593. **Map** p122 C4 ⑤

All *93 487 83 42/www.arenadisco.com.*
Metro Universitat. **Open** 12.30am-5am
Fri, Sat. **Admission** (incl 1 drink) €5
Fri; €10 Sat. No credit cards.

The four different Arena discos offer
variations on familiar, well-worn gay
themes; you can switch between them
freely after getting your hand stamped
at the entrance. Of the four, Classic is

the most light-hearted, playing classic
hits from the 1980s and '90s, with a
campy-kitsch atmosphere and a
healthy mix of the sexes. The cav-
ernous Madre is more full-on, with a
darkroom, pounding house music and
current chart hits. It attracts a younger
crowd, and is more of a cattle market.
VIP and Dandy are probably the tack-
iest and are also the most mixed; again,
they are youthful venues with lots of
space, but nonetheless heave at weekends. VIP does its bit for the Spanish
retro pop industry, while Dandy bangs
away with more house tunes.

Buda Restaurante

C/Pau Claris 92 (93 318 42 52/
www.budarestaurante.com). Metro
Catalunya. **Open** 9pm-3am daily.
Admission free. **Map** p123 D4 ⑤

The centre of Barcelona is strangely
devoid of glamorous nightspots, or at
least it was until Buda came along. The
place has lots of throne-style furniture
and gilded wallpaper, topped off with

Vinçon

Santa Locura

a colossal chandelier. The laid-back nature of the staff (dancing on the bar seems completely acceptable) and upbeat house music make it excellent for drinks and an ogle. Wednesday is flamenco night, Friday is Disco Fever, and Saturday is Bollywood.

City Hall

Rambla Catalunya 2-4 (93 317 21 77/ www.grupo-ottozutz.com). Metro Catalunya. **Open** midnight-6am Tue-Sun. **Admission** (incl 1 drink) €12. Credit cards on door only. **Map** p122 C4 ⑤⑤

Soul City on Thursdays at City Hall has made a name for itself among the local NY-capped, billowing trouser-wearing posses by bringing acts like Killa Kela and the Scratch Perverts to Barcelona. The rest of the week it's a little more mixed, with music from deep house to electro rock, and an older post-work (even pre-work?) crowd joining the young, tanned and skinny to show the dancefloors some love. Outside, the terrace is a veritable melting pot of tourists and locals.

Danzarama

Gran Via de les Corts Catalanes 604 (93 301 97 43/reservations 93 342 5070/www.gruposalsitas.com). Metro Universitat. **Open** 7pm-3am Mon-Sat. **Admission** free. **Map** p122 C4 ⑤⑥

Make your way past the flash restaurant upstairs – we're talking white sofas swinging from the ceiling – and down on to the brick-walled, loud dancefloor. With no entry charge and lots of tables, Danzarama has become a popular pre-party venue for Pacha (on Thursdays; p159) and Catwalk (on Sundays; p107), with a free shuttle bus and thumping tunes making up for the club-priced drinks.

Distrito Diagonal

Avda Diagonal 442 (mobile 607 113 602/www.distritodiagonal.com). Metro Diagonal. **Open** midnight-6am Fri, Sat. **Admission** free before 3am, €15 (incl 1 drink) after. No credit cards. **Map** p123 D2 ⑤⑦

With its easy-going atmosphere, Distrito Diagonal attracts a slightly older crowd. The venue's bathed in red light, there are sounds from nu jazz to deep house and plenty of chairs to sink into. It's become a sought-after place for small promoters and one-off parties, which means the music can veer from Bollywood to hip hop.

Luz de Gas

C/Muntaner 246 (93 209 77 11/ www.luzdegas.com). FGC Muntaner. **Open** 11.30pm-5am daily. Gigs 12.30am daily. **Admission** (incl 1 drink) €15. **Map** p122 B1 ⑤⑧

This lovingly converted old music hall, garnished with chandeliers and classical friezes, occasionally hosts gentle pop and rock concerts. Between these gig, you'll find nightly residencies: blues on Mondays, Dixieland on Tuesdays, disco on Wednesdays, rock covers on Thursdays and Fridays, and jazz on Saturdays and Sundays.

Metro

C/Sepúlveda 185 (93 323 52 27/ www.metrodisco.bcn). Metro Universitat. **Open** 1-5am Mon; midnight-5am Tue-Sun. **Admission** (incl 1 drink) €14. **Map** p122 B4 ⑤⑨

Metro has been fully refurbished. It has a redesigned bar and even what were the dingier corners have achieved a better shine. With stiffer competition around, it remains to be seen whether this will be enough to sustain it as the pre-eminent gay club in town. Latin beats prevail on the smaller dancefloor, with house on the main one to keep the boys entertained.

Raum

Gran Via 593 (mobile 600 422 318/ www.raum.es). Metro Universitat. **Open** midnight-5am Thur. **Admission** €10. No credit cards. **Map** p122 C4 ⑥⓿

Raum's cold industrial decor lends itself well to this weekly electronic night, during which the tunes run the gamut from minimal to hard techno to the occasional chunk of deep electro-house. The Thursday slot ensures the crowd – a chatty bunch of expats and locals – come for the tunes rather than to pose among the steel pillars and lunar-style projections.

Salvation

Ronda Sant Pere 19-21 (93 318 06 86/www.matineegroup.com). Metro Urquinaona. **Open** midnight-5am Thur-Sat. **Admission** (incl 1 drink) €15. No credit cards. **Map** p123 D5 ⑥①

It's been said of Salvation – one of the city's enduringly popular gay clubs – that 'everyone you see naked on Gaydar…you can see in here with their clothes on'. One room is full of said tanned, buff torsos lurching around to house; in the other room, sprightly young things bounce about to pop.

Santa Locura

C/Consell de Cent 294 (93 200 14 66). Metro Passeig de Gràcia. **Open** midnight-5.30am Thur-Sat. **Admission** (incl 1 drink) €10. No credit cards. **Map** p122 C4 ⑥②

Perhaps Barcelona's most extraordinary clubbing experience, Santa Locura has three floors filled with weird and wonderful nocturnal pleasures: get married at the bar; plead guilty at the confessional box; watch a Chippendale-style show; and hit the dancefloor to the music of Kylie and her ilk.

Space Barcelona

C/Tarragona 141-147 (93 426 84 44/ www.spacebarcelona.com). Metro Tarragona. **Open** midnight-6am Fri, Sat. **Admission** (incl 1 drink) €15; €12 with flyer. No credit cards. **Map** p122 A3 ⑥③

Space tries hard to cash in on Barcelona's Balearic party aspirations. A young crowd of pseudo-fashionistas and clubbers descends en masse to strike poses under the deep lights and pounding bass. Occasional appearances from the likes of Carl Cox keep the brand's reputation safe.

Arts & leisure

L'Auditori

C/Lepant 150 (93 247 93 00/www. auditori.org). Metro Marina. **Open** Information 8am-10pm daily. Box office noon-9pm Mon-Sat; 1hr before performance Sun. Closed Aug. **Map** p123 F5 ⑥④

Serious music lovers in Barcelona prefer concerts at Rafael Moneo's sleek L'Auditori. The 2,400-seat hall has provided the city with a world-class music venue and a home to its orchestra, the OBC. The Museu de la Música opened in 2007 (p126), as did a new 600-seat auditorium that will add more variety to an already impressive programme covering not just classical music, but jazz, contemporary and world music. Various night-buses connect the Auditori with Plaça Catalunya after evening performances.

Casablanca-Gràcia

C/Girona 173-175 (93 459 03 26). Metro Diagonal. **Tickets** €4.50 Wed; €6 Mon, Tue, Thur-Sun. No credit cards. **Map** p123 D2 **65**

A venerable three-screen cinema, opened in 1936. Independent Spanish and European films are mostly offered in their original language.

Casablanca-Kaplan

Passeig de Gràcia 115 (93 218 43 45). Metro Diagonal or Verdaguer. **Tickets** €4.50 Mon; €6 Tue-Sun. No credit cards. **Map** p123 D2 **66**

This cinema is the smallest in Barcelona, with two screens offering independent Spanish and European films. Films made in languages other than English or Spanish are dubbed.

FilmoTeca

Cinema Aquitania, Avda Sarrià 31-33 (93 410 75 90/http://cultura.gencat. net/filmo). Metro Hospital Clínic. Closed Aug. **Tickets** €2.70; €2 reductions; €18 for 10 films. No credit cards. **Map** p122 A2 **67**

Funded by the Catalan government, the Filmoteca is a little dry for some tastes, offering comprehensive seasons of cinema's more recondite auteurs, alongside better-known classics, plus screenings each spring of all films nominated in the Goya Awards. Overlapping cycles last two or three weeks, with each film screened at least twice at different times. Books of 20 and 100 tickets bring down the price per film to a negligible amount.

Méliès Cinemes

C/Villarroel 102 (93 451 00 51/ www.cinesmelies.net). Metro Urgell. **Tickets** €2.70 Mon; €4 Tue-Sun. No credit cards. **Map** p122 B4 **68**

A small, two-screen cinema that is the nearest Barcelona comes to an art-house, with the familiar idiosyncratic roster of accessible classics alongside more recent films that aren't quite commercial enough for general release.

Plaza de Toros Monumental

Gran Via de les Corts Catalanes 749 (93 245 58 04/93 215 95 70). Metro Monumental. **Open** *Bullfights* Apr-Sept 5.30-7pm Sun. *Museum* Apr-Sept 11am-2pm, 4-8pm Mon-Sat; 10.30am-1.30pm Sun. **Admission** *Bullfights* €20-€97. *Museum* €4; €3 reductions. No credit cards. **Map** p123 F4 **69**

In 2004 council voted the city to be *anti-taurino* (against bullfighting), but this was largely a symbolic gesture: 100 bulls are still killed every year at the city's single remaining bullring, although its future is in the balance. The *corridas* mostly take place in front of tourists and homesick Andalucians.

Renoir-Floridablanca

C/Floridablanca 135 (93 228 93 93/ www.cinesrenoir.com). Metro Sant Antoni. **Tickets** €4.80 Mon; €6.20 Tue-Thur; €6.50 Fri-Sun; €4.80 late show Fri, Sat. **Map** p122 B5 **70**

The closest first-run original-version cinema you'll find to the centre of town. Renoir-Floridablanca has four screens and shows up to eight independent, off-beat foreign and Spanish films per day.

Teatre Nacional de Catalunya (TNC)

Plaça de les Arts 1 (93 306 57 00/ www.tnc.cat). Metro Glòries. **Box office** 3-9pm Tue-Sun. **Tickets** €15-€25; €10-€15 reductions. **Map** p123 F4 **71**

The huge TNC has three superb performance spaces. Its main stage promotes Spanish classical theatre, while more contemporary European theatre is normally staged in the Sala Tallers.

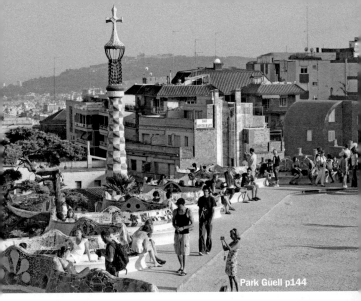
Park Güell p144

Gràcia

Gràcia was a mere village 150 years ago, centred around the 17th-century convent of Santa Maria de Gràcia, with just 2,608 inhabitants. By the time it was annexed to Barcelona in the late 19th century, however, the population had risen to 61,935, making it the ninth largest town in Spain. The effects of rapid industrial expansion brought about much political activity and it became a hotbed of Catalanism, republicanism and anarchism. Today, few vestiges of radicalism remain, though the *okupa* squatter movement inhabits a relatively high number of buildings in the area and it isn't uncommon to see the odd anarchist protest. Many streets still have telltale names such as Llibertat, Revolució and Fraternitat.

Nowadays, the *barri* is a favourite hangout of the city's bohemians. The numerous small, unpretentious bars are frequented by artists, designers and students. However, Gràcia really comes into its own for a few days in mid August, when its famous festa major grips the entire city. Residents spend months in advance preparing original home-made street decorations, and all of Barcelona converges on the tiny *barri* to party.

Sights & museums

Fundació Foto Colectània
C/Julián Romea 6, D2 (93 217 16 26/ www.colectania.es). FGC Gràcia. **Open** 11am-2pm, 5-8.30pm Mon-Sat. Closed Aug. **Map** p142 B4 ●
This private foundation is dedicated to the promotion of photography and has

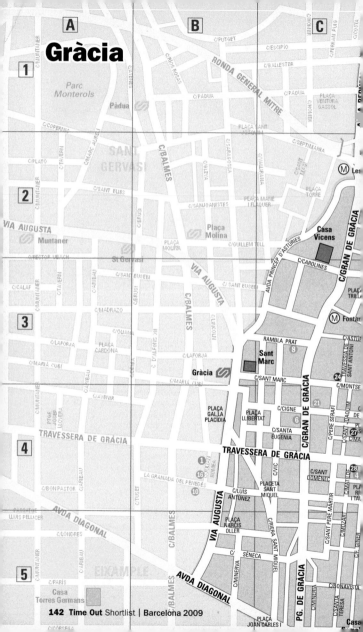

Gràcia

Parc Monterols

Pàdua

SANT GERVASI

C/PLATÓ

C/SANT EUES

Plaça Molina

Muntaner

VIA AUGUSTA

C/DIRECTOR UBACH

St Gervasi

Plaça Cardona

Gràcia

RONDA GENERAL MITRE

PLAÇA VENTURA GASSOL

PLAÇA SANT JOAQUIM

PLAÇA MANÉ I FLAQUER

PLAÇA TORRE

Casa Vicens

Fontana

RAMBLA PRAT

Sant Marc

C/SANT MARC

PLAÇA GAL·LA PLACÍDIA

PLAÇA LLIBERTAT

TRAVESSERA DE GRÀCIA

PLAÇA SANT MIQUEL

PLAÇA NARCÍS OLLER

Casa Torres Germans

EIXAMPLE

AVDA DIAGONAL

PG. DE GRÀCIA

PLAÇA JOAN CARLES I

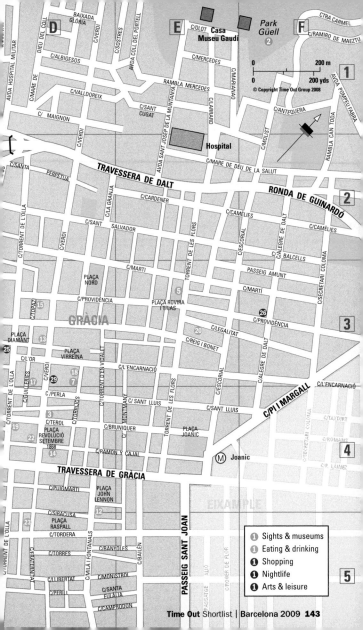

AVE Maria!

The high-speed train arrives, beleaguered and belated.

At last, three years late and 12 years since work began, Barcelona and Madrid are linked by high-speed train (AVE). The link, with a service of 17 trains a day running at up to 350kph (220mph), cuts journey times from six hours to two hours 38mins and should give the inter-city airlines a run for their money. Technically speaking, allowing for check-in, flying takes two hours, but then time has to be allowed for the trip to the airport, delays are frequent and many travellers will be prepared to pay over the odds to avoid using Madrid's difficult to navigate Barajas airport.

However, the AVE's journey to Barcelona has been dogged by controversy and it isn't over yet. At present the train arrives at Sants station, but for its next leg on to the French border, the plan is to tunnel under the city, close to the foundations of Gaudí's La Pedrera and the Sagrada Família. Not surprisingly, the plan faces considerable opposition from residents and the Church.

Commercially, politically and, above all, psychologically, the AVE will bring the capital and Barcelona closer together. Furthermore, Barcelona is now part of a high-speed network that, via Madrid, links it to Sevilla, Málaga, Toledo and Valladollid. Next stop, Perpignan, in 2012.

collections of major Iberian photographers from the 1950s to the present day. It also has an extensive library of Spanish and Portuguese photography books, including out-of-print editions.

Park Güell

C/Olot (Casa-Museu Gaudí 93 219 38 11). Metro Lesseps/bus 24, 25. **Open** 10am-sunset daily. *Museum* Apr-Sept 10am-7.45pm daily. Oct-Mar 10am-5.45pm daily. **Admission** *Park* free. *Museum* €4; €3 reductions; free under-9s. No credit cards. **Map** p143 F1 ②

Gaudí's brief for this spectacular project was to emulate the English garden cities so admired by his patron Eusebi Güell (hence the spelling of 'park'): to lay out a self-contained suburb for the wealthy, but also to design the public areas. The idea never took off and the Güell family donated the park to the city in 1922.

The fantastical exuberance of Gaudí's imagination is breathtaking. The visitor was previously welcomed by two life-sized mechanical gazelles – a religious reference to medieval Hebrew love poetry – although these were destroyed in the Civil War. The two gatehouses that do still remain were based on designs the architect made earlier for the opera *Hansel and Gretel*, one of them featuring a red and white mushroom for a roof. From here, walk up a splendid staircase flanked by multicoloured battlements, past the iconic mosaic lizard sculpture, to what would have been the marketplace. Here, 100 palm-shaped pillars hold up a roof, reminiscent of the hypostyle hall at Luxor. On top of this structure is the esplanade, surrounded by undulating benches in the form of a sea-serpent decorated with shattered tiles. The park's peak is marked by a large cross and offers an amazing panorama of Barcelona and the sea. Gaudí lived for a time in one of the two houses built on the site: it's since become the Casa-Museu Gaudí.

The best way to get to the park is by bus; if you go via Lesseps metro, be prepared for a steep uphill walk.

Flash Flash p147

Eating & drinking

La Baignoire

C/Verdi 6 (mobile 606 330 460). Metro Fontana or Joanic. **Open** *June-Sept* 8pm-2am Mon-Thur, Sun; 8pm-3am Fri, Sat. *Oct-May* 6pm-2am Mon-Thur, Sun; 6pm-3am Fri, Sat. No credit cards. **Bar.** Map p143 D4 ❸

The name means 'bathtub', which gives some idea of the size, but the staff are unfailingly friendly, and slide projections and lounge music complement the mellow vibe. Fresh fruit juices are served in summer; cocktails and decent wine are available year round.

Bo!

Plaça Rius i Taulet 11 (93 368 35 29). Metro Fontana. **Open** 10am-1am Mon-Thur; 10am-2.30am Fri-Sun. €€. **Café.** Map p142 C4 ❹

Decent tapas, creative sandwiches and generous portions, plus plenty of terrace tables, make this a favourite spot in one of Gràcia's most emblematic, lively squares. If Bo!'s black chairs are all taken, you'll do nearly as well on one of neighbouring bar Amelie's white ones.

Bodega Manolo

C/Torrent de les Flors 101 (93 284 43 77). Metro Joanic. **Open** 10am-6pm Tue, Wed; 10am-1am Thur, Fri; 12.30-6.30pm, 8.30pm-1am Sat; noon-3pm Sun. Closed Aug. No credit cards. €€. **Tapas.** Map p143 E3 ❺

Another old family bodega with faded, peeling charm, barrels on the wall and rows of dusty bottles, Manolo specialises not only in wine, but in classy food: we recommend the foie gras with port and apple. At the other end of the scale comes the 'Destroyer': egg, bacon, sausage and chips.

Botafumeiro

C/Gran de Gràcia 81 (93 218 42 30). Metro Fontana. **Open** 1pm-1am daily. €€€€. **Galician.** Map p142 C4 ❻

Love it or hate it (and the size, racket and overwhelmingly arriviste diners mean no one leaves undecided), there's no denying Botafumeiro's success, and its literally dozens of tables are rarely empty for very long. The speciality is excellent Galician seafood, served with military precision by the fleet of nautically clad waiters. Non-fishy dishes

Park Güell p144

include a rich *caldo gallego* (cabbage and pork broth) and *lacón con grelos* (gammon with turnip tops).

Cantina Machito

C/Torrijos 47 (93 217 34 14). Metro Fontana or Joanic. **Open** 1-4pm, 7pm-1.30am daily. **€€. Mexican**. **Map** p143 D3

Every day is Day of the Dead in this cheerily decked out little Mexican joint, hung with bunting and humming with conversation. The minuscule writing on the menu and low lighting make for some guesswork when placing your order, but the choi-ces are standard enough – quesadillas, tacos, ceviche and enchiladas – with a couple of surprises thrown in, such as the tasting platter of insects. Service can be slow and the kitchen can be heavy-handed with the sauces, but the portions are huge and prices reasonable.

Casa Quimet

Rambla de Prat 9 (93 217 53 27). Metro Fontana. **Open** 6.30pm-2am Tue-Sun. Closed Aug. No credit cards. **Bar**. **Map** p142 C3

Yellowing jazz posters cover every inch of wallspace, dozens of ancient guitars are suspended from the ceiling and a succession of ticking clocks compete to be heard over the voice of Billie Holiday. This other-worldly 'Guitar Bar' (as the place is invariably known to locals) occasionally springs to life with an impromptu jam session, but most of the time it remains a perfect study in melancholy.

Envalira

Plaça del Sol 13 (93 218 58 13). Metro Fontana. **Open** 1.30-4pm, 9pm-midnight Tue-Sat; 1.30-5pm Sun. Closed Aug. **€€. Spanish**. **Map** p142 C4

Old-school Spain lives on, as penguin-suited waiters solemnly hand out brown PVC menus at plastic teak-effect tables under austere lighting. But it's all worth it for the food: as traditionally brown as the drab decor, it runs the full gamut of hefty Iberian classics. Start with fish soups or lentils and go on to paellas, roast meats and seafood stews, followed by serious, own-made crema catalana or tarta de Santiago. Arrive early for the leather banquettes at the front.

Flash Flash

C/Granada del Penedès 25 (93 237 09 90). FGC Gràcia. **Open** 1.30pm-1.30am daily. **€€€. Tortillas/cocktails.** **Map** p142 B4 ⑩

Opened in 1970, this bar was a design sensation in its day, with its white leatherette banquettes and walls that are still imprinted with silhouettes of a life-size, frolicking, Twiggy-like model. They call it a *tortilleria*, which means there are 60 or so tortilla variations, alongside a list of child-friendly dishes and adult-friendly cocktails.

Folquer

C/Torrent de l'Olla 3 (93 217 43 95). Metro Diagonal or Verdaguer. **Open** 1-4pm, 9-11.30pm Mon-Fri; 9-11.30pm Sat. Closed 3wks Aug. **€€€. Catalan.** **Map** p143 D5 ⑪

Filled with an animated, older clientele Folquer is a welcoming space with daffodil yellow wood panelling and artworks. The food is well executed and priced, never more so than in the lunch deals: the 'Executive' is a sturdy main, such as entrecôte, with a salad, pudding and wine for €15, while the normal *menú* is cheaper and still creative.

Himali

C/Milà i Fontanals 68 (93 285 15 68). Metro Joanic. **Open** noon-4pm, 8pm-midnight Tue-Sun. **€€. Nepalese.** **Map** p143 D4 ⑫

Cocking a snook at the many mediocre Indian restaurants around, Barcelona's first Nepalese eaterie has become a hit. Faced with an alien and impenetrable menu, the set meals seem tempting, but they aren't always the best option: press the waiters for recommendations or try *mugliaco kukhura* (barbecued butter chicken in creamy tomato sauce) or *khasi masala tarkari* (baked spicy lamb). Meat cooked in the tandoori oven (*txulo*) is also worth a try, and there are plenty of vegetarian choices.

Mesopotamia

C/Verdi 65 (93 237 15 63). Metro Fontana. **Open** 8.30pm-midnight Tue-Sat. Closed 2wks Dec. **€€.** No credit cards. **Iraqi. Map** p143 D3 ⑬

The policy at Barcelona's only Iraqi restaurant is to have everything on the menu at the same price, so the cost won't hold people back from ordering what they want. Best value, though, is the enormous taster menu, which includes great Lebanese wines, a variety of dips for your *riqaq* bread, bulgur wheat with aromatic roast meats and vegetables, sticky baklawa and Arabic teas.

La Nena

C/Ramón y Cajal 36 (93 285 14 76). Metro Fontana or Joanic. **Open** *Oct-July* 9am-10pm daily. *Aug, Sept* 9am-2pm, 4-10pm daily. Closed 3wks Aug. **€€.** No credit cards. **Café. Map** p143 D4 ⑭

An oasis at breakfast time, La Nena (the little girl) is as cutesy as its name suggests, and the sweetness carries over into the menu: home-made cakes, biscuits, freshly whipped cream, ice-creams, and chocolate are what this little girl is made of. But the more health-minded can take refuge in home-made yoghurts, a wide range of mueslis, and freshly made juices from orange to papaya.

Noise i Art

C/Topazi 26 (93 217 50 01). Metro Fontana. **Open** 6pm-2.30am Tue-Thur, Sun; 7pm-3am Fri, Sat. Closed 1st wk Sept. No credit cards. **Bar/café.** **Map** p143 D3 ⑮

It's known locally as the 'IKEA bar', which, although some of the plastic fittings do look strangely familiar, does not really do justice to the colourful, pop art interior. A chilled and convivial atmosphere is occasionally livened up with a flamenco session, and all the usual Gràcia staples such as houmous and tabbouleh are served along with various salads and pasta dishes.

Octubre

C/Julián Romea 18 (93 218 25 18). FGC Gràcia/metro Diagonal. **Open** 1.30-3.30pm, 9-11pm Mon-Fri; 9-11pm Sat. Closed Aug. **€€. Catalan.** **Map** p142 B4 ⑯

Time stands still in this quiet little spot, with quaint old-fashioned decor, swathes of lace and brown table linen.

Time often stands still, in fact, between placing an order and receiving any food, but this is all part of Octubre's sleepy charm, along with a roll-call of reasonably priced and mainly Catalan dishes. The beef in mustard sauce is excellent, and wild mushroom risotto, while not outstanding, is decent enough for the price. The puddings also vary a fair bit, but Octubre is more about atmosphere than anything else.

Puku Café

C/Guilleries 10 (93 368 25 73). Metro Fontana. **Open** 7pm-1.30am Mon-Wed; 7pm-2am Thur; 7pm-3am Fri, Sat. **Bar/café. Map** p143 D3 ⑰

The Puku Café has two very different vibes. During the week it's a colourful meeting place, where the casually hip hang out over a bottle of wine and maybe some cactus and lime ice-cream. At weekends, however, the amber walls and deep orange columns prop up a younger, scruffier crowd, nodding along to some of the city's best DJs spinning an electropop playlist.

Salambó

C/Torrijos 51 (93 218 69 66). Metro Fontana or Joanic. **Open** noon-1am Mon-Thur, Sun; noon-3am Fri, Sat. **Café. Map** p143 D3 ⑱

The time-honoured meeting place for Verdi cinema-goers, Salambó is a large and ever so slightly staid split-level café that serves coffee, teas and filled ciabatta in the *barri*'s more conservative element. At night, those who are planning to eat are given preference when it comes to bagging a table.

Samsara

C/Terol 6 (93 285 36 88). Metro Fontana or Joanic. **Open** *June-Sept* 8.30pm-2am Mon-Thur; 8.30pm-3am Fri, Sat. *Oct-May* 1.30-4pm, 8.30pm-2am Mon-Thur; 1.30-4pm, 8.30pm-3am Fri; 8.30pm-3am Sat. **€€€. Tapas. Map** p143 D4 ⑲

With its combination of Moroccan-themed decor and intelligent cooking, Samsara has built up quite a following among Gràcia foodies. Its tapas are diminutive but don't want for flavour

or imagination: try monkfish ceviche with mango or watermelon gazpacho with basil oil. A DJ plays lounge and the smoothest of house later in the week.

San Kil

C/Legalitat 22 (93 284 41 79). Metro Fontana or Joanic. **Open** 1-4pm, 8.30pm-midnight Mon-Sat. Closed 2wks Aug. **€€. Korean. Map** p143 E3 ⑳

If you've never eaten Korean before, it pays to gen up before you head to this bright, spartan restaurant. *Panch'an* is the ideal starter: four little dishes containing vegetable appetisers, one of which will be tangy *kimch'i* (fermented cabbage with chilli). Then try mouth-watering *pulgogi* (beef served sizzling at the table and eaten rolled into lettuce leaves) and maybe *pibimbap* (rice with vegetables and occasionally meat) topped with a fried egg.

Shojiro

C/Ros de Olano 11 (93 415 65 48). Metro Fontana. **Open** 1.30-3.30pm Mon; 1.30-3.30pm, 9-11.30pm Tue-Sat. Closed 3wks Aug. **€€€. Catalan/Japanese. Map** p142 C4 ㉑

A curious but successful mix of Catalan and Japanese applies to the decor as much as the food, with original 'mosaic' flooring and dark green paintwork setting off a clean feng-shui look. There are only set meals, starting with an amuse-bouche, then offering sushi with strips of nori, sticky rice and salad, or courgette soup and pancetta as a starter, with salmon teriyaki or spring chicken confit with potato dauphinois as mains.

Sureny

Plaça de la Revolució 17 (93 213 75 56). Metro Fontana or Joanic. **Open** 8.30pm-midnight Tue-Thur; 8.30pm-1am Fri, Sat; 1-3.30pm, 8pm-midnight Sun. Closed last wk Sept, 1st wk Oct, 2nd wk Apr. **€€. Tapas. Map** p143 D4 ㉒

A well-kept gastronomic secret, Sureny boasts superb tapas and knowledgeable staff. As well as the usual run-of-the-mill tortilla 'n' calamares, look out for tuna marinated in ginger and soy, partridge and venison in season, and a sublime duck foie with redcurrant sauce.

La Tarantella

C/Fraternitat 37 (93 284 98 57). Metro
Fontana. **Open** 8.30pm-midnight Tue;
1.30-3.30pm, 8.30-11.30pm Wed-Sun.
€€. **Pizzeria**. **Map** p143 D5 ㉓
Forge your way through the brightly
lit tunnel of a bar into the cosy, low-
ceilinged back room, warmed with
beams and yellow paintwork. Here you
can dine on decent, budget Italian grub
(salads, pasta and pizzas).

Shopping

Hibernian Books

C/Montseny 17 (93 217 47 96/
www.hibernian-books.com). Metro
Fontana. **Open** 4-8.30pm Mon;
10.30am-8.30pm Tue-Sat. No credit
cards. **Map** p142 C4 ㉔
Hibernian Books stocks over 30,000 fiction and non-fiction books in English.
A children's corner, armchairs, packed
shelves, and tea and coffee furnish this
bookworm's lair, which operates a
part-exchange system for those keen
on offloading some suitcase ballast.

Vinus & Brindis

Torrent de l'Olla 147 (93 218 30 37/
www.vinusbrindis.com). Metro Fontana.
Open June-Oct 11am-2.15pm, 5-9.15pm
Mon-Sat. Nov-May 10.30am-2pm, 5-9pm
Mon-Sat. **Map** p143 D3 ㉕
This franchise of approachable wine
shops has a young, funky feel. It specialises in new and up-and-coming
wine areas, winemakers and wines. Its
staff are more than eager to advise, and
it always has a good range of easy
drinking wines for under €6, as well as
special monthly offers.

Nightlife

KGB

C/Alegre de Dalt 55 (93 210 59 06/
www.salakgb.net). Metro Joanic. **Open**
1-6am Thur-Sat. **Admission** free
before 3am with flyer; €12 (incl 1 drink)
after 3am or without flyer. **Gigs** varies.
Map p143 F3 ㉖
KGB is a cavern-like space that was, in
its heyday, the rock 'n' roll barn capital of the city and the 'after' where the
party kids would bolt to at 6am. It still
remains loud, whether featuring concerts or DJ sessions. The concerts tend
towards rock and hip hop, and the DJ
sets feature reggae, hip hop, techno,
electro and house. Thursdays have
rumba music to get you dancing.

Mond Club

Plaça del Sol 21 (93 272 09 10/
www.mondclub.com). Metro Fontana.
Open 8.30pm-3am daily. **Admission**
free. No credit cards. **Map** p142 C4 ㉗
This tiny two-level bar gets sweaty
and smoky as the coolest cats in Gràcia
pack in for an early drink. Recent problems with the neighbours saw the DJs
replaced with a jukebox.

Vinilo

C/Matilde 2 (mobile 626 464 759/
http://vinilus.blogspot.com). Metro
Fontana. **Open** 8pm-2.30am Mon-Thur,
Sun; 7pm-3am Fri, Sat. **Admission** free.
No credit cards. **Map** p142 C4 ㉘
Local musician Jordi opened this cosy
red-velveted bar/café a couple of years
ago and he's having rip-roaring success.
Doubling as a casual eating place that
serves up damn fine crêpes, Vinilo has
an immaculate music selection –
Sparklehorse, Coco Rosie and Rufus
Wainwright all get good runs here, as
do the Beatles and Pink Floyd.

Arts & leisure

Verdi

C/Verdi 32 (93 238 79 90/www.cines-
verdi.com). Metro Fontana. No credit
cards. **Map** p143 D3 ㉙
A long-standing champion of foreign
cinema, the original five-screen Verdi,
plus its four-screen annexe Verdi Park
on the next street over, offer a diverse
programme of interesting, accessible
cinema from around the world, concentrating on Asia and Europe, as well as
some Spanish repertoire. At peak times,
chaos reigns; arrive early and make sure
you don't mistake the queue of people
going in for the queue buying tickets.
Other locations Verdi Park,
C/Torrijos 49 (93 238 79 90).

Other Districts

Sants & Les Corts

The arrival of the new high-speed train (see box p148) has prompted a long overdue sprucing up of the area around Sants station, but for now it remains a depressing introduction to the city. The adjacent **Plaça dels Països Catalans** looks like it was designed with skateboard tricks in mind and is still crying out for some greenery or perhaps a bench or two.

High-rise streets of mismatching apartment blocks now obscure any trace of the rustic origins of **Les Corts** (literally, 'cowsheds' or 'pigsties'), as the village itself was swallowed up by Barcelona in the late 19th century. One pocket of tranquillity is the **Plaça de la Concòrdia**, a quiet square dominated by a 40-metre (131-foot) bell tower. This is an anachronistic oasis housing the civic centre Can Deu, formerly a farmhouse and now home to a great bar that hosts jazz acts every other Thursday. The area is much better known, though, for what happens every other weekend, when tens of thousands pour in to watch FC Barcelona, whose Nou Camp stadium takes up much of the west of the *barrio*.

Sights & museums

Parc de l'Espanya Industrial

Passeig de Antoni (no phone). Metro Sants-Estació. **Open** 10am-sunset daily. A puzzling and futuristic space, with ten other-worldly watchtowers looking over a boating lake with a statue of Neptune in the middle, flanked by a stretch of mud that is used mainly for walking dogs. By the entrance, children are encouraged to clamber over Andrés Nagel's *Drac*, a massive and sinister black dragon.

Monestir de Pedralbes p156

Eating & drinking

Icho

C/Deu i Mata 69-95, Les Corts (93 444 33 70/www.ichobcnjapones.com). Metro Maria Cristina. **Open** *1.30-3.30pm, 9-11.30pm Tue-Sat. Closed 2wks Aug.* **€€€€. Japanese/Spanish.**
In a coolly designed space under the NH Constanza, Icho (in Japanese it means gingko tree – of which three graceful examples sit outside) fuses Japanese with Spanish cooking. This really shouldn't work, but does – perhaps because you can offset the digestive demands of tender suckling pig and pumpkin purée with a platter of sushi, or balance a starter of foie and eel with tuna tartare and creamed tofu with wasabi. The portions aren't especially large, and diners are encouraged to order several and share.

Shopping

Enric Rovira Shop

Avda Josep Tarradellas 113, Les Corts (93 419 25 47/www.enricrovira.com). Metro Entença. **Open** *10am-2pm, 5-8pm Tue-Fri; 10am-2.30pm Sat. Closed Aug.*

Perhaps the best place in town for designer chocolates, this is where substance actually keeps up with style. Rovira's Gaudí-esque chocolate tile is an iconic gift for any choc lover, and his pink peppercorn truffles make great after-dinner conversation pieces.

L'Illa

Avda Diagonal 545-557, Les Corts (93 444 00 00/www.lilla.com). Metro Maria Cristina. **Open** *10am-9.30pm Mon-Sat. Supermarket 9.30am-9.30pm Mon-Sat.*
This monolithic mall features all the usual fashion favourites but also has a good range of Catalan brands such as Camper, Custo and Antonio Miró. It has been gaining a good reputation lately for its food offerings, with specialist gourmet food stalls and interesting eateries such as sushi and oyster bars.

Nightlife

Bikini

C/Déu i Mata 105, Les Corts (93 322 08 00/www.bikinibcn.com). Metro Les Corts or Maria Cristina. **Open** *Club midnight-5am Wed-Sat; 8.30pm-5am Sun. Gigs varies.* **Admission** *(incl 1 drink) €15.*

BARCELONA BY AREA

It's not easy to find Bikini in the non-descript, soulless streets behind the L'Illa shopping centre. But it's worth making the effort to seek it out, as you'll find top-flight gigs here by serious musicians of every conceivable stripe, from Femi Kuti to Thievery Corporation, and from Marianne Faithfull to Amp Fiddler. After the gigs, stay for club nights with house, funk and hip hop on the turntables. On Sunday watch Barça football matches on the big screen from 8.30pm, then party on to the latest dance sounds from 10.30pm.

Arts & leisure

Auditori Winterthur

L'Illa, Avda Diagonal 547, Les Corts (93 290 11 02/www.winterthur.es). Metro Maria Cristina. **Open** *Information* 8.30am-1.30pm, 3-5.30pm Mon-Fri. Closed Aug.
A charming, intimate venue in the unlikely setting of L'Illa shopping centre. Though it hosts few concerts, they're generally of high quality; the Schubert cycle and series of song recitals, both annual events, are well worth catching.

Nou Camp – FC Barcelona

Nou Camp, Avda Aristides Maillol, Les Corts (93 496 36 00/08/www. fcbarcelona.com). Metro Collblanc or Palau Reial. **Ticket office** *Sept-June* 9am-1.30pm, 3.30-6pm Mon-Thur; 9am-2.30pm Fri; from 11am match days. *Aug* 8.30am-2.30pm Mon-Fri. Tickets available from 2wks before each match. **Tickets** €19-€125. **Museum** *Open* 10am-6.30pm Mon-Sat; 10am-2pm Sun. *Admission* €5.30; €3.70 reductions; free under-5s. *Guided tour* €9.50; €6.60 reductions. No credit cards.
Current president Joan Laporta presides over Barça's most successful spell since the Dream Team of Johan Cruyff in the early 1990s, although the 2007/8 season represents some falling back from previous heights, and there are now whispers about the future of manager Frank Rijkaard. But this should not diminish Rijkaard's achievement in building the best Barcelona team since Johan Cruyff's version of the ultimate club line up. Barça complemented back-to-back league titles in 2005 and 2006 with a Champions League win, also in 2006. After that, the 2006/7 season proved a disappointment, with Barça losing La Liga in its final moments to hated rivals Real Madrid, and 2007/8, a season that began with hopes fuelled by the high-profile transfer of Thierry Henry from Arsenal, proved even worse. Real Madrid won La Liga and, even worse, did the double over their rivals in El Clásico: Barcelona lost 1-0 at home in December and then were thrashed 4-1 at the Bernabéu stadium in May. No manager, no matter how successful his record, could survive such blows and Rijkaard was sacked.

Getting to see a game, though, can be something of a lottery. Around 4,000 tickets usually go on sale on the day of the match: phone to find out when, and join the queue an hour or so beforehand at the intersection of Travessera de les Corts and Avenida Aristides Maillol. 'Rented out' seats go on sale from these offices and can also be bought through Servi-Caixa ATMs. If there are none left, buy a *reventa* ticket from touts at the gate. The 'B' team plays in the mini-stadium over the road.

Tibidabo & Collserola

Tibidabo is the dominant peak of the Collserola massif, with its sweeping views of the whole of the Barcelona conurbation stretching out to the sea. The neo-Gothic Sagrat Cor church crowning it has become one of the city's most recognisable landmarks; thousands of people head to the top of the hill at weekends to whoop and scream their way around the creaky, old-fashioned **funfair**.

Getting up to the top on the clanking **Tramvia Blau** (Blue Tram) and then the funicular railway is part of the fun; Plaça

Doctor Andreu between the two is a great place for an alfresco drink. For the best view of the city, either take a lift up the needle of Norman Foster's communications tower, the **Torre de Collserola**, or up to the *mirador* at the feet of Christ atop the Sagrat Cor.

The vast **Parc de Collserola** is more a series of forested hills than a park; its shady paths through holm oaks and pines open out to spectacular views. Take the FGC train on the Terrassa–Sabadell line from Plaça Catalunya or Passeig de Gràcia, getting off at Baixador de Vallvidrera station.

Sights & museums

Funicular de Tibidabo
Plaça Doctor Andreu to Plaça Tibidabo (93 211 79 42). FGC Avda Tibidabo, then Tramvia Blau. **Open** As funfair (see below), but starting 30mins earlier. **Tickets** *Single* €2; €1.50 reductions. *Return* €3; €2 reductions. No credit cards.
This art deco vehicle offers occasional glimpses of the city below as it winds through the pine forests up to the summit of Tibidabo. The service has been running since 1901, but only according to a timetable too complicated for just about anyone to figure out. For those who are feeling energetic, it's nearly an hour's (mostly pleasant) hike up from Plaça Doctor Andreu.

Tibidabo funfair
Plaça del Tibidabo, Tibidabo (93 211 79 42/www.tibidabo.es). FGC Avda Tibidabo, then Tramvia Blau, then funicular. **Open** *Nov-mid Dec, mid Jan-Feb* noon-6pm Sat, Sun. *Mar, Apr* noon-7pm Sat, Sun. *May, June* noon-8pm Sat, Sun. *July* noon-8pm Wed-Fri; noon-11pm Sat; noon-10pm Sun. *Aug* noon-10pm Mon-Thur; noon-11pm Fri-Sun. *1st 2wks Sept* noon-8pm Wed-Fri; noon-9pm Sat, Sun. *2nd 2wks Sept* noon-9pm Sat, Sun. *Oct* noon-7pm Sat, Sun. Closed mid Dec-mid Jan. **Admission** *Unlimited rides* €24; €9-€19 reductions; free children under 90cm.

After years of falling profits and slowing turnstiles, Tibidabo funfair has invested millions and boomed in popularity again – thanks, in part, to various new attractions calculated to draw the thrill-seeking punter: a terrifying freefall ride called the Pendulum and a hot-air balloon style ride for smaller children, to be joined at the end of 2008 by a rollercoaster that will reach 522m (1,713ft) above sea level. Other attractions includes everything from a house of horrors and bumper cars to the Avió, the world's first popular flight simulator built in 1928. Don't miss the antique mechanical puppets at the Museu d'Autòmats or the hourly puppet shows at the Marionetàrium (from 1pm). At the weekends, there are circus parades and, in the summer, *correfocs* (fire runs) and street theatre.

Torre de Collserola
Ctra de Vallvidrera al Tibidabo, Tibidabo (93 211 79 42/www.torre decollserola.com). FGC Peu Funicular, then funicular. **Open** *Apr-June, Sept* 11am-2.30pm, 3.30-7pm Wed-Fri; 11am-7pm Sat, Sun. *July, Aug* 11am-2.30pm, 3.30-8pm Mon-Fri; 11am-8pm Sat, Sun. *Oct-Mar* 11am-2.30pm, 3.30-6pm Mon-Fri; 11am-6pm Sat, Sun. **Admission** €5; €4 reductions; free under-4s.
Norman Foster's communications tower was built in 1992 to transmit images of the Olympics around the world. Visible from just about anywhere in the city and always flashing at night, the tower is loved and hated in almost equal measure, but its extraordinary views of Barcelona and the Mediterranean are unbeatable.

Eating & drinking

Merbeyé
Plaça Doctor Andreu, Tibidabo (93 417 92 79). FGC Avda Tibidabo, then Tramvia Blau/bus 60. **Open** 11am-2.30am Tue-Thur; noon-3.30am Fri, Sat; noon-2am Sun. **Bar**.
Merbeyé is a cocktail bar straight from central casting: moodily lit and plush with red velvet. In summer there's also a peaceful, stylish terrace for alfresco

CosmoCaixa

fun. The clientele runs from the shabbily genteel to flashy Barça players and their bling-encrusted wives.

La Venta

Plaça Doctor Andreu, Tibidabo (93 212 64 55). FGC Avda Tibidabo, then Tramvia Blau. **Open** 1.30-3.15pm, 9-11.15pm Mon-Sat. €€€.
Mediterranean.

Perched high above the city, La Venta's Moorish-influenced interior plays second fiddle to the terrace for every season: shaded by day and uncovered by night in summer, sealed and warmed with a wood-burning stove in winter. Starters include lentil and spider crab salad; sea urchins au gratin; and langoustine ravioli, filled with leek and foie mousse. Simpler but high-quality mains run from rack of lamb to delicate monkfish in filo pastry with pesto.

Nightlife

Danzatoria

Avda Tibidabo 61, Tibidabo (93 211 62 61/www.danzatoria-barcelona.com). FGC Avda Tibidabo, then 10min walk. **Open** 11pm-2.30am Tue, Wed; 11.30pm-3am Thur-Sat.
Admission free.

The uptown location attracts an upscale crowd to this spectacular converted manor house on a hill overlooking Barcelona. The hipness factor goes up as you climb the club's glamour-glutted storeys. Preened *pija* flesh is shaken on hot-house dancefloors, or laid across sofas hanging from the ceiling in the chill-out lounges. We've had reports of snotty staff, but who cares when you're lounging in one of the layers of palm-filled gardens, accompanied by some gorgeous creature and some (very expensive) champagne.

Mirablau

Plaça Doctor Andreu 1, Tibidabo (93 418 58 79). FGC Avda Tibidabo, then Tramvia Blau. **Open** 11am-4am Mon-Thur; 11am-5.30am Fri-Sun.
Admission free.

It doesn't get any more uptown than this, either geographically or socially.

Located at the top of Tibidabo, this small bar is packed with the high rollers of Barcelona, from local footballers living on the hill to international businessmen on the company card, as well as young *pijos* stopping by for a drink before heading off to nearby Danzatoria on daddy's ride. Apart from the cheesy Spanish pop, its real attraction is the breathtaking view.

Zona Alta

Zona Alta (the 'upper zone') is the name given to a series of smart neighbourhoods, including Sant Gervasi, Sarrià, Pedralbes and Putxet, that stretch out across the lower reaches of the Collserola hills. The centre of Sarrià and the streets of old Pedralbes around the **convent** retain a whiff of the sleepy country towns that these once were.

Gaudí fans are rewarded by a trip up to the **Pavellons de la Finca Güell** at Avda Pedralbes 15; its extraordinary wrought-iron gate features a dragon into whose gaping mouth the foolhardy can fit their heads. Once inside the gardens, accessed via the main gate on Avda Diagonal, be sure to look out for a delightful fountain designed by the master himself. Across near Putxet is Gaudí's relatively sober **Col·legi de les Teresianes** (C/Ganduxer 85-105), while up towards Tibidabo, just off Plaça Bonanova, rises his remarkable Gothic-influenced **Torre Bellesguard**.

Sights & museums

CosmoCaixa

C/Teodor Roviralta 47-51 (93 212 60 50/www.fundacio.lacaixa.es). Bus 60/ FGC Avda Tibidabo, then Tramvia Blau. **Open** 10am-8pm Tue-Sun.
Admission €3; €2 reductions; free under-3s. *Planetarium* €2; €1.50 reductions; free under-3s.

The long and eagerly awaited revamp of the Fundació La Caixa's science museum and planetarium, creating the biggest in Europe, was only partially successful. First off, its size is a little misleading: apart from a couple of spaces – the Flooded Forest, a reproduction of a bit of Amazonia complete with flora and fauna, and the Geological Wall – the collection has not been proportionally expanded to fit the new building. A glass-enclosed spiral ramp runs down an impressive six floors, but actually represents quite a long walk to reach the main collection five floors down. What's more, for all the fanfare made by the museum about taking exhibits out of glass cases and making scientific theories accessible, many of the displays look very dated.

On the plus side, the installations for children are excellent: the Bubble Planetarium pleases kids aged three to eight, and the wonderful Clik (aimed at ages three to six) and Flash (for ages seven to nine) introduce children to science through games. Toca Toca! ('Touch! Touch!') educates youngsters about which animals and plants are safe and which should be avoided. One of the real highlights, for children and adults, remains the hugely entertaining sound telescope, which is situated outside on the Plaça de la Ciència.

Event highlights The relationship between numbers, science and mathematics through the ages (Oct 2008-Mar 2009).

Monestir de Pedralbes

Baixada del Monestir 9 (93 256 21 22). FGC Reina Elisenda. **Open** *Oct-Mar* 10am-2pm Tue-Sat; 10am-3pm Sun. *Apr-Sept* 10am-5pm Tue-Sat; 10am-3pm Sun. **Admission** (*combined ticket with Museu d'Història de la Ciutat & Refugi 307*) €6; €4 reductions; free under-16s. Free 1st Sun of mth.

In 1326 the widowed Queen Elisenda of Montcada used her inheritance to buy this land and build a convent for the 'Poor Clare' order of nuns, which she soon joined. The result is a veritable jewel of Gothic architecture, with

an understated single-nave church with fine stained-glass windows and a beautiful three-storey 14th-century cloister. The place was out of bounds to the general public until 1983 when the nuns, a closed order, opened it up as a museum in the mornings (they themselves escape to a nearby annexe).

The site offers a fascinating insight into life in a medieval convent, taking you through the kitchens, pharmacy and refectory with its huge vaulted ceiling. To one side is the tiny chapel of Sant Miquel, with murals dating to 1343 by Ferrer Bassa, a Catalan painter and student of Giotto. In the former dormitory next to the cloister is a selection of hitherto undisplayed objects belonging to the nuns. Among them are illuminated books, furniture and objects reflecting the artistic and religious life of the community.

Museu de les Arts Aplicades

Palau Reial de Pedralbes, Avda Diagonal 686 (93 256 34 65/ www.museuceramica.bcn.cat/ www.museuartsdecoratives.bcn.cat/ www.museutextil.bcn.cat). Metro Palau Reial. **Open** 10am-6pm Tue-Sat; 10am-3pm Sun. **Admission** €4.20; €2.40 reductions; free under-16s. Free 1st Sun of mth. No credit cards.

In July 2008 the Museu Tèxtil, which was previously located in the Born, joined the ceramic and decorative arts museums in the Palau Reial de Pedralbes, built in the 1920s and briefly used as a royal palace. The Textile Museum provides a chronological tour of clothing and fashion, from its oldest piece, a Coptic man's tunic from a seventh-century tomb, through to Karl Lagerfeld. Among curiosities such as the world's largest collection of kid-skin gloves or an 18th-century bridal gown in black figured silk, the real highlight is the fashion collection – from Baroque to 20th-century – one of the finest of its type anywhere.

The Museum of Decorative Arts is informative and fun, and looks at the different styles influencing the design

Hisop p158

of artefacts in Europe since the Middle Ages, from Romanesque to art deco and beyond. A second section shows post-war Catalan design of objects as diverse as urinals and inflatable pens.

The Ceramics Museum is equally fascinating, showing how Moorish ceramic techniques from the 13th century were developed after the Reconquista with the addition of colours (especially blue and yellow) in centres such as Manises (in Valencia) and Barcelona. Upstairs is a section on 20th-century ceramics, which includes a room dedicated to Miró and Picasso. The three museums, along with several smaller collections, are to be merged in the future in a Museu de Disseny (Design Museum) as part of the cultu-ral overhaul of the Plaça de les Glòries.

Parc de la Creueta del Coll

C/Mare de Déu del Coll *(no phone).* Metro Penitents. **Open** 10am-sunset daily. **Admission** free.
This park was created from a quarry in 1987 by Josep Martorell and David Mackay, the team that went on to design the Vila Olímpica. It boasts a sizeable swimming pool, complete with its own 'desert island', and an interesting sculpture by Eduardo Chillida.

Tramvia Blau (Blue Tram)

Avda Tibidabo (Plaça Kennedy) to Plaça Doctor Andreu (93 318 70 74/www.tramvia.org/tramviablau). FGC *Avda Tibidabo.* **Open** *Mid June-mid Sept* 10am-8pm daily. *Mid Sept-mid June* 10am-6pm Sat. **Frequency** 20mins. **Tickets** €2.20 single; €3.30 return. No credit cards.
Barcelonins and tourists have been clanking 1,225m (4,000ft) up Avda Tibidabo in the 'blue trams' since 1902. In the winter months, when the tram only operates on Saturdays, a rather more prosaic bus takes you up (or you can walk it in 15 minutes).

Eating & drinking

Artkuisine

NEW *C/Madrazo 137 (93 202 31 46/www.artkuisine.blogspot.com).* FGC *Sant Gervasi.* **Open** 1.30-3.45pm Mon; 1.30-3.45pm, 8.30-11.45pm Tue-Sat. **€€€. French.**
Artkuisine's French credentials do not leap out sporting berets and strings of

Barcelona's other club

Second banana is never a happy position – just ask FC Espanyol. Even the name of Barça's lesser rivals has been Catalanised since the original 'Español' formed in 1900. On the other hand, Espanyol was Spain's first club set up by Spaniards alone, while the looming presence that is FC Barcelona was founded by Swiss Joan Gamper and it has relied ever since on foreign talent – even its colours are said to come from abroad.

Sadly, followers of Los Periquitos, 'The Parakeets', have endured disappointment through the years. Goalkeeping hero Ricardo Zamora went to Real Madrid in 1930. Sixty years later, leading Bayer Leverkusen 3-0 in the first leg, Los Periquitos lost the UEFA Cup in a penalty shoot-out. Soon afterwards, they had their Sarrià stadium bulldozed to repay debts and now play out 'home' games at the soulless Olympic Stadium.

But this is changing. Under president Daniel Sánchez Libre, Espanyol have won two Spanish cups and reached the UEFA Cup final in 2007, losing to Sevilla only on penalties. A Champions League spot looks possible in 2008-09. With ex-FCB Ivan de la Peña leading graduates of Espanyol's football academy on the pitch, off it Espanyol are building a 39,000-capacity stadium at Cornellà near the airport. Perhaps the Parakeets can fly high at last.

onions. Instead, they make themselves known in other, more subtle ways: the buttermilk Regency furniture, the charming and *soigné* waiting staff, and the classical approach underpinning the chef's wilder flights of fancy. Who would have thought, for example, that cocoa and banana compôte would complement oxtail stew, or that tonka bean and vanilla ice-cream would work with tarte tatin? The French, apparently.

Café Berlin

C/Muntaner 240-242 (93 200 65 42). Metro Diagonal. **Open** *Sept-July* 10am-2am Mon-Wed; 10am-3am Thur-Sat. *Aug* 5.30pm-2am Mon-Wed; 5.30pm-3am Thur-Sat. **€€. Café.**
Downstairs, low sofas fill up with couples while upstairs all is sleek and light, with brushed steel, dark leather and a Klimtesque mural. A rack of newspapers and plenty of sunlight make it popular for coffee or snacks all day; as well as tapas there are pasta dishes, *bocadillos* and cheesecake, but beware the 20% surcharge for pavement tables.

Hisop

Passatge Marimon 9 (93 241 32 33/ www.hisop.com). Metro Hospital Clínic. **Open** 1.30-3.30pm, 9-11pm Mon-Fri; 9-11pm Sat. **€€€. Mediterranean.**
Run by two young, enthusiastic and talented chefs, Hisop aims to bring serious dining to the non-expense account masses by keeping its prices on the low side and its service approachable. The €52 tasting menu is a popular choice among diners, with dishes that vary according to the season, but often includes their rich 'monkfish royale' (served with its liver, a cocoa-based sauce and tiny pearls of saffron essence) and a pistachio soufflé with kaffir lime ice-cream.

Nightlife

Elephant

Passeig dels Til·lers 1 (93 334 02 58/ www.elephantbcn.com). Metro Palau Reial. **Open** 11.30pm-4am Wed, Thur; 11.30pm-5am Fri, Sat. **Admission** free Wed; €12 Thur-Sat.

If you have a Porsche and a model girl-friend, this is where you meet your peers. Housed in a converted mansion, Elephant is as elegant and high-design as its customers. The big attraction is the outdoor bar and terrace dancefloor, though the low-key and low-volume (due to neighbours' complaints) house music doesn't inspire a great deal of hands-in-the-air action.

Otto Zutz

C/Lincoln 15 (93 238 07 22/www.grupo-ottozutz.com). FGC Gràcia. **Open** midnight-5am Tue, Wed; midnight-5.30am Thur-Sat. **Admission** (incl 1 drink) €15.
Run by the same people as City Hall, Otto Zutz was once *the* nightclub in Barcelona. The space hasn't changed much, but the models, film people and poseurs have moved on. It would do well to be a little less wrapped up in its pretensions and a little more concerned with the music. Three floors of an old textile factory feature R&B, hip hop and some electro, but the main focus is on the same old not-so-funky house.

Pacha

Avda Doctor Marañon 17 (93 334 32 33/www.clubpachabcn.com). Metro Zona Universitaria. **Open** June-Sept midnight-6am daily. Oct-May midnight-6am Thur-Sun. **Admission** (incl 1 drink) €15.
When the news broke that Pacha was set to open in Barcelona a few years back, the queues of potential barstaff were so long that they made the evening news. Such is the power of the global clubbing giant that armies of tourists, out-of-towners and locals continue rolling up for fair sound quality, a so-so venue and heaps of attitude.

Sala BeCool

Plaça Joan Llongueras (93 362 04 13/www.salabecool.com). Metro Hospital Clínic. **Open** Gigs 10pm Thur-Sat. Club midnight-5am Thur-Sat. **Admission** Gigs varies. Club €10.
The latest minimal electro sounds from Berlin reach Barcelona via this chic uptown concert hall. After the live

shows by local rock stars, young urbanites throb to Euro techno and electro-pop. In an adjacent red room, DJs provide melodic indie pop alternatives to pounding beats.

Universal

C/Marià Cubí 182 bis-184 (93 201 35 96/www.grupocostaeste.com). FGC Muntaner. **Open** 11pm-3.30am Mon-Thur; 11pm-5am Fri, Sat. **Admission** free.
One of a very few clubs in the city that caters to an older crowd, Universal doesn't charge admission to get in, but the drink prices are steep as a result. As it gets later, the music moves from downtempo to soft house, which works the crowd up to a gentle shimmy.

Arts & leisure

Boliche

NEW Avda Diagonal 508 (93 218 17 88). Metro Diagonal. **Tickets** €5.20 Wed; €6.40 Mon, Tue, Thur; €6.70 Fri-Sun. No credit cards.
A four-screen cinema, offering mostly mainstream fare, which has recently made the switch from dubbed to original version films.

Poblenou

Poblenou has been many things in its time: a farming community, a fishing port, the site of heavy industry and a trendy post-industrial suburb. Now it's also a burgeoning technology and business district, snappily tagged '22@'. The factories around here closed down in the 1960s; these days the buildings that haven't been torn down or converted into office blocks are used as schools, civic centres, workshops or, increasingly, coveted lofts.

On its northern edge, Plaça de les Glòries holds the area's most striking landmark, French architect Jean Nouvel's hugely phallic **Torre Agbar**. The *plaça* has become the gateway to a new commercial and leisure area on the shoreline, known as the Fòrum after the cultural symposium in 2004 for which it was created. Many critics of the Fòrum felt its real purpose was to regenerate this post-industrial wasteland, and certainly part of its legacy is a slew of enormous conference halls and hotels intended to draw wealthy business clients into the city.

Eating & drinking

Els Pescadors

Plaça Prim 1 (93 225 20 18/ www.elspescadors.com). Metro Poblenou. **Open** 1-3.45pm, 8.30pm-midnight daily. €€€. **Catalan**.
In a forgotten, almost rustic square lies this first-rate fish restaurant, with tables under the canopy formed by two huge and ancient ombú trees. Suspend your disbelief with the crunchy sardine skeletons that arrive as an aperitif (trust us, they're delicious), and move on to tasty fried chipirones, followed by cod and pepper paella or creamy rice with prawns and smoked cheese. Desserts include strawberry gelatine 'spaghetti' in a citric soup, and the waiters are exceptionally professional and friendly.

Shopping

Barcelona Glòries

Avda Diagonal 208 (93 486 04 04/ www.lesglories.com). Metro Glòries. **Open** Shops 10am-10pm Mon-Sat.
This mall, office and leisure centre has a seven-screen cinema (the films are mostly dubbed into Spanish) and over 220 shops, including a Carrefour supermarket, an H&M, a Mango and a Disney Store, facing on to a large, café-filled square decorated with jets of coloured water. Family-orientated attractions include play areas and entertainment such as bouncy castles and trampolines.

Diagonal Mar

Avda Diagonal 3 (93 567 76 37/ www.diagonalmar.com). Metro El Maresme-Forum. **Open** Shops 10am-10pm Mon-Sat. Food court & entertainment 10am-midnight Mon-Thur; 10am-2am Fri, Sat; 11am-midnight Sun.
This mall has a marine theme and a sea-facing roof terrace filled with cafés and restaurants of the fast-food variety. Business is a little slow (except at the giant Alcampo supermarket), so it's a good queue-free option. Other anchor stores include Zara, Mango and FNAC. There is also a bowling alley, exhibitions, concerts and, every Sunday at 12.30pm, children's entertainment.

Els Encants

C/Dos de Maig 177-187, Plaça de les Glòries (93 246 30 30). Metro Glòries. **Open** 9am-6pm Mon, Wed, Fri, Sat. Auctions 7.30-9am Mon, Wed, Fri. No credit cards.
It's increasingly hard to find a bargain at Barcelona's old flea market, but it's a diverting way to pass the time: the buyers and sellers are as varied and curious as the bric-a-brac, Barça memorabilia, cheap electrical gadgets, religious relics and ancient Spanish school books that make up the majority of the stalls' booty. If you want to buy furniture come to the auctions at 7.30am with the commercial buyers or at noon, when unsold stuff drops in price.

Nightlife

Razzmatazz

C/Almogàvers 122 (93 320 82 00/ www.salarazzmatazz.com). Metro Bogatell or Marina. **Open** 1-5am Fri, Sat. **Admission** varies.
Skinny jeans, battered Converse and a heavy dose of party-rock dominate this warehouse superclub, and while some of the punters are a bit young and the toilets a bit vile, line-ups are on the ball. As it's essentially five clubs in one, if you're tired of 2manydjs or Miss Kittin in the main Razz Room, you can head upstairs to check out Queens of Noize, Fourtet or Tiga playing the Loft. Razzmatazz is also one of the city's best venues for live music, with acts from the Arctic Monkeys to Queens of the Stone Age to, er, Bananarama.

Essentials

Hotels

While Barcelona has seen phenomenal growth on its hotel scene of late, the increase is limited to four- and five-star hotels, as the council pushes the city as a conference centre. While this has eased the difficulty of finding accommodation in a city with year-round high occupancy, there is still a real dearth of more modest hotels that offer fewer frills but provide all the facilities most travellers need.

There is now quite a good range of boutique hotels, but again, they are mostly at the top end of the scale. If you look hard enough, however, there is plenty of charm at the budget end too, as many *hostales* (or *pensiones*) are situated in fabulous old buildings with elaborate doorways, grand staircases and beautiful tiled floors. A new generation of hoteliers is transforming gloomy, old-style *hostales* into bright and friendly establishments with en-suite bathrooms, internet access and other 21st-century essentials.

Booking in advance is strongly recommended, though many of the cheaper hotels won't accept reservations. Hotels often require you to guarantee your booking with credit card details or a cash deposit; whether or not you've provided either, it's always worth calling a few days before your arrival to reconfirm the booking (get it in writing if you can; many readers have reported problems), and check the cancellation policy too – often you will lose at least the first night.

To be sure of getting a room with natural light or a view, ask for an outside room (*habitació/habitación exterior*), which will usually face the street. Many of Barcelona's buildings are built around a

Gran Hotel La Florida p176

central airshaft or patio, and the inside rooms (*habitació/habitación interior*) around them can be quite dark, albeit quieter. In some cases, though, these inward-facing rooms are blessed with a view over gardens or open-air patios.

Apartments

Renting a flat can be a great way of experiencing the city, but it pays to do your research. Holiday apartments are normally designed to house a lot of people in a small space. But if you intend to be out all day and most of the night you could end up saving money. There is no shortage of horror stories, and it pays to use a little common sense. Check the small print (payment, deposits, cancellation fees and so on) and exactly what is included before booking.

The following offer apartments: www.rentthesun.com; www.inside-bcn.com; www.oh-barcelona.com; www.rentaflatinbarcelona.com; www.barcelonaliving.com;

ESSENTIALS

www.friendlyrentals.com;
www.1st-barcelona.com;
www.apartmentsbcn.net;
www.flatsbydays.com.

Barri Gòtic & La Rambla

H10 Racó del Pi

C/Pi 7 (93 342 61 90/www.h10 hotels.es). Metro Liceu. €€€.
Part of the H10 chain, the Racó del Pi offers spacious rooms with parquet floors, handsome terracotta-tiled bathrooms and an elegant glass conservatory on the ground floor. It can be a bargain out of season.

H1898

La Rambla 109 (93 552 95 52/ www.nnhotels.es). Metro Catalunya or Liceu. €€€€.
H1898 is a luxury hotel in a splendid 19th-century building right on La Rambla. Rooms are subject to Henley Regatta-type colour schemes; one floor is all perky green-and-white stripes, another red-and-white, and so on. The more expensive rooms have sizeable wooden-decked terraces, while some of the suites have plunge pools.

Hostal Fontanella

Via Laietana 71, 2° (93 317 59 43/ www.hostalfontanella.com). Metro Urquinaona. €€.
The splendid Modernista lift lends an aura of grandeur to this 11-room hostal, where devotees of Laura Ashley will feel at home amid the chintz. The downside of the Fontanella's central location is that outward-facing rooms are abuzz with the sound of traffic. But it's clean and comfortable, and double-glazing has recently been installed.

Hostal Jardí

Plaça Sant Josep Oriol 1 (93 301 59 00). Metro Liceu. €€.
There is a somewhat institutional feel about both the rooms and the lobby of Hostal Jardí, but the location is excellent, overlooking a pretty square, although it is only really worth staying

here if you get one of the rooms with a balcony. Some rooms are dark, but all have en-suite bathrooms, and the place is sparkling clean. It's advisable to book well in advance.

Hostal Lausanne

Portal de l'Angel 24, 1° 1ª (93 302 11 39/www.hostallausanne.com). Metro Catalunya. €. No credit cards.
This *hostal* feels spacious, with light pouring in from both ends of the building. Of the 17 basic rooms, four have en-suite bathrooms and some have balconies. It may be a bit dated, but it's a friendly and safe place, with a fun backpacker vibe. The street is as quiet at night as it is busy during the day.

Hostal Noya

La Rambla 133, 1° (93 301 48 31). Metro Catalunya. €. No credit cards.
Cheap and cheerful, the Noya is at the top of three flights of stairs. Rooms are basic, to say the least, but some have balconies looking out on to La Rambla and there are handsome old tiles on the floor. The lone bathroom is weathered and worn, and it can get busy since it's shared between 15 rooms (there is a separate WC), but all bedrooms do have their own washbasins.

Hostal Rembrandt

C/Portaferrissa 23, pral 1ª (93 318 10 11/www.hostalrembrandt.com). Metro Liceu. €.
A charming 27-room *hostal*: fairly stylish (for the price) with lots of wood panelling, soft lighting and a lift. The pretty interior courtyard makes for a pleasant chill-out zone/eating area. Rooms out front can be a little noisy.

Hotel Colón

Avda Catedral 7 (93 301 14 04/ www.hotelcolon.es). Metro Jaume I. €€€.
If you have had it with minimalism, stay here. With thick carpets and walls bedecked in bright floral prints, the Colón is all about making guests feel comfortable. The best rooms are those overlooking the cathedral, some of which have balconies.

Designer dreams

Prestige Forest

Barcelona loves nothing more than a name to drop, plastering the walls of its restaurants with photos of visiting celebs and broadcasting their every move in the news. The latest in this star-fuelled obsession is to ensure that every new building project comes with a name attached.

French architect Dominique Perrault designed the 120-metre (390-foot) high **Sky** (p176). Opened in June 2008, it has been described somewhat romantically, if not hyperbolically, as a 'tree of tempered steel', piercing the heavens like a needle along the Diagonal's increasingly Manhattan-esque skyline. Each room promises eye-popping views, while the random distribution of red, green and blue glass rather cleverly makes it look like a giant stained-glass window when viewed from afar.

Regeneration plans for L'Hospitalet meanwhile are straight out of Gotham city, all futuristic lines and crazy lights. Enric Ruiz-Geli's **Prestige Forest** eco-hotel (www.prestigehotels. com) is scheduled to open sometime in 2010. Shrouded in a spectacular web of 5,000 LEDs or 'leaves' as they are known, it registers sunlight and temperatures by day to cut energy costs and glows pretty colours at night.

Not all projects have been as positively received as these two, however. Out on the breakwater at the top of Passeig Joan de Borbó, Ricardo Bofill's sail-shaped **W Hotel** (www.starwoodhotels.com/ whotels), due to open in September 2009, fell flat when first presented. Critics went to town on its uncanny resemblance to the Burj Al Arab in Dubai, followed quickly by residents complaining, not unreasonably, about their lost sea views. A rethink has produced an uglier, squatter version of the original and the grumbling continues.

More squeals of protest erupted at the **Barceló Raval** (Rambla del Raval 17-21, 902 101 001, www.barcelo.com), a unique cylindrical hotel that will be bathed in a diaphanous light: brilliant, providing you're not trying to blot out the glow from your rather more humble abode opposite. A muted version was agreed and scheduled to open in July 2008. The hotel has promised to provide services that are attractive to the local population as well as guests, but what those five-star services might be – in one of the more rundown areas of Barcelona – remains to be seen.

Hotel Le Meridien Barcelona

*La Rambla 111 (93 318 62 00/
www.barcelona.lemeridien.com).
Metro Liceu.* €€€€.

Le Meridien is a great place for spotting celebrities. It has revamped its genteel image with wood floors and leather furnishings, along with rain showers and plasma-screen TVs. Despite its size (it has 233 rooms), it manages to retain an air of intimacy thanks to its helpful, friendly staff.

Hotel Neri

*C/Sant Sever 5 (93 304 06 55/www.
hotelneri.com). Metro Jaume I.* €€€€.

A sumptuous boutique hotel, located in an 18th-century palace. After the lobby, which teams flagstone floors and wooden beams with designer fixtures, red velvet and gold leaf, the 22 rooms can seem a little serious, with neutral tones, natural materials and rustic finishes, sharp design and high-tech perks (hi-fis, plasma-screen TVs).

Hotel Oriente

*La Rambla 45 (93 302 25 58/
www.husa.es). Metro Liceu.* €€€.

Barcelona's first-ever 'grand hotel' was built in 1842. All bedrooms now have pale wood floors, minimalist design and sleek electrical gadgetry, in striking contrast to the ritzy ballroom and dining room. Sadly, no amount of renovation can do away with the noise from La Rambla; light sleepers should ask for a room at the back of the hotel.

Hotel Petit Palace Opera Garden

*C/Boqueria 10 (93 302 00 92/www.
hthoteles.com). Metro Liceu.* €€€.

A private mansion was thoroughly gutted to create this minimalist haven in 2006. The 61 rooms are white and futuristic, with a different zingy colour on each floor and opera scores printed on the walls above the beds. Lamps and chairs lend a swinging '60s air. Some bathrooms have massage showers. The best thing, perhaps, is the secret (though public) garden out back.

Pensió Alamar

*C/Comtessa de Sobradiel 1, 1° 2ª
(93 302 5012/www.pensioalamar.com).
Metro Jaume I or Liceu.* €.

Eight of the basic, yet tasteful, rooms at this family-run *hostal* have plant-filled balconies overlooking the street. Beds are new and excellent quality, with crisp cotton sheets, and windows are double-glazed to keep noise to a happy minimum. The downside is that the 12 rooms share two bathrooms. There are good discounts for longer stays, use of a kitchen, and larger rooms for families.

Pensión Hostal Mari-Luz

*C/Palau 4 (93 317 34 63/www.
pensionmariluz.com). Metro Jaume
I or Liceu.* €.

The entrance and staircase of this 18th-century stone building are certainly imposing, but the downside is the several flights of stairs. The effort is well worth it, however, for the smiling service and homely atmosphere. Stripped wood doors and old floor tiles add character to the 15 otherwise plain but quiet rooms, some of which face a plant-filled inner courtyard. No.4 and no.6 have good en-suite bathrooms.

Born & Sant Pere

Banys Orientals

*C/Argenteria 37 (93 268 84 60/
www.hotelbanysorientals.com).
Metro Jaume I.* €€.

Banys Orientals exudes cool, with the deeply stylish shades-of-grey minimalism of its rooms, along with such well thought out touches as complimentary mineral water placed on the landings. The only drawback to the place is the smallish size of some of the guestrooms. Plans to create a luxurious new service by tapping into the eponymous thermal baths that lie underneath the hotel are in the pipeline.

Chic&basic

*C/Princesa 50 (93 295 46 52/
www.chicandbasic.com). Metro
Arc de Triomf or Jaume I.* €€€.

A monochrome space-age theatrical vibe reigns supreme here: if you've ever dreamed of entering your room through a shimmering curtain of transparent plastic twirls, as if you were walking into a waterfall, then welcome home. The building retains its original grand staircase, now attractively furnished with oversized chairs and sofas. A chill-out room has coffee- and tea-making facilities, a fridge and a microwave, as well as sofas and pouffes.

Ciutat Barcelona

C/Princesa 35 (93 269 74 75/www. ciutathotels.com.) Metro Jaume I. €€€.
The Ciutat Barcelona opened in 2006 and has gone to town on the colour co-ordination front – even the plastic cups in the bathrooms match the red, blue or green colour scheme of the rooms. Retro shapes prevail in the stylish furnishings and decoration, distracting from the fact that rooms are rather small. There is a great roof terrace with a plunge pool.

Grand Hotel Central

Via Laietana 30 (93 295 79 00/www. grandhotelcentral.com). Metro Jaume I. €€€.
The Grand Hotel Central is another of the recent wave of Barcelona hotels to adhere to the unwritten rule that grey is the new black. The Central's shadowy corridors open up on to sleekly appointed rooms that come with flat-screen TVs, DVD players and Molton Brown toiletries. The real charm of the hotel lies on its roof. Here you can sip a cocktail and admire the fabulous views while floating comfortably in the vertiginous infinity pool.

Pensió 2000

C/Sant Pere Més Alt 6, 1º (93 310 74 66/www.pension2000.com). Metro Urquinaona. €€.
One of Barcelona's best-value *pensiones*, Pensió 2000 is in a charming old building opposite the Palau de la Música Catalana. Only two of its six bright and airy rooms are en suite, but the communal facilities are sparkling. Its tall windows, buttercup-yellow walls and a lounge peppered with books and toys make it a cheery place, with a warm, relaxed atmosphere. The large rooms also make it a good bet for holidaying families.

Raval

Abba Rambla Hotel

C/Rambla del Raval 4 (93 505 54 00/ www.abbahoteles.com). Metro Liceu or Sant Antoni. €€€.
Overlooking the Rambla del Raval, an open space flanked by bars and restaurants, the Abba Rambla is a comfortable and friendly base for nightlife and sightseeing, although rooms are a bit bland. More stylish are the ground-floor lounge and breakfast bar.

Barceló Raval

`NEW` *Rambla del Raval 17-21 (902 101 001/www.barceloraval.com). Metro Liceu.* €€€€.
See box p166.

Casa Camper

C/Elisabets 11 (93 342 62 80/www. casacamper.com). Metro Catalunya. €€€€.
Devised by the Mallorcan footwear giant, this is a holistic concept-fest of a boutique hotel where Mediterranean simplicity meets contemporary cool. You get a pair of plastic Camper clogs to shuffle around in and your own personal sitting room across the corridor, complete with TV and hammock. There is nothing as naff as a minibar, but you can help yourself to free snacks in the café whenever you want.

Hostal Gat Raval

C/Joaquín Costa 44, 2º (93 481 66 70/ www.gataccommodation.com). Metro Universitat. €€.
Gat Raval embodies everything that 21st-century budget accommodation should be: smart, clean and funky, with bright, sunshiny rooms. Each contains a work by a local artist, and some have balconies. The only downsides are that nearly all the bathrooms are communal (although they are very clean) and there is no lift.

ESSENTIALS

Aboard and lodging

Picture the scene: a private wood deck with a straight view to sea, the amber glow of sunset on the horizon, the gentle rocking of water beneath, and a glass of wine in hand. You could be on an island, yet you're perfectly placed between Barcelona's old town and the beach, a million miles from the tourist throng. Here you have some idea of the experience that is Willowmoon: arguably the most romantic accommodation in town.

Willowmoon is a 65-year-old wooden ketch that has been lovingly restored to provide an intimate two-person cabin of wooden beams, polished portholes and white linen. A smaller annexe is suitable for one or two children (over-10s only), and amazingly, the en-suite bathroom has managed to squeeze in an oval shaped tub beneath a skylight that is perfect for stargazing.

So what of the facilities? Well there's no TV or WiFi – the point is total escape – though charming owner Steve Lodge does provide a full breakfast on deck in the mornings. If the weather's grim, it's served in his living room in front of a woodburning stove, adding to a unique atmosphere, light years from boutique boredom.

Willowmoon

Berth F57, Marina Port Vell, C/Escar 26, Port Vell (93 484 2365/www.willowmoon.uk.com). Metro Barceloneta. €€.

Hostal Gat Xino

C/Hospital 155 (93 324 88 33/ www.gataccommodation.com). Metro Sant Antoni. €€.
This 'Gat' has a bright and breezy breakfast room complete with apple-green polka-dot walls, a wood-decked patio and a roof terrace with black beanbags for chilling out. There's more bright green in the rooms, all of which are en suite, with good-quality beds, crisp white linen and the regulation flat-screen TVs. The best have balconies.

Hosteria Grau

C/Ramelleres 27 (93 301 81 35/www. hostalgrau.com). Metro Catalunya. €€.
This charming, family-run *hostal* oozes character, with a tiled spiral staircase and fabulous 1970s-style communal areas, including a funky café next door. The open fireplace is a luxury if you visit in the winter. Rooms are basic, comfortable and fairly quiet. There are also some apartments available on the top floor. Book well in advance.

Hotel Ambassador

C/Pintor Fortuny 13 (93 342 61 80/ www.rivolihotels.com). Metro Catalunya. €€€€.
The Ambassador has been refur-bished, and now boasts a heady blend of water features, gold paint and smoked glass, a colossus of a chande-lier and a freestanding Modernista bar that dominates the lounge area. Rooms are straightforwardly decorated, with no scary designer features, and there's also a pool and a jacuzzi on the rooftop.

Hotel España

C/Sant Pau 9-11 (93 318 17 58/ www.hotelespanya.com). Metro Liceu. €€€.
The lower floors at this Modernista landmark were designed by Domènech i Montaner in 1902. The main restau-rant is decorated with floral tiling and elaborate woodwork, while the larger dining room beyond features dreamy murals of mermaids by Ramon Casas, and the bar boasts a sculpted marble fireplace. After all this grandeur, how-ever, the bedrooms are unexciting.

Hotel Claris p174

Hotel Mesón Castilla

*C/Valldonzella 5 (93 318 21 82/www.
mesoncastilla.com). Metro Universitat.*
€€€.
If you want a change from contemporary design, check into this chocolate-box hotel, which opened in 1952. Before then, it was a private house belonging to an aristocratic family. Public areas are full of antiques, while the guestrooms are all different and decorated with hand-painted furniture, with tiled floors. The best have tranquil terraces, with a delightful plant-packed one off the breakfast room.

Hotel Principal

*C/Junta de Comerç 8 (93 318 89 74/
www.hotelprincipal.es). Metro Liceu.*
€€€.
After an impressive revamp, the Principal offers rooms of a good standard, with flat-screen TVs, original artworks and marble bathrooms. Guests can relax on loungers on the roof, where there is also a suite with a private terrace. The buffet breakfast is served in a pleasant, light room.

Hotel Sant Agustí

*Plaça Sant Agustí 3 (93 318 16 58/
www.hotelsa.com). Metro Liceu.* **€€€**.
With its sandstone walls and huge, arched windows looking on to the plaça, not to mention the pink marble lobby filled with forest-green furniture, this imposing hotel is the oldest in Barcelona. Housed in the former convent of St Augustine, it was converted into a hotel in 1840. Rooms are spacious and comfortable, but there's no soundproofing. Good buffet breakfast.

Barceloneta & the Ports

Hostal Poblenou

*C/Taulat 30, pral (93 221 26 01/
www.hostalpoblenou.com). Metro
Poblenou.* **€€**.
Poblenou is a delightful *hostal* in an elegant restored building a short walk from the beach. The five rooms are all light and airy, with their own bathrooms, and breakfast is served on a lovely, sunny terrace.

Hotel Arts

*C/Marina 19-21 (93 221 10 00/www.
ritzcarlton.com). Metro Ciutadella-Vila
Olimpica.* €€€€.

The 44-storey, Ritz-Carlton-run Arts
has redesigned all its rooms, and scores
top marks for exemplary service. CD
players, interactive TV, sea and city
views and a 'Club' floor for VIPs are
just some of the hedonistic perks await-
ing guests. The spectacular duplex
apartments have butlering round-the-
clock and chef services. The luxurious
Six Senses Spa has fabulous views and
is open to non-guests.

Hotel Duquesa de Cardona

*Passeig Colom 12 (93 268 90 90/
www.hduquesadecardona.com). Metro
Drassanes or Jaume I.* €€€€.

This elegantly restored 16th-century
palace retains lots of original features
and is furnished with natural materials, complemented by a soft colour
scheme. The cosy bedrooms make it
ideal for a romantic stay, particularly
the deluxe rooms and junior suites on
the higher floors with views out across
the harbour. The beach is a ten-minute
walk away, but guests can sunbathe on
the decked roof terrace and then cool
off afterwards in the plunge pool.

Hotel Medinaceli

*Plaça del Duc de Medinaceli 8 (93 481
77 25/www.gargallo-hotels.com). Metro
Drassanes.* €€€€.

The 44 rooms in this restored palace
near the harbour are done out in sooth-
ing rusty shades. Some of the bathrooms have jacuzzi baths, while others
come with massage showers. Repro
versions of the sofa Dalí created
inspired by Mae West's lips decorate
the lobby, to match the crimson velvet
thrones in the first-floor courtyard.

Montjuïc

AC Miramar

*Plaza Carlos Ibáñez 3, Passeig de
Miramar (93 281 16 00/www.ac-
hotels.com). Metro Paral·lel, then
funicular.* €€€€.

A controversial remodelling of a villa
built for the 1929 International
Exhibition, the Miramar has an unde-
niably spectacular location, high on
the hill, looking out to sea. Local architect Oscar Tusquet's champagne-
coloured marble lobby gives a suitably
lofty air to the place, enhanced by a
stairwell built to resemble the ramparts
of a castle. A casual lounge area and
cocktail bar give on to an ample terrace
with views over a richly speckled
orange patio. Rooms at the top are
smaller, but some have large private
terraces with a hot tub. Be sure to specify a sea view.

Hostal BCN Port

*Avda Paral·lel 15, entl (93 324 95
00/www.hostalbcnport.com). Metro
Drassanes or Paral·lel.* €€.

A smart new *hostal* near the ferry port,
the BCN Port has rooms that are furnished in a chic contemporary style
with not a hint of the kitsch decor
prevalent in more traditional budget
places. All the 19 rooms have en-suite
bathrooms, as well as televisions and
air-conditioning. Check the website for
last-minute discounts.

Eixample

Hostal Central Barcelona

*C/Diputació 346, pral 2ª (93 245 19
81/www.hostalcentralbarcelona.com).
Metro Tetuán.* €€.

Lodging at the Central, spread across
two floors of an old Modernista building, is like staying in a rambling flat
rather than an *hostal*. Rooms have kept
their original tiling and high ceilings,
but are kitted out with air-conditioning
and double glazing; walls painted in a
wide palette, from duck-egg blue to
daffodil yellow, jolly things up.

Hostal d'Uxelles

*Gran Via de les Corts Catalanes 688,
pral (93 265 25 60/www.hotelduxelles.
com). Metro Tetuán.* €€.

D'Uxelles is a tastefully decorated
hostal, with pretty tiles and antique furnishings. Pastel colours rule, and

ESSENTIALS

drapes hang romantically above the bedsteads. The best rooms have plant-filled balconies with tables and chairs, where you can have breakfast. It's a bargain, and staff are friendly too.

Hostal Eden

C/Balmes 55, pral 1ª (93 454 66 20/ www.hostaleden.net). Metro Passeig de Gràcia. €€.

Located on three floors, this warm and relaxed *hostal* with friendly, helpful staff offers free internet access and has a sunny patio with a shower. The best rooms have marble bathrooms with corner baths, and nos.114 and 115, at the rear, are quiet and have large windows overlooking the patio. Room 103 is dark but good-sized and quirky, with a sprawling bathroom.

Hostal Girona

C/Girona 24, 1º 1ª (93 265 02 59/ www.hostalgirona.com). Metro Urquinaona. €€.

This gem of an *hostal* is filled with antiques, chandeliers and oriental rugs. The rooms may be on the simple side, but they all have charm. The outward-facing rooms have small balconies overlooking C/Girona; darker rooms with bigger balconies face on to a quiet patio. Gorgeous and good value.

Hostal Goya

C/Pau Claris 74, 1º (93 302 25 65/ www.hostalgoya.com). Metro Urquinaona. €€.

Located in a typical Eixample building with fabulous tiled floors, the bedrooms are done out in chocolates and creams, with comfy beds, chunky duvets and cushions; the bathrooms are equally luxurious. The best rooms either give out on to the street or the terrace at the back. Excellent value for money.

Hostal Palacios

Rambla de Catalunya 27, 1º (93 301 30 79/www.hostalpalacios.com). Metro Catalunya. €€.

Situated in a sumptuous building, the 11 rooms at the Palacios are well equipped and decorated in a tasteful style, more typical of a four-star, with good bathrooms, air-con, digital TV and internet connection. Rates may seem high for an *hostal*, but the standard of the rooms, together with the location, make it good value.

Hostal San Remo

C/Ausiàs Marc 19, 1º 2ª (93 302 19 89/www.hostalsanremo.com). Metro Urquinaona. €.

The friendly owner, Rosa, and her fluffy white dog live on site and take good care of their guests. All seven of the rooms are equipped with air-con, blue-and-white striped bedspreads and modern wooden furniture; five out of seven have en-suite bathrooms, and most of them have a little balcony and double glazing. A good place to stay.

Hotel Axel

C/Aribau 33 (93 323 93 93/www. axelhotels.com). Metro Universitat. €€€.

The buzzy Axel is a cornerstone of the 'Gaixample', as the area around the hotel is known and good-looking staff sport T-shirts with the logo 'hetero-friendly'. Huge beds come as standard, as does free mineral water. 'Superior' rooms have stained-glass gallery balconies and hydro-massage bathtubs. The Sky Bar on the rooftop is where it all happens, with a little pool, jacuzzi, sun deck, sauna and steam room.

Hotel Claris

C/Pau Claris 150 (93 487 62 62/ www.derbyhotels.es). Metro Passeig de Gràcia. €€€€.

Antiques and contemporary design merge behind the neoclassical exterior of the Claris, which contains the largest private collection of Egyptian art in Spain. Some bedrooms are on the small side, while others are duplex, but all have Chesterfield sofas and plenty of art. The rooftop has a small pool, a cocktail bar and DJ.

Hotel Condes de Barcelona

Passeig de Gràcia 73-75 (93 445 00 00/www.condesdebarcelona.com). Metro Passeig de Gràcia. €€€€.

Prestige Paseo de Gràcia p176

Renowned for its good service, the Condes is made up of two buildings. The older occupies a 19th-century palace and has a plunge pool on the roof. In the newer, rooms on the seventh floor have terraces and a view of La Pedrera.

Hotel Constanza

C/Bruc 33 (93 270 19 10/www. hotelconstanza.com). Metro Urquinaona. €€€.
The lobby has boxy, white sofas, lots of dark wood and Japanese silk screens painted with giant white lilies. Upstairs, wine-coloured corridors lead to sumptuous bedrooms with dark wood and leather furnishings, huge pillows and quality cotton sheets.

Hotel Granados 83

C/Enric Granados 83 (93 492 96 70/ www.derbyhotels.es). Metro Diagonal. €€€.
The original ironwork structure of this former hospital lends an industrial feel to the Granados 83. The 77 rooms, with brickwork walls, include duplex and triplex versions, some with their own terraces and plunge pools. There is a rooftop pool and sun deck.

Hotel Jazz

C/Pelai 3 (93 552 96 96/www.nn hotels.es). Metro Catalunya. €€€.
The rooms at the Hotel Jazz are super-stylish in calming tones of grey, beige and black, softened with parquet floors and spiced up with dapper pinstripe cushions. The beds are larger than usual for hotels, and bathrooms feature polished black tiles. A rooftop pool and sun deck top things off.

Hotel Majestic

Passeig de Gràcia 68 (93 488 17 17/ www.hotelmajestic.es). Metro Passeig de Gràcia. €€€€.
The Majestic has long been one of Barcelona's grandest hotels. Behind a neoclassical façade lies a panoply of perks, such as a service that allows you to print a selection of the day's newspapers from all over the world. Rooms are suitably opulent, decorated with classical flair. The Drolma restaurant is one of the finest in the city.

Hotel Omm

C/Rosselló 265 (93 445 40 00/ www.hotelomm.es). Metro Diagonal. €€€€.

ESSENTIALS

Feng shui goes space age at the drop-dead cool Omm. Bedrooms are soothingly stylish, with lacquer screens and every gadget imaginable. Get a corner room and spend all day watching the urban scene below. Up on the roof, the plunge pool offers fabulous views of Gaudí's landmark buildings.

Hotel Pulitzer

C/Bergara 8 (93 481 67 67/www.hotelpulitzer.es). Metro Catalunya. €€€.
A discreet façade reveals an impressive lobby that's stuffed with comfortable white leather sofas, a reading area and a swanky bar and restaurant. The rooms are small, but sumptuously decorated with cool elephant-grey marble and leather trim.

Market Hotel

Passatge Sant Antoni Abat 10 (93 325 12 05/www.markethotel.com.es). Metro Sant Antoni. €€€.
The people who brought us the wildly successful Quinze Nits chain of restaurants apply their low-budget, high-design approach to this hotel, although prices have crept up since it opened. The monochrome rooms are comfortable and stylish, and downstairs is a keenly priced restaurant.

Prestige Paseo de Gràcia

Passeig de Gràcia 62 (93 272 41 80/www.prestigehotels.com). Metro Passeig de Gràcia. €€€€.
The rooms are equipped with plasma-screen TVs, intelligent lighting, free minibars and even umbrellas. Outside their rooms, the hotel's guests hang out in the cool Zeroom lounge-bar-library, where expert concierges (of the funky rather than the fusty variety) are constantly on hand.

the5rooms

C/Pau Claris 72 (93 342 78 80/www.thefiverooms.com). Metro Catalunya or Urquinaona. €€€.
A chic and comfortable B&B in a handsome building, where the delightful Jessica Delgado makes every effort to ensure guests feel at home. Books and

magazines are dotted around the stylish sitting areas and bedrooms, and breakfast is served at any time of day.

Gràcia

Casa Fuster

Passeig de Gràcia 132 (93 255 30 00/www.hotelcasafuster.com). Metro Diagonal. €€€€.
Designed by Lluís Domènech i Montaner as a family home, this has regained its former glory as a swanky hotel with both art nouveau and art deco features. The 96 opulent rooms have original architectural details, along with flat-screen TVs and remote-controlled lighting.

Hostal HMB

C/Bonavista 21, 1º (93 368 20 13/www.hostalhmb.com). Metro Diagonal. €€.
The HMB opened in 2006 and it feels every bit as crisp and clean as you might hope. Situated on the first floor, with a lift, it has 12 rooms, which have high ceilings and are fairly spartan but enlivened with fabrics in blue and green with wood floors, flat-screen TVs and good lighting.

Other districts

Gran Hotel La Florida

Carretera de Vallvidrera al Tibidabo 83-93, Tibidabo (93 259 30 00/www.hotellaflorida.com). €€€€.
From 1925 through to the 1950s, this was Barcelona's grandest hotel, frequented by royals and film stars. It has lavish suites designed by artists, private terraces and gardens, a summer outdoor nightclub, breathtaking views from its infinity pool, and a luxury spa. A good choice if you want to relax in opulent style, but getting a cab from town at night can be tricky.

Sky H&R

NEW *C/Pere IV 272, Poblenou (93 492 93 94/www.skybarcelonahotel.com). Metro Glòries or Selva de Mar.* €€€€.
See box p166.

Getting Around

Arriving & leaving

By air

Aeroport de Barcelona

91 393 60 00/www.aena.es/
www.barcelona-airport.com
Barcelona's airport is at El Prat, just
south-west of the city. Each airline
works from one of the three main terminals (A, B or C), with a fourth due for
completion in 2009. There are tourist
information desks and currency
exchanges in terminals A and B.

Aerobús

The airport bus (information 93 415
60 20) runs from each terminal to
Plaça Catalunya, with stops at
Plaça d'Espanya, C/Urgell and Plaça
Universitat. Buses to the airport
go from Plaça Catalunya (in front
of El Corte Inglés), stopping at
Sants station and Plaça d'Espanya.
Buses run every 8-10mins, leaving
the airport from 6am-1am Mon-Fri
and 6.30am-1am at weekends,
returning from Plaça Catalunya
5.30am-12.15pm Mon-Fri and 6am-
12.15pm at weekends. The trip
takes 35-45mins; a single is €4.05.
At night the N17 runs every hour, on
the hour, between the airport (from
10pm) and Plaça Catalunya (from
11pm), with several stops on the
way, including Plaça d'Espanya
and Plaça Universitat. Last
departures are at 5am. Journey
time is 45 mins; the cost is a
single metro fare.

Airport trains

A long overhead walkway between
terminals A and B leads to the airport
train station. The Rodalies line C10
leaves the airport at 29 and 59 mins
past the hour, 6.29am-10.59pm, with
an extra train at 11.44pm daily,
stopping at Sants, Passeig de Gràcia
and Estació de França. Trains to the

airport leave Sants at 25 and 55 past
the hour, 5.25am-11.55pm daily (13
mins earlier from Estació de França
and 5 mins earlier from Passeig de
Gràcia). The journey takes 20-30mins
and costs €2.60 each way. Be aware
that tickets are valid only for 2hrs
after purchase. A little-publicised
fact is that the T-10 metro pass
can also be used.

Taxis from the airport

The basic taxi fare from the airport to
central Barcelona should be €18-€26,
including a €3 airport supplement.
Fares are about 15 per cent higher
after 9pm and at weekends. There is
a 90¢ supplement for each large piece
of luggage placed in the car boot. All
licensed cab drivers use the ranks
outside the terminals.

By bus

Most long-distance coaches
(both national and international)
stop or terminate at **Estació
d'Autobusos Barcelona-Nord**
(C/Ali Bei 80, Eixample, 902 26
06 06, www.barcelonanord.com).
Some international Eurolines
services (information 93 490 40
00, www.eurolines.es) begin and
end journeys at Sants.

By train

Most long-distance services
operated by the Spanish state
railway company **RENFE** run from
Barcelona-Sants station, easily
reached by metro. A few services
from the French border, or south
to Tarragona, stop at the **Estació
de França** in the Born, near the
Barceloneta metro, but it's otherwise
sparsely served. Many trains stop at
Passeig de Gràcia, which can be
the handiest for the city centre.

RENFE

National 902 24 02 02/international 902 24 34 02/www.renfe.es. **Open** *National* 5am-10pm daily. *International* 7am-midnight daily.

RENFE tickets can be bought online, at train stations, travel agents or reserved over the phone and delivered to an address or hotel for a small extra fee. They have some English-speaking phone operators.

Public transport

Although it's run by different organisations, Barcelona's public transport is highly integrated, with the same tickets valid for up to four changes of transport on bus, tram, local train and metro lines as long as you do it within 75 minutes. The **metro** is generally the quickest and easiest way of getting around the city. For a map of the metro lines, turn to the inside back cover of this book. All metro lines operate from 5am to midnight Monday to Thursday, Sunday and public holidays; 5am to 2am Friday, and all through Saturday night. **Buses** run throughout the night and to areas not covered by the metro system. Local buses and the metro are run by the city transport authority (**TMB**). Two underground train lines connect with the metro but are run by Catalan government railways, the **FGC**. One runs north from Plaça Catalunya; the other runs west from Plaça d'Espanya to Cornellà. Two tramlines are of limited use to visitors.

FGC information

Vestíbule, Plaça Catalunya FGC station, Barri Gòtic (93 205 15 15/www.fgc.net). **Open** 7am-9pm Mon-Fri.
Other locations FGC Provença (open 9am-7pm Mon-Fri, closed Aug); FGC Plaça d'Espanya (open 9am-2pm, 4-7pm Mon-Fri).

TMB information

Main vestíbule, Metro Universitat, Eixample (93 318 70 74/www.tmb.net). **Open** 8am-8pm Mon-Fri.
Other locations vestíbule, Metro Sants Estació & Sagrada Família (both 7am-9pm Mon-Fri; Sants also opens 9am-7pm Sat, 9am-2pm Sun); vestíbule, Metro Diagonal (8am-8pm Mon-Fri).

Buses

Many city bus routes originate in or pass through the city centre, at Plaça Catalunya, Plaça Universitat and Plaça Urquinaona. However, they often run along different parallel streets, due to the city's one-way system. Not all stops are labelled and street signs are not always easy to locate. Most routes run 6am-10.30pm daily except Sundays. There's usually a bus every 10-15mins, but they're less frequent before 8am, after 9pm and on Saturdays. On Sundays, buses are less frequent still; a few do not run at all.

Board at the front and disembark through the middle or rear doors. Only single tickets can be bought from the driver; if you have a *targeta,* insert it into the machine behind the driver as you board.

Fares and tickets

Travel in the Barcelona urban area has a flat fare of €1.30 per journey, but multi-journey tickets or *targetes* are better value. The basic ten-trip *targeta* is the **T-10** (Catalan *Te-Deu,* Spanish *Te-Diez*) for €7.20, which can be shared by any number of people travelling simultaneously; the ticket is validated in the machines on the metro, train or bus once per person per journey. The T-10 offers access to all five of the city's main transport systems (local RENFE and FGC trains within the main metropolitan area, the metro, tram and buses). To transfer, insert your card into a machine a second time; unless 75 minutes have elapsed since your last journey, another unit will not be deducted. Single tickets don't allow free transfers.

You can buy T-10s in newsagents and Servi-Caixa cashpoints as well as metro and train stations, but not on buses.

Trams

Lines **T1**, **T2** and **T3** go from Plaça Francesc Macià, Zona Alta to the outskirts of the city. T1 goes to Cornellà via Hospitalet and Esplugues de Llobregat; T2 goes the same way, but contines further to Sant Joan Despí; and T3 runs to Sant Just Desvern. **T4** runs from Ciutadella-Vila Olímpica (also a metro stop), via Glòries and the Fòrum, on to Sant Adrià (also a RENFE train station).

All trams are fully accessible for wheelchair-users and are part of the integrated TMB *targeta* system: simply insert the ticket into the machine as you board. You can buy integrated tickets and single tickets from the machines at tram stops.

Tram information

Trambaix (902 19 32 75/www.tram bcn.com). **Open** 9am-2pm, 4-7pm Mon-Thur; 9am-2pm Fri.

Taxis

It's usually easy to find one of the 10,300 black and yellow taxis. There are ranks at railway and bus stations, in main squares and throughout the city, but taxis can also be hailed on the street when they show a green light on the roof and a sign saying '*lliure/libre*' (free) behind the windscreen. Information on taxi fares, ranks and regulations can be found at www.emt-amb.com.

Fares

Rates and supplements are shown inside cabs on a sticker in the rear side window (in English). The basic fare for a taxi hailed in the street to pick you up is €1.80 (or €1.90 at night, weekends and holidays), which is what the meter should register when you set off. The basic rate, 82¢/km, applies 8am-8pm Mon-Fri; at other times, including public holidays, the rate is €1.04/km, plus a €4 supplement after midnight. There are supplements for luggage (€1), the airport (€3.10) and the port (€2.10), and for 'special nights' such as New Year's Eve (€3.10), as well as a waiting charge. Taxi drivers are not required to carry more than €20 in change; few accept credit cards.

Radio cabs

These companies take bookings 24 hours daily. Phone cabs start the meter when a call is answered but, by the time it picks you up, it should not display more than €3.09 during weekdays and €3.86 at night, at weekends or public holidays.

Autotaxi Mercedes Barcelona
93 307 07 07.
Barnataxi
93 357 77 55.
Fono-Taxi
93 300 11 00.
Ràdio Taxi '033'
93 303 30 33.
Servi-Taxi
93 330 03 00.
Taxi Groc
93 322 22 22.
Taxi Miramar
93 433 10 20.

Driving

Car & motorbike hire

Car hire is relatively pricey, but it's a competitive market so shop around. Check carefully what's included: ideally, you want unlimited mileage, 16% VAT (IVA) included and full insurance cover (*seguro todo riesgo*) rather than the third-party minimum (*seguro obligatorio*). You'll need a credit card as a guarantee. Most

ESSENTIALS

companies require you to have had a licence for at least a year; many also enforce a minimum age limit.

Pepecar *807 41 42 43, www.pepecar.com.*
Europcar *93 491 25 65, reservations 902 10 50 30, www.europcar.com.*
Motissimo *93 490 84 01, www.motissimo.es.*
Vanguard *93 439 38 80, www.vanguardrent.com.*

Parking

Parking is fiendishly complicated, and municipal police are quick to hand out tickets or tow away cars. In some parts of the old city, access is limited to residents for much of the day. In some Old City streets, time-controlled bollards pop up, meaning your car may get stuck. Wherever you are, don't park in front of doors signed '*Gual Permanent*', indicating an entry with 24-hour right of access.

Pay and display areas

The Area Verda contains zones exclusively for residents' use (most of the old city), and 'partial zones' (found in Gràcia, Barceloneta and the Eixample) where non-residents pay €2.80 an hour with a one- or two-hour maximum stay, as indicated on the meter.

If you overstay by no more than an hour, you can cancel the fine by paying an extra €6; to do so, press *Anul·lar denúncia* on the machine, insert €6, then press *Ticket*. Some machines accept credit cards (MC, V); none accepts notes or gives change. For information, call 010 or see www.bcn.cat/areaverda.

Car parks

Car parks ('*parkings*') are signalled by a white 'P' on a blue sign. **SABA** (Plaça Catalunya, Plaça Urquinaona, Rambla Catalunya, Avda Catedral, airport and elsewhere; 93 230 56 00, 902 28 30 80, www.saba.es) costs around €2.40/hr, while **SMASSA**

car parks (Plaça Catalunya 23, C/Hospital 25-29, Avda Francesc Cambó 10, Passeig de Gràcia 60, and elsewhere; 93 409 20 21, www.bsmsa.es/mobilitat) cost €2-€2.45/hr. The €5.50 fare at the **Metro-Park** park-and-ride facility (Plaça de les Glòries, Eixample, 93 265 10 47, open 4.30am-12.30am Mon-Sat) includes a day's unlimited travel on the metro and buses.

Towed vehicles

If the police have towed your car, they should leave a triangular sticker on the pavement where it was. The sticker should let you know to which pound it's been taken. If not, call 901 513 151; staff generally don't speak English. Recovering your vehicle within 4hrs costs €141.90, with each extra hour costing €1.85, or €18.50 per day. You'll also have to pay a fine to the police, which varies. You'll need your passport and documentation, or the rental contract, to prove ownership.

Petrol

Most *gasolineres* (petrol stations) have unleaded (*sense plom/sin plomo*), regular (*super*) and diesel (*gas-oil*). Petrol is cheaper in Spain than it is in most northern European countries.

Cycling

There's a network of bike lanes (*carrils bici*) along major avenues and by the seafront; local authorities are keen to promote cycling. However, weekday traffic can be risky, despite legislation that states that drivers must slow down near cyclists. No more than two bikes may ride side by side. Cycling information can be found at www.bcn.es/bicicleta.

Bicicleta Barcelona (bicycle hire)

C/Esparteria 3, Born (93 268 21 05). Metro Barceloneta or Jaume I. **Open** 10am-7pm Mon-Sat; 10am-2pm Sun.

Resources A-Z

Accident & emergency

The following lines are available 24 hours a day.

Emergency services *112. Police, fire or ambulance.*
Ambulance/Ambulància *061*
In a medical emergency, go to the casualty department (*Urgències*) of any of the main public hospitals. All are open 24 hours daily.
Centre d'Urgències Perecamps *Avda Drassanes 13-15, Raval (93 441 06 00). Metro Drassanes or Paral·lel.*
Hospital Clínic *C/Villarroel 170, Eixample (93 227 54 00). Metro Hospital Clínic.*
Hospital del Mar *Passeig Marítim 25-29, Barceloneta (93 248 30 00). Metro Ciutadella-Vila Olímpica.*
Hospital Dos de Maig *C/Dos de Maig 301, Eixample (93 507 27 00). Metro Hospital de Sant Pau.*
Hospital de Sant Pau *C/Sant Antoni Maria Claret 167, Eixample (93 291 90 00). Metro Hospital de Sant Pau.*

Pharmacies

Pharmacies (*farmàcies/farmacias*) are signalled by large green and red neon crosses. Most are open 9am-1.30pm and 4.30-8pm weekdays, and 9am-1.30pm on Saturdays. About a dozen operate around the clock, while many more have late opening hours; some of the most central are detailed below. The full list of chemists that stay open late (usually until 10pm) and overnight on any given night is posted daily outside every pharmacy door and given in the day's newspapers. You can also call the 010 and 098 information lines. At night, duty pharmacies often appear closed, but knock on the shutters and you'll be attended to.

Farmàcia Alvarez *Passeig de Gràcia 26, Eixample (93 302 11 24). Metro Passeig de Gràcia.* **Open** 8am-10.30pm Mon-Thur; 8am-midnight Fri; 9am-midnight Sat.
Farmàcia Cervera *C/Muntaner 254, Eixample (93 200 09 96). Metro Diagonal.* **Open** 24hrs daily.
Farmàcia Clapés *La Rambla 98, Barri Gòtic (93 301 28 43). Metro Liceu.* **Open** 24hrs daily.
Farmàcia Vilar *Vestíbul, Estació de Sants, Sants (93 490 92 07). Metro Sants Estació.* **Open** 7am-10.30pm Mon-Fri; 8am-10.30pm Sat, Sun.

Consulates

A full list of consulates can be found in the phone book under '*Ambaixades i consolats/ Embajadas y consulados*'.

Australian Consulate *Plaça Gal·la Placidia 1-3, 1°, Gràcia (93 490 90 13/ www.spain.embassy.gov.au). FGC Gràcia.* **Open** 10am-noon Mon-Fri. Closed Aug.
British Consulate *Avda Diagonal 477 13°, Eixample (93 366 62 00/ www.ukinspain.com). Metro Hospital Clínic.* **Open** *Mid Sept-mid June* 9.30am-2pm Mon-Fri. *Mid June-mid Sept* 8.30am-1.30pm Mon-Fri.
Canadian Consulate *C/Elisenda de Pinós 10, Sarrià (93 204 27 00/www. canada-es.org). FGC Reina Elisenda.* **Open** 10am-1pm Mon-Fri.
Irish Consulate *Gran Via Carles III 94, Les Corts (93 491 50 21). Metro Maria Cristina.* **Open** 10am-1pm Mon-Fri.
New Zealand Consulate *Travessera de Gràcia 64, 2°, Gràcia (93 209 03 99). Metro Diagonal.* **Open** 9am-2pm, 4-7pm Mon-Fri.
South African Consulate *Parque Empresarial Mas Blau II, Alta Ribagorza 6-8, El Prat de Llobregat (93 506 91 00).* **Open** 9.30am-noon Mon-Fri.
US Consulate *Passeig Reina Elisenda 23, Sarrià (93 280 22 27/www. embusa.es). FGC Reina Elisenda.* **Open** 9am-1pm Mon-Fri.

Credit card loss

Each of these lines has English-speaking staff and is open 24 hours a day.

American Express *902 11 11 35.*
Diners Club *901 10 10 11.*
MasterCard *900 97 12 31.*
Visa *900 99 11 24.*

Customs

Customs declarations are not usually necessary if you arrive in Spain from another EU country and are carrying only legal goods for personal use. The amounts given below are guidelines only: if you approach these maximums in several different categories, you may still have to explain your personal habits.

■ 800 cigarettes, 400 small cigars, 200 cigars or 1kg loose tobacco

■ 10 litres of spirits (over 22% alcohol), 90 litres of wine (under 22% alcohol) or 110 litres of beer

From a non-EU country or the Canary Islands, you can bring:

■ 200 cigarettes, 100 small cigars, 50 regular cigars or 250g (8.82oz) of tobacco

■ 1 litre of spirits (over 22% alcohol) or 2 litres of wine or beer (under 22%)

■ 50g (1.76oz) of perfume

■ 500g coffee; 100g tea

Visitors can also carry up to €6,000 in cash without having to declare it to customes. Non-EU residents are able to reclaim VAT (IVA) on some purchases when they leave.

Disabled travellers

Run by a British expat wheelchair-user who now lives in Barcelona, **www.accessiblebarcelona.com** is a very useful resource for disabled travellers.

Institut Municipal de Persones amb Disminució

Avda Diagonal 233, Eixample (93 413 27 75/www.bcn.cat/accessible). Metro Glòries or Monumental/56, 62 bus. **Open** 9am-2pm Mon-Fri.
The city's organisation for the disabled has information on access to venues and can provide a useful map with wheelchair-friendly itineraries.

Transport

Access for disabled people to local transport still leaves quite a lot to be desired. For wheelchair-users, buses and taxis are usually the best bets, since only the Purple line on the Metro is completely accessible to wheelchair-users. For transport information, call **TMB** (93 318 70 74) or 010. Transport maps, which can be picked up from transport information offices and some metro stations, indicate wheelchair access points and adapted bus routes. For a list of accessible metro stations and bus lines, check **www.tmb.net** and click on 'Transport for everyone'.

Electricity

The standard voltage in Spain is 220V. Plugs are of the type that have two round pins. Thus, you'll need a plug adaptor to use three-pin British-bought electrical devices. If you have US (110V) equipment, you will need a transformer as well as an adaptor.

Estancs/estancos

Government-run tobacco shops, known as an *estanc/estanco* (or at times, just as '*tabac*') and identified by a brown and yellow sign, are very important institutions in Spain. As well as tobacco, they will supply postage stamps and envelopes, public transport *targetes* and phonecards.

Internet

There are internet centres all over Barcelona. Libraries have free internet access, but there is often a queue.

Bornet Internet Café

C/Barra de Ferro 3, Born (93 268 15 07/www.bornet-bcn.com). Metro Jaume I. **Open** 10am-10pm Mon-Fri; 3pm-10pm Sat, Sun. No credit cards.

There are ten terminals in this small café and six more for laptops. One hour is €2.60; but you're really paying for atmosphere.

easyEverything

La Rambla 31, Barri Gòtic (93 301 75 07/www.easyeverything.com). Metro Drassanes or Liceu. **Open** 8am-2am daily. No credit cards.

There are 330 terminals here and 240 at Ronda Universitat 35 (open 8am-2am daily). Buy credit from the machines; the price then increases with demand.

Police

If you're robbed or attacked, report the incident as soon as possible at the nearest police station (*comisaría*), or dial 112. In the centre, the most convenient is the 24hr **Guàrdia Urbana** station (La Rambla 43, 092 or 93 256 24 30), which often has English-speaking officers on duty; they may eventually transfer you to the **Mossos d'Esquadra** (C/Nou de la Rambla 76, 088 or 93 306 23 00) to formally report the crime.

To do this, you'll need to make an official statement (*denuncia*). It's highly improbable that you will recover your property, but you need the *denuncia* to make an insurance claim. You can also make this statement over the phone or online (902 10 21 12, www.policia.es) except for crimes involving physical violence, or if the perpetrator has been identified. You'll still have to go to the *comisaría* within 72 hours to sign the *denuncia*, but you'll skip some queues.

Post

Letters and postcards weighing up to 20g cost 31¢ within Spain; 60¢ to the rest of Europe; 78¢ to the rest of the world – though anything in a non-rectangular envelope costs more. Prices normally rise on 1 January. It's usually easiest to buy stamps at *estancs* (p182). Mail sent abroad is slow: 5-6 working days in Europe, 8-10 to the USA. Postboxes in the street are yellow, sometimes with a white or blue horn insignia. Postal information is available at www.correos.es or on 902 197 197.

Correu Central

Plaça Antonio López, Barri Gòtic (93 486 80 50). Metro Barceloneta or Jaume I. **Open** 8.30am-9.30pm Mon-Fri; 8.30am-2pm Sat. **Other locations** Ronda Universitat 23, Eixample; C/Aragó 282, Eixample (both 8.30am-8.30pm Mon-Fri, 9.30am-1pm Sat).

Poste restante

Poste restante letters should be sent to Lista de Correos, 08080 Barcelona, Spain. Pick-up is from the main post office; you'll need your passport.

Smoking

Laws were passed in 2006 that required all bars and restaurants over 100sq m (1,080sq ft) to have a non-smoking area; smaller establishments can elect to be non-smoking or not, but those that are not can no longer admit under-18s. The application of this law is rather hit-or-miss. Most hotels have non-smoking rooms or floors, although if you ask for

ESSENTIALS

a non-smoking room, some hotels may just give you a room that has had ashtrays removed. Smoking bans in cinemas, theatres and on trains are generally respected, but smoking in banks, offices and on station platforms is still common.

Telephones

Normal Spanish phone numbers have nine digits; the area code (93 in the province of Barcelona) must be dialled with all calls, both local and long-distance. Spanish mobile numbers always begin with 6. Numbers starting 900 are freephone lines, while other 90 numbers are special-rate services.

International calls

To make an international call, dial 00 and then the country code, followed by the area code (omitting the first zero in UK numbers), and then the number you wish to call. Country codes are as follows: Australia 61; Canada 1; Irish Republic 353; New Zealand 64; South Africa 27; United Kingdom 44; USA 1. To phone Spain from abroad, you should dial the international access code, followed by 34, followed by the required number.

Public phones

The most common type of payphone accepts coins (5¢ up), phonecards and credit cards. There is a multilingual digital display (press 'L' to change language) and written instructions in English and other languages. Calls to directory enquiries on 11818 are free from payphones, but you'll usually have to insert a coin to make the call (it will be returned when you hang up).

Telefónica phonecards (*targetes telefònica/tarjetas telefónica*) are sold at newsstands and *estancs* (p182). Other cards sold at phone centres, shops and newsstands give cheaper rates on all but local calls. This latter type of card contains a toll-free number to call from any phone.

Tickets

FNAC (p135) has an efficient ticket desk on its ground floor: it sells tickets to theme parks and sights, but it's especially good for contemporary music concerts and events. Concert tickets for smaller venues are often sold in record shops and at the venues themselves; check posters for further details. If you want to get tickets to the football, see the listings on p152.

Servi-Caixa – La Caixa

902 33 22 11/www.servicaixa.com.
Use the special Servi-Caixa ATMs (most larger branches of La Caixa have them), dial 902 33 22 11 or check the website to purchase tickets for cinemas, concerts, plays, museums, amusement parks and Barça games. You'll need the card with which you made the payment when you collect the tickets.

Tel-entrada – Caixa Catalunya

902 10 12 12/www.telentrada.com.
Through Tel-entrada you can purchase tickets for theatre performances, cinemas (including the IMAX), concerts, museums and sights over the phone, online or over the counter at any branch of the Caixa Catalunya savings bank. Tickets can be collected from Caixa Catalunya ATMs or the tourist office at Plaça Catalunya (below).

Time

Spain is one hour ahead of London, six hours ahead of New York, eight hours behind Sydney and ten hours behind Wellington. In

ESSENTIALS

all EU countries clocks are moved forward one hour in early spring and back again in late autumn.

Tipping

There are no fixed rules for tipping in Barcelona, but locals generally don't tip much. It's fair to leave 5-10 per cent in restaurants, but if you think the service has been bad, don't feel you have to. People sometimes leave a little change in bars: not expected, but appreciated. In taxis, tipping is not standard, but many people will round up to the nearest euro. It's usual to tip hotel porters.

Tourist information

Centre d'Informació de la Virreina

Palau de la Virreina, La Rambla 99 (93 316 10 00/www.bcn.cat/cultura). Metro Liceu. **Open** 10am-8pm Mon-Sat; 11am-3pm Sun. *Ticket sales* 11am-8pm Tue-Sat; 11am-3pm Sun.
The information office of the city's culture department, with details of shows, exhibitions and special events.

Oficines d'Informació Turística

Plaça Catalunya, Eixample (information 807 11 72 22/from outside Spain +34 93 285 38 34/www.bcn.cat/ www.barcelonaturisme.com). Metro Catalunya. **Open** *Office* 9am-9pm daily. *Call centre* 9am-8pm Mon-Fri.
The main office of the city tourist board is underground on the Corte Inglés side of the square: look for big red signs with 'i' in white. It has information, money exchange, a shop and a hotel booking service, and sells phonecards, tickets for shows, sights and public transport. **Other locations** C/Ciutat 2, Barri Gòtic; C/Sardenya (located opposite the Sagrada Familia), Eixample; Plaça Portal Pau (located opposite Monument a Colom), Port Vell; Sants station; La Rambla 115; corner of Plaça d'Espanya and Avda Maria Cristina; airport.

Palau Robert

Passeig de Gràcia 107, Eixample (93 238 80 91/www.gencat.net/probert). Metro Diagonal. **Open** 10am-7pm Mon-Sat; 10am-2.30pm Sun.
The Generalitat's lavishly equipped centre has maps and other essentials for the whole of Catalonia.

010 phoneline

Open 8am-10pm Mon-Sat.
This city-run information line is aimed mainly at locals, but it manages to do an impeccable job of answering all kinds of queries. There are sometimes English-speaking operators.

Visas

EU nationals and citizens of the US, Canada, Australia and New Zealand do not need visas for stays of up to three months. For EU citizens a passport or national ID card valid for travel abroad is sufficient; non-EU citizens must have full passports.

What's on

The main papers all have daily 'what's on' events listings, with entertainment supplements on Fridays (most run TV schedules on Saturdays). For monthly listings, see *Metropolitan* and the freesheets such as *Mondo Sonoro* and *AB* (these can be found in bars and music shops).

Guía del Ocio

This is a weekly listings magazine. Available at any kiosk in the city, its listings aren't always 100% up to date or accurate but it is a useful starting point. You can also consult their website at www.guiadelociobcn.es.

Time Out Barcelona

A new and comprehensive weekly listings magazine, published in Catalan. There are plans in place to add a monthly pull-out section in English (www.timeout.cat).

ESSENTIALS

Spanish Vocabulary

Although many locals prefer to speak Catalan, everyone in the city can speak Spanish. The Spanish familiar form for 'you' (*tú*) is used very freely, but it's safer to use the more formal *usted* with older people and strangers (verbs below are given in the *usted* form).

Useful expressions

hello *hola*; **good morning** *buenos días*; **good afternoon, good evening** *buenas tardes*; **good evening** (after dark), **good night** *buenas noches* **goodbye** *adiós*
please *por favor*; **very good/OK** *muy bien* **thank you (very much)** *(muchas) gracias*; **you're welcome** *de nada*; **do you speak English?** *¿habla inglés?* **I don't speak Spanish** *no hablo castellano*; **I don't understand** *no lo entiendo*; **OK/fine** *vale*
what's your name? *¿cómo se llama?* **Sir/Mr** *señor (sr)*; **Madam/Mrs** *señora (sra)*; **Miss** *señorita (srta)*
excuse me/sorry *perdón*; **excuse me, please** *oiga* (to attract someone's attention, politely; literally, 'hear me')
where is…? *¿dónde está…?* **why?** *¿por qué?* **when?** *¿cuándo?* **who?** *¿quién?* **what?** *¿qué?* **where?** *¿dónde?* **how?** *¿cómo?* **who is it?** *¿quién es?* **is/are there any…?** *¿hay…?*
very *muy*; **and** *y*; **or** *o*; **with** *con*; **without** *sin*; **enough** *bastante* **open** *abierto*; **closed** *cerrado*; **entrance** *entrada*; **exit** *salida*
I would like *quiero*; **how many would you like?** *¿cuántos quiere?* **how much is it** *¿cuánto es?*
I like *me gusta*; **I don't like** *no me gusta*
good *bueno/a*; **bad** *malo/a*; **well/badly** *bien/mal*; **small** *pequeño/a*; **big** *gran, grande*; **expensive** *caro/a*; **cheap** *barato/a*; **hot** (food, drink) *caliente*; **cold** *frío/a*; **something** *algo*; **nothing** *nada* **more/less** *más/menos*; **more or less** *más o menos* **toilets** *los baños/los servicios/los lavabos*

Getting around

a ticket *un billete*; **return** *de ida y vuelta*; **the next stop** *la próxima parada*; **left** *izquierda*; **right** *derecha* **here** *aquí*; **there** *allí*; **straight on** *todo recto*; **to the end of the street** *al final de la calle*; **as far as** *hasta*; **towards** *hacia*; **near** *cerca*; **far** *lejos*

Time

now *ahora*; **later** *más tarde*; **yesterday** *ayer*; **today** *hoy*; **tomorrow** *mañana*; **tomorrow morning** *mañana por la mañana* **morning** *la mañana*; **midday** *mediodía*; **afternoon/evening** *la tarde*; **night** *la noche*; **late night** (roughly 1-6am) *la madrugada* **at what time…?** *¿a qué hora…?* **at 2** *a las dos*; **at 8pm** *a las ocho de la tarde*; **at 1.30** *a la una y media*; **at 5.15** *a las cinco y cuarto*; **in an hour** *en una hora*

Numbers

0 *cero*; 1 *un, uno, una*; 2 *dos*; 3 *tres*; 4 *cuatro*; 5 *cinco*; 6 *seis*; 7 *siete*; 8 *ocho*; 9 *nueve*; 10 *diez*; 11 *once*; 12 *doce*; 13 *trece*; 14 *catorce*; 15 *quince*; 16 *dieciséis*; 17 *diecisiete*; 18 *dieciocho*; 19 *diecinueve*; 20 *veinte*; 21 *veintiuno*; 22 *veintidós*; 30 *treinta*; 40 *cuarenta*; 50 *cincuenta*; 60 *sesenta*; 70 *setenta*; 80 *ochenta*; 90 *noventa*; 100 *cien*; 200 *doscientos*; 1,000 *mil*

Days & months

Monday *lunes*; **Tuesday** *martes*; **Wednesday** *miércoles*; **Thursday** *jueves*; **Friday** *viernes*; **Saturday** *sábado*; **Sunday** *domingo* **January** *enero*; **February** *febrero*; **March** *marzo*; **April** *abril*; **May** *mayo*; **June** *junio*; **July** *julio*; **August** *agosto*; **September** *septiembre*; **October** *octubre*; **November** *noviembre*; **December** *diciembre*

Catalan Vocabulary

Catalan phonetics are significantly different from those of Spanish, with a wider range of vowel sounds and soft consonants. Catalans use the familiar (*tu*) rather than the polite (*vostè*) second-person forms very freely, but for convenience verbs are given here in the polite form.

Useful expressions

hello *hola*; **good morning** *bon dia*; **good afternoon** *bona tarda*; **good evening/night** *bona nit*; **goodbye** *adéu*
please *si us plau*; **very good/OK** *molt bé*; **thank you (very much)** *(moltes) gràcies*; **you're welcome** *de res*
do you speak English? *parla anglés?*
I'm sorry, I don't speak Catalan *ho sento, no parlo català*
I don't understand *no ho entenc*
what's your name? *com es diu?*
Sir/Mr *senyor (sr)*; **Madam/Mrs** *senyora (sra)*; **Miss** *senyoreta (srta)*
excuse me/sorry *perdoni/disculpi*; **excuse me, please** *escolti* (literally, 'listen to me'); **OK/fine** *val/d'acord*
how much is it? *quant val?*
why? *perquè?* **when?** *quan?* **who?** *qui?* **what?** *què?* **where?** *on?* **how?** *com?* **where is...?** *on és...?* **who is it?** *qui és?* **is/are there any...?** *hi ha...?/n'hi ha de...?*
very *molt*; **and** *i* or *o*; **with** *amb*; **without** *sense*; **enough** *prou*
open *obert*; **closed** *tancat*
entrance *entrada*; **exit** *sortida*
I would like *vull*; **how many would you like?** *quants en vol?* **I like** *m'agrada*; **I don't like** *no m'agrada*
good *bo/bona*; **bad** *dolent/a*; **well/badly** *bé/malament*; **small** *petit/a*; **big** *gran*; **expensive** *car/a*; **cheap** *barat/a*; **hot** (food, drink) *calent/a*; **cold** *fred/a*
something *alguna cosa*; **nothing** *res*; **more** *més*; **less** *menys*; **more or less** *més o menys*
toilets *els banys/els serveis/els lavabos*

Getting around

a ticket *un bitllet*; **return** *de anada i tornada*; **left** *esquerra*; **right** *dreta*; **here** *aquí*; **there** *allí*; **straight on** *tot recte*; **at the corner** *a la cantonada*; **as far as** *fins a*; **towards** *cap a*; **near** *a prop*; **far** *lluny*; **is it far?** *és lluny?*

Time

now *ara*; **later** *més tard*; **yesterday** *ahir*; **today** *avui*; **tomorrow** *demà*; **tomorrow morning** *demà pel matí*; **morning** *el matí*; **midday** *migdia*; **afternoon** *la tarda*; **evening** *el vespre*; **night** *la nit*; **late night** (roughly, 1-6am) *la matinada*; **at what time...?** *a quina hora...?* **in an hour** *en una hora*; **at 2** *a les dues*; **at 8pm** *a les vuit del vespre*; **at 1.30** *a dos quarts de dues/a la una i mitja* (can also be referred to as quarters of the next hour); **at 5.15** *a un quart de sis/a las cinc i quart*; **at 22.30** *a vint-i-dos-trenta*

Numbers

0 *zero*; **1** *u, un, una*; **2** *dos, dues*; **3** *tres*; **4** *quatre*; **5** *cinc*; **6** *sis*; **7** *set*; **8** *vuit*; **9** *nou*; **10** *deu*; **11** *onze*; **12** *dotze*; **13** *tretze*; **14** *catorze*; **15** *quinze*; **16** *setze*; **17** *disset*; **18** *divuit*; **19** *dinou*; **20** *vint*; **21** *vint-i-u*; **22** *vint-i-dos, vint-i-dues*; **30** *trenta*; **40** *quaranta*; **50** *cinquanta*; **60** *seixanta*; **70** *setanta*; **80** *vuitanta*; **90** *noranta*; **100** *cent*; **200** *dos-cents, dues-centes*; **1,000** *mil*

Days & months

Monday *dilluns*; **Tuesday** *dimarts*; **Wednesday** *dimecres*; **Thursday** *dijous*; **Friday** *divendres*; **Saturday** *dissabte*; **Sunday** *diumenge*
January *gener*; **February** *febrer*; **March** *març*; **April** *abril*; **May** *maig*; **June** *juny*; **July** *juliol*; **August** *agost*; **September** *setembre*; **October** *octubre*; **November** *novembre*; **December** *desembre*

Menu Glossary

Basics

Catalan	Spanish	English
una cullera	una cuchara	a spoon
una forquilla	un tenedor	a fork
un ganivet	un cuchillo	a knife
una ampolla de	una botella de	a bottle of
vi negre	vino tinto	red wine
vi rosat	vino rosado	rosé
vi blanc	vino blanco	white wine
una altra	otra	another (one)
més	más	more
pa	pan	bread
oli d'oliva	aceite de oliva	olive oil
sal i pebre	sal y pimienta	salt and pepper
amanida	ensalada	salad
truita	tortilla	omelette

(note: *truita* refers to either an omelette or a trout.)

Catalan	Spanish	English
la nota	la cuenta	the bill
un cendrer	un cenicero	ashtray
bon profit	aproveche	enjoy your meal
sóc…	soy…	I'm a…
vegetarià/ana	vegetariano/a	vegetarian
diabètic/a	diabético/a	diabetic

Cooking terms

Catalan	Spanish	English
a la brasa	a la brasa	char-grilled
a la graella/ planxa	a la plancha	grilled on a hot metal plate
a la romana	a la romana	fried in batter
al forn	al horno	baked
al vapor	al vapor	steamed
fregit	frito	fried
rostit	asado	roast
ben fet	bien hecho	well done
a punt	medio hecho	medium
poc fet	poco hecho	rare

Carn/Carne/Meat

Catalan	Spanish	English
bou	buey	beef
cabrit	cabrito	kid
conill	conejo	rabbit
embotits	embotidos	cold cuts
fetge	higado	liver
garrí	cochinillo	suckling pig
llebre	liebre	hare
llengua	lengua	tongue
llom	lomo	loin (usually pork)
pernil (serrà)	jamón serrano	dry-cured ham
pernil dolç	jamón york	cooked ham
peus de porc	manos de cerdo	pigs' trotters
porc	cerdo	pork
porc senglar	jabalí	wild boar
vedella	ternera	veal
xai/be	cordero	lamb

Aviram/Aves/Poultry

Catalan	Spanish	English
ànec	pato	duck
gall dindi	pavo	turkey
guatlla	codorniz	quail
oca	oca	goose
ous	huevos	eggs
perdiu	perdiz	partridge
colomí	pichón	pigeon
pintada	gallina de Guinea	guinea fowl
pollastre	pollo	chicken

Peix/Pescado/Fish

Catalan	Spanish	English
anxoves	anchoas	anchovies
bacallà	bacalao	salt cod
besuc	besugo	sea bream
caballa	verat	mackerel
llenguado	lenguado	sole
llobarro	lubina	sea bass
lluç	merluza	hake
moll	salmonete	red mullet

rap	*rape*	monkfish
rèmol	*rodaballo*	turbot
salmó	*salmón*	salmon
sardines	*sardinas*	sardines
tonyina	*atún*	tuna
truita	*trucha*	trout

(note: *truita* can also mean omelette.)

Marisc/Mariscos/Shellfish

Catalan	Spanish	English
calamarsos	*calamares*	squid
cloïsses	*almejas*	clams
cranc	*cangrejo*	crab
escamarlans	*cigalas*	crayfish
escopinyes	*berberechos*	cockles
espardenyes	*espardeñas*	sea cucumbers
gambes	*gambas*	prawns
llagosta	*langosta*	spiny lobster
llagostins	*langostinos*	langoustines
llamàntol	*bogavante*	lobster
musclos	*mejillones*	mussels
navalles	*navajas*	razor clams
percebes	*percebes*	barnacles
pop	*pulpo*	octopus
sípia	*sepia*	squid
tallarines	*tallarinas*	wedge clams

Verdures/Legumbres/Vegetables

Catalan	Spanish	English
albergínia	*berenjena*	aubergine
all	*ajo*	garlic
alvocat	*aguacate*	avocado
bolets	*setas*	wild mushrooms
carbassós	*calabacines*	courgettes
carxofes	*alcachofas*	artichokes
ceba	*cebolla*	onion
cigrons	*garbanzos*	chickpeas
col	*col*	cabbage
enciam	*lechuga*	lettuce
endivies	*endivias*	chicory
espinacs	*espinacas*	spinach
mongetes blanques	*judías blancas*	haricot beans
mongetes verdes	*judías verdes*	French beans
pastanagues	*zanahorias*	carrots

patates	*patatas*	potatoes
pebrots	*pimientos*	peppers
pèsols	*guisantes*	peas
porros	*puerros*	leeks
tomàquets	*tomates*	tomatoes
xampinyons	*champiñones*	mushrooms

Postres/Postres/Desserts

Catalan	Spanish	English
flam	*flan*	crème caramel
formatge	*queso*	cheese
gelat	*helado*	ice-cream
música	*música*	dried fruit and nuts served with muscatel
pastís	*pastel*	cake
tarta	*tarta*	tart

Fruïta/Fruta/Fruit

Catalan	Spanish	English
figues	*higos*	figs
gerds	*frambuesas*	raspberries
maduixes	*fresas*	strawberries
pera	*pera*	pear
pinya	*piña*	pineapple
plàtan	*plátano*	banana
poma	*manzana*	apple
préssec	*melocotón*	peach
prunes	*ciruelas*	plums
raïm	*uvas*	grapes
taronja	*naranja*	orange

ESSENTIALS

Index

Sights & Areas

a
Ajuntament (City Hall) p56
Antic Hospital de la Santa
  Creu & La Capella p88

b
Barceloneta p98
Barri Gòtic p54
Barrio Chino p94
Born p73
Bus Montjuïc Turistic p110

c
CaixaForum p110
Casa Àsia p121
Casa Batlló p124
Catamaran Orsom p103
Cathedral p56
CCCB (Centre de Cultura
  Contemporània de
  Barcelona) p88
Cementiri del Sud-oest
  p110
Collserola p152
Corts, Les p150
CosmoCaixa p155

e
Eixample p121

f
Font Màgica de Montjuïc
  p110
Fundació Antoni Tàpies
  p124
Fundació Foto Colectània
  p141
Fundació Joan Miró p110
Fundación Francisco Godia
  p125
Fundació Suñol p125
Funicular de Tibidabo p153

g
Golondrinas, Las p103
Gràcia p141

h
Hospital de la Santa Creu
  i Sant Pau p125

j
Jardí Botànic p111
Jardins Mossèn Costa
  i Llobera p112

l
Lower Raval p94

m
MACBA (Museu d'Art
  Contemporani de
  Barcelona) p89
MNAC (Museu Nacional
  d'Art de Catalunya) p112
Monestir de Pedralbes p156
Montjuïc p108
Monument a Colom p104
Museu Barbier-Mueller
  d'Art Precolombí p73
Museu d'Arqueologia de
  Catalunya p113
Museu de Carrosses
  Fúnebres p125
Museu de Cera p71
Museu de Ciències Naturals
  de la Ciutadella p74
Museu de la Música p126
Museu de la Xocolata p74
Museu del Calçat (Shoe
  Museum) p56
Museu de les Arts
  Aplicades p156
Museu del Perfum p126
Museu d'Història de
  Catalunya p104
Museu d'Història de la
  Ciutat p56
Museu Egipci de Barcelona
  p127
Museu Etnològic p114
Museu Frederic Marès p56
Museu Marítim p104
Museu Militar p114
Museu Olímpic I de l'Esport
  p114
Museu Picasso p76

p
Palau de la Generalitat p57
Palau de la Música Catalana
  p76
Palau de la Virreina p71
Palau Güell p95
Paral·lel p118
Parc de la Ciutadella p77
Parc de la Creueta del Coll
  p157
Parc de l'Espanya Industrial
  p150
Parc de l'Estació del Nord
  p127
Parc Joan Miró (Parc de
  l'Escorxador) p127

Park Güell p144
Pavelló Mies van der Rohe
  p114
Pedrera, La (Casa Milà)
  p127
Poble Espanyol p114
Poblenou p159
Poble Sec p118
Port Vell p103

r
Rambla, La p70
Raval p86
Refugi 307 p118

s
Sagrada Família p127
Santa Maria del Mar p77
Sant Pau del Camp p95
Sant Pere p73
Sants p150

t
Telefèric de Montjuïc p116
Tibidabo p152
Tibidabo funfair p153
Torre de Collserola p153
Tramvia Blau p157
Transbordador Aeri p104

u
Upper Raval p86

v
Vila Olímpica p106

z
Zona Alta p155
Zoo de Barcelona p78

Eating & Drinking

a
Agua p106
Alkimia p129
Artkuisine p157

b
Baignoire, La p145
Bar Bodega Teo p57
Bar Celta p58
Bar Colombo p105
Bar Kasparo p90
Bar Lobo p90
Bar Mendizábal p91
Bar Mut p129
Bar Seco p118
Baraka p91

ESSENTIALS

Kennedy

irish sailing club
The Little Corner of Ireland in Barcelona

Enjoy a real Irish Pub in the
PORT OLIMPIC, BARCELONA

Live music everyday at midnight. Great bands
playing covers, pop-rock, and irish pub songs.
5 huge screens, to enjoy all sports events.
**For timetable and information visit our
website www.kennedybcn.com**

KENNEDY IRISH SAILING CLUB
PORT OLIMPIC - BARCELONA
Open every day from 6pm to 3.30am

Where to find us:

Open every day from 6pm to 3.30am
Metro linea 4 "Vila Olimpica"
Bus Line 10-157-36-45-57-59 -71-92 - Bus turistic "Vila Olimpica"

Moll Mestral 26-27-28, Port Olimpic - Barcelona - Spain
Tel. Number: +34 932 210 039 - e-mail: hello@kennedybcn.com